Restaurant Management in Hotel

Restaurant Management in Hotel

B.K. Kochhar

CYBER TECH PUBLICATIONS
4264/3, Ansari Road, Daryaganj, New Delhi-110002 (India)
Ph.: 011-23244078. Fax: 011-23280028
E-Mail: cyberpublicationsdelhi@yahoo.com

RESTAURANT MANAGEMENT IN HOTEL

B.K. Kochhar

First Edition 2009

Published by :

G.S. Rawat for **Cyber Tech Publications**
4264/3, Ansari Road, Daryaganj, New Delhi-110002 (India)
Ph.: 011-23244078. Fax: 011-23280028
E-Mail: cyberpublicationsdelhi@yahoo.com

Printed at . Asian Offset Printers

Preface

Hotel chains have flourished because they offer consumers a reliable and predictable visit. Each hotel in a chain offers similar facilities and services. Many are adding services from nationally known franchises such as pizzerias or Starbucks coffee shops. This similarity makes them popular because travellers going to an unfamiliar city know what to expect if they have stayed in another hotel or motel in the same chain. The hotel industry faces fierce competition due to an oversupply of hotel rooms. A construction boom in the 1980s was followed by a decline in the number of travellers during the early 1990s. Hotel occupancy fell from a high of 72 percent in 1979 to just 59.2 percent in 2003, leaving more than one-third of all hotel rooms empty on any given night. The result of this oversupply has been increased market segmentation. Rather than running huge, five-hundred-room hotels to fit the needs of every traveler, many hotels today target one market segment such as business or budget travellers.

Some innovative hotel designs have also captured markets successfully. One popular trend has been the all-suite hotel. Each unit in an all-suite hotel provides a living area and a separate bedroom. Some also offer a cooking area. Another development is the environmentally conscious "ecohotel," which highlights features such as low-flush toilets, refillable containers for toiletries, and recycled stationery.

The growth of the global economy has also affected the hotel industry. Many hotel chains based in the United States have expanded overseas. At home the hotel industry made a slow recovery from 9/11 but was still coping with the effects of the recession through the first decade of the new century.

— *Author*

CONTENTS

1

Introduction

Location is one of the most important factors in choosing a hotel. Whether they travel for business or pleasure, people need a place to stay when they are away from home.

Some very special hotels-New York's Waldorf-Astoria or San Francisco's Ritz-Carlton, for example-become destinations in themselves. But most travellers know where they want to go and then select a hotel that fits their needs.

Many travellers prefer to stay at "branded" hotels-places that offer the familiarity of well-known franchises in both accommodations and food services regardless of the location. Other travellers believe that branded hotels lack uniqueness and seek out smaller, independent hotels when they travel. Hotel locations are closely linked to transportation. America's earliest hotels were small public inns that catered to passengers who arrived in horse-drawn wagons. They were built along major roads and at river crossings.

Then railroads built a travel network across the country, and new, larger hotels sprang up near the main stations. The travel and tourism industry is by its very nature global in scope. By the beginning of the twenty-first century, however, travel destinations and vacation activities were changing.

Perhaps the hottest trend in travel is the rise of "ecotourism." According to the Quebec Declaration on Ecotourism, ecotourism "includes local and indigenous communities in its planning, interprets the natural and cultural heritage of the destination to the visitor, and lends itself better to independent travellers."

Not so long ago many of the now-popular ecotourism destinations were either unknown to the outside world or fairly inaccessible. For most people places such as the Amazon rain forest, Africa's savannas, and the Himalaya and Andes mountains were simply out of reach. But many countries are now promoting their remote environmental treasures to travellers looking for something out of the ordinary. Tour operators are developing special packages for the environmentally minded traveler, and local groups are organizing tourism associations that attract tourists to out-of-the-way places. Archaeological tourism is another growing trend.

Ancient sites in destinations such as Egypt, Israel, and various other places in the Middle East are attracting visitors who only a short time ago had little knowledge of that region of the world. In 2005 Archaeological Tours in New York City offered packages that allowed travellers to explore the ancient Silk Road of China, the Byzantine monuments in southern Italy, and the legendary statues of Easter Island. Most of the tours were led by archeologists or university professors. The development of ecotourism and archaeological tourism has coincided with an increase in travel to the United States by foreign tourists.

Along with a global economy has come a growing middle class in Asia and Latin America. Latin America's outbound travel market has grown almost 33 percent since the mid-1990s, according to a 2004 on-line article by the Travel Industry Association of America. A good number of these newly prosperous travellers will eventually make their way to the United States. Another travel trend has its roots in America's history as a country of immigrants.

In recent years many Americans have begun searching for relatives or ancestors both at home and abroad. As distant parts of the world grow closer together, travellers are finding more opportunities for what has come to be called "heritage travel" to Europe, Asia, Africa, and Central and South America. No innovation has affected the hotel industry more than the automobile. With the invention of the automobile, locations throughout the country became far more accessible to travellers.

Motels, or "motor hotels," were built to accommodate drivers as they explored America.

Early motels were usually small, family-owned businesses with a few roadside cabins. Air travel has further expanded the possible locations to which people can travel. Moreover, the Internet has had a profound impact on tourism. Potential travellers can explore vacation packages and make reservations online. According to a 2005 article published in Revenue, travel researcher PhoCusWright noted that half of flight and hotel reservations were made online by the end of 2005.

Trends in the Hotel Industry

In the first five years of the twentieth century hotel chains dominated the industry. In 2000 chains controlled nearly 70 percent of the hotel market share in the United States while less than 40 percent of all hotels were independently owned and operated. Just ten years earlier in 1990 nearly 55 percent of all hotels were independent.

Hotel chains have flourished because they offer consumers a reliable and predictable visit. Each hotel in a chain offers similar facilities and services. Many are adding services from nationally known franchises such as pizzerias or Starbucks coffee shops. This similarity makes them popular because travellers going to an unfamiliar city know what to expect if they have stayed in another hotel or motel in the same chain. The hotel industry faces fierce competition due to an oversupply of hotel rooms. A construction boom in the 1980s was followed by a decline in the number of travellers during the early 1990s. Hotel occupancy fell from a high of 72 percent in 1979 to just 59.2 percent in 2003, leaving more than one-third of all hotel rooms empty on any given night. The result of this oversupply has been increased market segmentation. Rather than running huge, five-hundred-room hotels to fit the needs of every traveler, many hotels today target one market segment such as business or budget travellers.

Some innovative hotel designs have also captured markets successfully. One popular trend has been the all-suite hotel. Each unit in an all-suite hotel provides a living area and a separate bedroom. Some also offer a cooking area. Another development is the environmentally conscious "ecohotel," which highlights features such as low-flush toilets, refillable containers for toiletries, and recycled stationery. One of the most popular promotions in resort locations is the all-inclusive package, which offers travellers not only lodging but all meals, drinks, and entertainment for one price.

The growth of the global economy has also affected the hotel industry. Many hotel chains based in the United States have expanded overseas. At home the hotel industry made a slow recovery from 9/11 but was still coping with the effects of the recession through the first decade of the new century. According to a March 2005 report in the Fairfield County Business Journal, the typical U.S. hotel achieved an estimated 13.3 percent increase in yearly profits in 2004. Moreover, an increased confidence in airport security, a decreased fear of a terrorist attack, and a weak U.S. dollar has led to an increase in foreign travel to the United States. During the first half of 2004 international spending in America rose for the first time since 9/11.

In 2004 the U.S. Commerce Department estimated that foreign tourism accounted for over $71 billion in economic activity in the United States-a figure larger than the profits from U.S. automobile, engine, and parts exports. With that much at stake, it is little surprise that President George W. Bush approved a $50 million ad campaign aimed at tourists in England, Japan, Germany, Canada, and Mexico.

Hotels make foreign travellers feel welcome by serving international cuisine in their restaurants and by providing room directories and menus printed in several languages.

Some hotels now employ multilingual concierges to help guests with making reservations, arranging tours, and answering questions about the region. This trend increases the demand for workers who speak several languages and who have experience with different cultures. In April 2005 Wyndham Hotels announced it would implement an English language education program for its Spanish-speaking employees.

BUSINESS TRAVELLERS

One major market segment for the hotel industry is business travel. Hotels in all price ranges compete to attract these guests and keep them as clients. Employees who have sales and marketing experience can help a hotel compete successfully.

Hotels seek business travellers by providing special features or services designed to make it easier to work away from home. During the 1980s many hotels built business centers that included computers and copiers. Portable technology has lessened the popularity of these centers, and now many business travellers prefer to work in their rooms using their own notebook computers. By the early 2000s popular hotel amenities included free newspapers, a complimentary breakfast, a large work desk, high-speed or WiFi Internet access, and exercise facilities.

Efficiency is a primary concern for all business travellers whose tight schedules require quick service. Many hotels provide computerized services for speedy check-in and check-out. Employees are trained to help visits run smoothly and to handle problems swiftly. As in any service industry, pleasing the customer is of foremost importance.

Some business-oriented hotels offer facilities for companies to conduct extended staff meetings. It is also common for businesses to schedule "retreats" where employees stay at the same hotel and discuss business strategies in designated meeting rooms, then spend time together participating in leisure activities such as golf, tennis, or swimming. Many hotels are designed to cater to these meetings, especially those at popular resort destinations.

Earning customer loyalty is a key feature of serving business travellers. If a hotel satisfies a business client, the long-term return can be great. One way that hotels promote customer loyalty is through frequent-guest programs. Travellers earn points for every dollar they spend at the hotel. When they have accumulated enough points, they can redeem them for gifts such as free lodging or a vacation at an exotic resort. Like all aspects of the hospitality industry, business and convention travel was hit hard by 9/11 and the sagging economy. From 1998 to 2003, business and convention travel experienced a 14 percent drop-off; however, business travel grew more than 4 percent in 2004 and should experience even more growth in the next few years, according to the Travel Industry Association of America.

CONVENTIONS

Guest rooms are only one source of revenue for many hotels. They can make large profits by renting meeting rooms and exhibition space and by hosting banquets and receptions. Trade shows and conventions draw hundreds of customers at a time to a hotel.

Many different industries and business organizations hold trade shows and conventions each year. Political, civic, religious, and social organizations also have annual meetings. Hotels hire convention planners to attract conventions, to help businesses plan events, and to negotiate prices. During a convention service managers supervise every stage of the event. Because a hotel's reputation for efficiency and good service is often the key to its success in attracting conventions, the work of the convention staff is critical.

HOTEL WORKER TEAMS

The workers in a large hotel generally are organized into teams according to the department in which they work. There are currently more than 170 different careers in the hospitality industry. Common departments include sales, food and beverage, housekeeping, and accounting. Each department is run by a manager, who usually reports to a general manager in charge of the hotel.

Hotel workers are traditionally described as "front-of-the-house" or "back-of-the-house" employees, depending on whether they have direct contact with the guests. Front-of-the-house workers include bellhops, desk clerks, and concierges. Back-of-the-house workers are the behind-the-scenes employees who keep the hotel running smoothly. They include kitchen workers, housekeepers, and accountants.

FOOD SERVICE INDUSTRY

Any business that prepares and serves meals, snacks, or beverages is part of the food service industry. The largest segment of the industry includes restaurants serving full menus and offering table service. The second-largest segment is limited-menu, or fast food, outlets. Although large fast food chains are a familiar sight all across the United States, more than seven out of ten eating and drinking places are single-unit, independent operations. Other segments of the food service industry include school and employee cafeterias, catering businesses, hotel restaurants, and vendors at sporting events and concerts.

The food service industry in the United States is booming and appears to be immune from the weak economy of the twenty-first century's first decade. Sales have increased from about $43 billion in 1970 to $426 billion in 2003. The National Restaurant Association estimates that more than 54 billion meals were eaten in restaurants and school and work cafeterias in 2002. Social scientists suggest that the boom is the result of people's busy schedules. They also point out that dual-income families have limited time for cooking. Although the rapid food service boom of the 1970s and 1980s may be slowing, the employment outlook is still very good. In 2002 the food service industry employed about 11.7 million workers, making it the largest U.S. employer besides the government. Food and beverage service employment is expected to reach 13.3 million by 2012.

Trends in Food Service

The growth of the take-out food market is a major trend in the food service industry. This market segment is called the "off-premises sector" because food is eaten away from the restaurant where it is cooked. It includes take-out, delivery, and drive-through restaurants. Many traditional restaurants that offer table service attempt to cash in on this expanding market by offering delivery service. Take-out and delivery accounted for 51 percent of total restaurant business in 2002. The Internet has also had a profound influence on the food service market; many workers now order their lunches online.

After rapid expansion in the 1980s the number of fast food restaurants remained stable through the 1990s. New restaurants are likely to be full-service restaurants, which cater more successfully to America's older population.

In fact, the full-service sector is expected to be the fastest-growing sector in the industry. The number of Americans between the ages of fifteen and thirty-four-the age group that generally thrives on fast food-is decreasing, whereas the food service industry includes any business that prepares and serves meals, snacks, or beverages. Many older diners have more time for a leisurely meal and do not seek out fast food.

Like any other business, fast food restaurants must adapt to changing times. Many fast-food chains are offering a wider range of choices and emphasizing low-fat items such as salads and grilled foods to appeal to health-conscious Americans. Another significant trend is the growth of the ethnic food sector. Whereas many Americans once limited their exploration of ethnic foods to Italian or Chinese cuisine, today they seek out traditional foods of Latin America, India, Africa, the Caribbean, and other cultures.

Food Service Workers

The people who work in the food service industry include food and beverage managers, restaurant managers, bartenders, chefs and cooks, bakers, dining room and cafeteria attendants, hostesses and hosts, waiters and waitresses, fast food franchise workers, caterers, stewards, dishwashers, and other kitchen workers. The food service industry employs large numbers of relatively unskilled workers. Restaurants traditionally have depended on young people to fill these positions; however, low birthrates in the 1970s and 1980s limited the number of youths looking for employment in the 1990s.

The food service industry was forced to attract workers from other age groups. It became common for food service businesses to offer more full-time employment, higher wages and bonuses, and more training for career advancement than before. The industry also began recruiting more women and minorities, as well as nontraditional workers such as seniors and mentally and physically challenged individuals.

RECREATION INDUSTRY

From aerobics and hiking to rock climbing and parachuting, the recreation industry helps millions of Americans enjoy their leisure time. Workers in this industry organize and lead activities, provide instruction and equipment, and maintain facilities.

SUMMER JOBS IN HOSPITALITY AND RECREATION

FOOD SERVICE

Summer jobs are available for kitchen and dining room workers, particularly servers, dishwashers, kitchen helpers, cooking staff, cashiers, and hosts and hostesses. Contact:

- hotels
- restaurants
- caterers
- amusement parks
- employment agencies

HOTELS

Summer positions in hotels include housekeepers, bellhops, porters, desk clerks, and doorkeepers. Hotels with other amenities such as room service, tourist information desks, and social programs need additional staff. Contact:

- hotels
- motels
- summer resorts
- cruise operators
- employment agencies

RECREATION

Summer jobs in this area include camp counsellors, lifeguards, and recreation workers. Some parks and museums offer summer internships. Guides are needed for parks, historic sites, and public monuments. Contact:

- local parks and recreation departments
- historic sites
- camps
- tourism offices
- museums
- community centers

Trends in Recreation

In the 1990s sociologists identified a trend called "cocooning." If this trend continues more and more Americans will stay at home for relaxation and recreation. Climbing sales of home gym equipment and rentals of DVDs suggest that cocooning will continue for at least the first decade of the twenty-first century. However, some U.S. consumers still seek out a diverse range of activities offered by the recreation industry. Because many Americans have a limited amount of leisure time, they are very selective about how they spend it. Instead of participating in several leisure activities, many people prefer to focus on just one. More and more people are choosing to take shorter vacations as well; for example, weekend and getaway trips are becoming more popular than traditional two-week vacations.

Physical Fitness Programs and Participatory Sports

The physical fitness movement of the 1980s was led by baby boomers-people born from 1946 to 1964. As members of this generation have reached middle age and become more interested in maintaining their physical fitness, they have devoted more time to working out in gyms, health clubs, and community centers.

The interest in physical fitness continues, but the focus has shifted from workouts to wellness. In addition to building their muscles and toning their bodies, aging baby boomers seek to improve their total mental and emotional well-being. "Total care" health clubs are responding to this trend by offering seminars and counselling in nutrition, stress management, smoking cessation, weight loss, and self-esteem.

Baby boomers seem to have turned to less strenuous sports that can be practiced safely throughout life. Within this age group, "lifetime" sports such as hiking, bicycling, walking, golf, and doubles tennis are increasing in popularity as more strenuous or hazardous sports such as running, jogging, downhill skiing, and singles tennis decline. Sporting goods stores employ instructors to teach customers basic skills and safety precautions pertaining to their sport of choice.

Movie Theatres

For decades the only place anyone could see a movie was in a theater. By the dawn of the twenty-first century theatres were competing fiercely with cable television and DVD sales and rentals. Movie theatres try to attract audiences by offering amenities such as improved audio and projection systems and concession stands that sell a wide range of food and drinks. Some chains are experimenting with special ultra-large screens that produce a thrilling and vivid viewing experience, and many theatres have added online information, reservation, and prepay ticket sales systems to make ticket purchasing easier. Such improvements are designed to attract an older, more affluent crowd.

Another continuing trend is the multiplex, a theater complex with many screens. Each theater offers In addition to providing traditional exercise facilities, many health clubs offer seminars and classes in nutrition, stress management, and self-esteem. Multiplexes encourage impulse viewing and increase customer satisfaction. By showing a popular film on more than one screen, multiplexes can increase the size of the audience and avoid the risk of selling out while patrons are still waiting for tickets. Movie theatres provide jobs for managers, projectionists, cashiers, ushers, and concession-stand workers.

Museums

The rich cultural history of the United States is reflected in its variety of museums. In addition to museums of art, many

American cities support museums devoted to history, science, culture, and children's studies. According to the 2004 Museum Attendance Report compiled by Morey and Associates, the average total attendance at more than eighty museums in the United States increased 2.6 percent between 2003 and 2004.

Most museums are seeking to attract wider, more diverse audiences. One common strategy is to plan exhibits that reflect the ethnic or cultural interests within a community. Some museums are dedicated entirely to particular themes, such as the Charles H. Wright Museum of African American History in Detroit, the Museum of Tolerance in Los Angeles, and the Holocaust Memorial Museum in Washington, D.C.

Many museums now use interactive technology-once limited to children's museums-to increase accessibility and encourage more active, hands-on experiences for visitors. This technology includes displays and kiosks that provide museum maps and helpful information about museum displays.

As Americans' travel habits shift from long family vacations to shorter, more frequent outings, museums need to find new ways to attract visitors. According to a 2002 report by the New England Museum Association, museums that "have diversified their offerings to include changing attractions along with special events and new experiences" have been the most successful.

Museums hire curators to plan and maintain exhibits. In a large museum a curator is usually in charge of one department such as photography or African American art. Updating museums requires the services of professional designers and educational specialists. Museums also hire clerks who sell tickets and work in museum stores, as well as tour guides, guards, maintenance workers, and fund-raising experts.

Spectator Sports

Millions of fans regularly attend professional and amateur sporting events. Baseball, basketball, ice hockey, and football grew in popularity during the 1980s. Spurred by Americans' interest in professional sports, many leagues have expanded in recent years or plan future expansion. At the beginning of the twenty-first century women's professional sports were attracting many new fans as well. The Women's National Basketball Association was founded in 1997, the U.S. women's soccer team enjoyed national attention when it won the 1999 Women's World Cup, and women's professional tennis maintained a decades-long period of popularity. However, men's professional organizations like the National Football League, National Basketball Association, National Hockey League, and Major League Baseball continue to be so popular that they have cultural significance as well as entertainment value.

Top-Earning Jobs in Hospitality and Recreation

These are some of the high-paying jobs described in this volume. The figures represent typical salaries or earnings for experienced workers.

$100,000-$25,000,000	* Professional Athlete
	* Professional Athletic Coach
$30,000-$80,000	* Athletic Trainer
	* Caterer
	* Corporate Travel Manager
	* Lodging Manager
	* Meeting and Convention Planner
	* Museum Conservator
	* Museum Curator
	* Property, Real Estate, and Community Association Manager
	* Restaurant Manager

Professional athletes are the highly paid stars of spectator sports, but many other people work in this sector of the recreation industry, including coaches, managers, trainers, ticket sellers, and stadium workers. Sales and marketing personnel create special promotions and events that help get fans into the stands. Even the steroid scandal that rocked American baseball could not drown fan interest: advance ticket sales for the 2005 season were up 6.5 percent from 2004. Sports still has its problematic economic issues, however, as evidenced by the lockout that cancelled the 2004-05 National Hockey League season. The lockout affected many local businesses and left thousands of employees out of work.

Community Recreation

Community recreation is the most widespread recreation field in the United States. Just about every community and county in the nation has a public recreation center where residents can swim, learn arts and crafts, put on a play, or participate in sports. Many "controlled" communities such as retirement centers also employ recreation staffs. Jobs available in community recreation facilities include recreation director, program director, lifeguard, playground supervisor, and recreation aide. Opportunities also exist for people who can teach activities such as dancing, crafts, drama, and sports.

Zoos

The Bronx Zoo in New York is a prime example of the changing role and function of American zoos. Its official name-the Wildlife Conservation Park-emphasizes its ties to the Wildlife Conservation Society, formerly known as the New York Zoological Society. Stressing their role in the preservation of animals and their ecosystems, modern zoos have replaced the old-fashioned animals-behind-bars environment with wildlife parks where animals roam free in replicas of their natural habitats.

The pioneering and best-known of these zoos, the San Diego Zoo, is noted for its breeding programs for endangered animals. Wildlife park directors feel that today's zoos play a vital role in helping to conserve endangered animals, as well as in teaching the public about the importance of conservation efforts throughout the world. Wildlife conservation parks require many skilled workers, including directors, curators, veterinarians, and zoologists. Zoos also hire animal caretakers, guides, maintenance workers, and public relations personnel.

State and National Parks

The United States has a well-developed system of county, state, and national parks. The National Park Service administers many frequently visited parks throughout the nation, from Gulf Islands National Seashore in Florida to Yosemite National Park in California. Since the 1950s visits to national parks Zoos are increasingly providing habitats for animals have jumped 500 percent. The park system employs thousands of workers to maintain the parks and help visitors enjoy camping, hiking, picnics, historical tours, and nature studies.

THE SNAPSHOTS

Hotels

Competition in the hotel industry is intense. Many hotels are targeting their services to particular market segments such as business-people or budget travellers. Expansion of smaller budget hotels is expected through 2014. Other trends include the all-suite hotel and the ecohotel. Increased international tourism makes cultural sensitivity and adaptability especially important in this field.

Food Services

Busy Americans rely heavily on the restaurant industry to provide satisfying meals. Although the fast food boom has slowed, take-out establishments that offer a wider and healthier selection of foods are still experiencing growth. A rise in the number of parents and children who dine out, combined with a more affluent population of diners age fifty-five and older, are expected to spur growth in restaurants offering traditional table service. Franchise outlets will continue to be a significant part of the industry, but small, independently owned businesses will still hold the largest market segment.

Recreation

Americans are being more selective when deciding how to spend their limited amounts of leisure time. All forms of recreation-movies, museums, zoos, parks, sporting events, and so on-compete to attract consumers. Recreation that meets the needs of an aging and culturally diverse population will be important in the first two decades of the twenty-first century.

Travel

An increase in both business and leisure travel is expected to continue, though it may not reach pre-9/11 levels until the end of 2006, according to the Office of Travel and Tourism Industries. Many travellers are opting for shorter but more frequent trips. With the broadening scope of choices and decisions to be made when planning a trip, some travellers will continue to seek out the services of travel industry workers. The increase in the number of senior citizens-many of whom have the free time and disposable income to devote to travel-will most likely spur the growth of leisure travel designed to appeal to older Americans.

Technology

Workers throughout the field of hospitality and recreation rely on computers. Museums and zoos feature multimedia exhibits and interactive displays. Travel agents and reservations clerks use computers to determine the availability of flights and accommodations. Restaurants use computers to keep track of inventory and table charges. Hotel managers can use computers for yield management-a process that reveals when to discount rates rather than have empty rooms.

Training

Many hotel and restaurant managers find that hospitality training is beneficial to their employees and their establishment. Employees who have completed training in the hospitality field are said to feel empowered and more capable of meeting their clients' needs. These programs go beyond teaching specific skills-they cover broad topics such as setting goals, developing communication skills, reducing stress, and building self-confidence. By promoting a good working environment, hospitality training contributes to worker and customer satisfaction. These programs need trainers as well as people to develop computerized training programs and instructional videos. According to the National Park Service Office of Communications, in 2004 more than 276 million people visited America's national parks. Since then many parks have faced a crippling budget crisis. In an April 17, 2006 article, WashingtonPost.com contributor Matt Stearns reported: "The Bush administration has ordered America's national parks to show that they can function at 80 percent or less of their operating budgets." National park superintendents have to make some hard choices concerning ranger staffs, services, and visitor center hours, according to an article in National Geographic News. Prior to President Bush's budget-cutting announcement, environmentalists and conservationists were urging the government to purchase more land for parks-a proposal that seemed unlikely to gain acceptance in light of the 20 percent cut in park funding set for 2007.

Camps

Summer camps are changing to adjust to new population and cultural trends. Camps still offer traditional activities such as swimming, boating, and hiking, but many also offer unique learning opportunities. Some camps focus on developing skills in specific areas, including computers, tennis, music, drama, and foreign languages. Others cater to children with special needs such as those with chronic illnesses or disabilities. Modern camps provide job opportunities for instructors and therapists, as well as directors, counsellors, lifeguards, nurses, and cooks.

The characteristics of camp-age children are expected to shift in the twenty-first century, with far more attendees coming from urban areas and different cultural backgrounds. The goal for the future is to find new ways to attract an increasingly diverse range of campers.

EMPLOYMENT OUTLOOK

The health of the hospitality and recreation industry and the coinciding employment outlook is greatly affected by fluctuations in the U.S. economy. During a recession such as the one that began in 2000, consumers have less income for travel and leisure pursuits and they are usually more cautious about spending money for nonessential items. They also are less likely to contribute money to support historic sites, museums, and zoos. As less money is spent on hospitality and recreation, fewer workers are hired and the number of available jobs decreases. This scenario characterized the beginning of the twenty-first century. On the other hand, during strong economic times, people have more discretionary income (extra money) and the hospitality and recreation industry generally flourishes. Consequently, the employment outlook for the field becomes favourable.

Changing demographics and lifestyles also have a major impact on employment in hospitality and recreation. As the United States entered the twenty-first century, about 25 percent of the population was over the age of fifty-five. This growing market segment has the money and the time to travel and pursue leisure activities. For this reason many analysts predict strong growth in leisure travel designed to appeal to retirees; this in turn will spur employment growth in the field. Technology and training will be vital for workers in the hospitality and recreation industry. As in all fields, new technology will help people work more efficiently. Training programs can help workers keep pace with new trends and changing needs.

Despite continued economic problems and the aftereffects of the 9/11 tragedy, employment opportunities in hospitality and recreation still exist. Candidates committed to the principles of customer service-those who display patience, knowledge, enthusiasm, and a willingness to go the extra mile for a client-are in the best position to enter, succeed, and advance in this field.

GETTING INTO HOSPITALITY AND RECREATION

Good jobs do not magically appear. Anyone who has been in the job market knows that landing the right job takes planning, preparation, perseverance, and patience. This is true whether you are looking for your first job, reentering the job market, trying to get a new job, or planning a mid-career change. This essay is designed to guide you through the process of finding a job, from helping you define your career objectives to suggesting ways to prepare yourself for interviews. Use the advice and checklists below to help identify the kind of work that fits your personality, skills, and interests. Then learn how to locate job openings that match your criteria. Finally, use these tips to help you create a resume and prepare for the interview that helps you land the job that's right for you.

Planning your Career

What are your unique skills? What kind of workplace appeals to you? What do you find most rewarding in your daily life? Answering these questions can help you identify a career path that will enrich your life, financially and otherwise. Most people enjoy doing a job well. There is an inner satisfaction that comes from taking on a challenge and accomplishing something worthwhile. Whether you are just starting out in the working world or you are at the midpoint of a career, it is worth taking some time to consider whether or not you are in the right kind of work-or looking for the right kind of job. If you are unhappy or dissatisfied in your daily work and are just trying to do enough to get by, you may not be in the right job or the right field. The following ideas can help you match your skills and interests with the kind of work you will find most rewarding.

Evaluate Yourself

Before you make any career decisions, think about subjects or topics that interest you and tasks you do well. This can help you pinpoint the kind of work you would be happy doing. One way to go about this is to compile a self-inventory chart. Such a chart will be helpful as you decide which jobs you want to consider. Including details about your work history and educational background will also make the chart useful to you as you compile your resume, write cover letters, complete job application forms, and prepare for job interviews.

Begin your self-inventory chart by listing all the jobs you have ever had, including summer employment, part-time jobs, volunteer work, and any freelance or short-term assignments you have done. Include the dates of employment, the names and addresses of supervisors, and the amount of money you earned. Then compile a similar list of your hobbies and other activities, including any special experiences you have had, such as travel. Next, do the same for your educational history, listing schools attended, major courses of study, grades, special honours or awards, courses you particularly enjoyed, and extracurricular activities.

At this point, you may see a career pattern emerging: perhaps your list is already suggesting a direction for your career search. If the picture still lacks detail or focus, expand your self-inventory chart by compiling a list of standard workplace aptitudes, and rate yourself above average, average, or below average for each one. Some skill categories to include in your list are administrative, analytic, athletic, clerical, language, leadership, managerial, manual, mathematical, mechanical, sales, and verbal abilities. Also rate your willingness to accept responsibility and your ability to get along with people. In combination with your educational background, work history, and list of personal interests, this information should help you understand why some kinds of work appeal to you and others do not.

Evaluate Workplace Characteristics

Another tool to help you find a rewarding job is the "Work Characteristics Checklist" below. Some of these characteristics will be attractive to you. Some will not. Perhaps you will discover that having a workplace with flexible hours, for example, is more important to you than being able to work outdoors. Or maybe you will find that these are both very significant issues in your quality of life.

This checklist can be useful as a guide as you compile your own list of what is important to you in a job or workplace. Do not expect a job to meet all your requirements, however. Focusing on the job characteristics that are most important to you will help you identify the type of work you would find most rewarding. It will also be helpful when it is time to decide whether or not to apply for jobs you discover during the search process.

Evaluate Career Options

Now that you've evaluated your personal skills, aptitudes, interests, and experience, and you've identified the kinds of workplace characteristics that are important to you, do you feel confident that you know what kinds of jobs you'd be good at? If not, you may wish to consult an experienced career counsellor or take advantage of online resources that can help you find a good career field match.

Most high schools, vocational schools, and colleges provide vocational testing and career counselling guidance for students and alumni. Some local offices of the state employment services affiliated with the federal employment service offer free counselling. Commercial career centers also offer guidance services. There are many tools available to test your interests and aptitudes for the purpose of career counselling. The personal profile that emerges from a skills inventory can be matched with potential career fields to show you what kinds of jobs might be good matches for your interests. These assessment tools will also show you what kind of training is necessary to qualify for jobs in these career fields. You may find programs like this online that you can try for yourself.

For a more comprehensive approach, you may prefer to look into aptitude tests that are administered and interpreted by a career counselor. Most major cities have professional career consultants and career counselling firms. You should make sure to check their reputations before paying for their services. A list of counselling services in your area is available from the American Counselling Association in Alexandria, Virginia.

You can also search the Internet for many services that career counsellors provide. Some sites have online counsellors who can help you with a variety of tasks, such as obtaining information on jobs, careers, and training. They may be able to provide information on available services, including housing assistance, day care facilities, and transportation. A list of career planning resources, including Web sites, is available at the end of this volume.

Evaluate Specific Jobs

After you have considered what you do well and what you enjoy doing, and identified some career options that provide a good match with your interests and abilities, you're ready to focus on the specific types of jobs that may be available to you. First, make a note of all the jobs in this volume that interest you. Then examine the education and training required for these jobs. Decide whether you qualify or would be able to gain the qualifications. If possible, talk with people who have the kinds of jobs you are considering. Firsthand information can be invaluable. Also look through the appropriate trade and professional journals listed at the end of this essay and check the section at the end of the volume called "Resources" for books and Web sites that contain more detailed information about the jobs. In addition, counsellors usually are helpful.

Once you have found out all you can about a particular type of job, compare the features of the job with your work characteristics checklist. See how many characteristics of the job match your work preferences. By completing these steps for all the jobs that appeal to you, you should be able to come up with a list of jobs that match your interests and abilities.

Work Characteristics Checklist

Do you want a job in which you can

- work outdoors?
- be physically active?
- work with your hands?
- be challenged mentally?
- work with machines?
- work independently?
- work on a team?
- follow clear instructions?
- earn a lot of money?
- have a chance for rapid advancement?
- have good benefits?
- travel in your work?
- work close to home?
- work regular hours?
- have a flexible schedule?

- have a variety of tasks?
- have supervisory responsibilities?
- express your own ideas?
- be a decision maker?

Finding Job Opportunities

Once you've decided what kind of job suits you, the next step is to look for available positions. Obviously, the more openings you can find, the better your chance of landing a job. People usually apply for many job openings before they find the right employment match. There are many ways to find out about or apply for job openings. Some of these job-hunting techniques are explained on the pages that follow, along with information about how to follow up on job leads.

Applying in Person

For some jobs, especially part-time or entry-level jobs, you may be able to find employment by visiting the company or companies for which you would like to work. This works best when a company is expanding or jobs are plentiful for other reasons, or when a "help wanted" sign is posted at the company. Applying in person can sharpen your interviewing techniques and give you a chance to see a variety of workplaces. This direct approach is best for hourly labour or service jobs; when applying for other types of work, it is not the method to use unless you are directed to do so. Applicants for professional or supervisory jobs should always send a letter and resume to the company.

Phone and Letter Campaigns

To conduct a phone campaign, use the business listings of your telephone directory to build a list of companies for which you might like to work. Call their personnel departments and find out whether they have any openings. This technique is not useful in all situations, and it has its drawbacks: you may not be able to make a strong impression by phone, and you will not have a written record of your contacts.

Letter writing campaigns can be very effective if the letters are well thought out and carefully prepared. Your letters should always be typed. Handwritten letters and photocopied letters convey a lack of interest or motivation.

You may be able to compile a good list of company addresses in your field of interest by reading the trade and professional publications listed at the end of this essay.

Many of the periodicals publish directories or directory issues. Other sources you can use to compile lists of companies are the trade unions and professional organizations listed at the end of each job profile in this volume. The reference librarian at your local library can also help you find appropriate directories.

You can also e-mail letters to human resource departments of many companies. Be sure to follow all the same guidelines as you would for traditional letter correspondence.

Job Finder's Checklist

The following list of job-hunting tips may seem obvious, but getting all the bits and pieces in order beforehand helps when you're looking for a job.

Resume

Find out whether you will need a resume. If so, bring your resume up to date or prepare a new one. Assemble a supply of neatly printed copies and have an electronic version ready to e-mail to prospective employers.

References

Line up your references. Ask permission of the people whose names you would like to use. Write down their addresses, phone numbers, and job titles.

Contacts

Put the word out to everyone you know that you are looking for a job.

Job Market

Find out where the jobs are. Make a list of possible employers in your field of interest.

Research

Do a little homework ahead of time-it can make a big difference in the long run. Find out as much as you can about a job, the field, and the company before you apply. A knowledgeable job applicant makes a good impression.

Organization

Keep a file on your job-hunting campaign with names and dates of employers contacted, ads answered, results, and follow-up.

Appearance

Make sure that the clothes you plan to wear to an interview are neat and clean. You may need to dress more formally than you would on the job, particularly if you are visiting a personnel office or meeting with a manager. Keep in mind that people will form an opinion of you based on their first impressions. Whether they are paper or electronic, your letters should be addressed to the personnel or human resources department of the organization. If possible, send the letter to a specific person. If you don't know who the correct person is, try to find the name of the personnel director through the directories in the library. You can also call on the phone and say, "I'm writing to ask about employment at your company. To whom should I address my letter?" If you can't find a name, use a standard salutation. It's a good idea to enclose a resume (described later in this essay) with the letter to give the employer a brief description of your educational and work experience.

Keep a list of all the people you write to, along with the date each letter was mailed, or keep a photocopy of each letter. Then you can follow up by writing a brief note or calling people who do not reply within about three weeks.

Job Databases Online

The World Wide Web can be an excellent resource for job hunters. The Internet currently has thousands of career-related sites where you can read about job openings or post your resume in a database for a possible match with available jobs.

Some sites, such as The Monster Board, help you build a resume and post it online as well as allow you to search through a massive database of help-wanted listings. Others employ a search engine to find jobs that match your background, then post your resume online for employers.

The Web site called CareerBuilder uses an interactive personal search program that lets you select job criteria such as location, title, and salary; you are then notified by e-mail when a matching position is posted in the database.

Many companies post job openings in their human resource Web pages. You can usually access these lists by visiting the Web site of a company and clicking on a link called "jobs," "careers," or "employment opportunities." If you find a job that interests you during your online search, whether it's posted at a company's own Web site or on a general listing of jobs, follow the directions given for applying for the position. Some online ads will provide the contact information you need to send your resume Many career-related Web sites can be found on the Internet. This hypothetical site allows job-seekers to search for a position by location and by job description (for illustration purposes only) and cover letter directly to the employer, either by e-mail or by traditional mail, but other ads direct job hunters to apply directly through a link at the job description.

Job hunters can often find job listings through the Web sites of the professional associations in their career fields. State government Web sites may also provide links to job listings- or to non-government sites that list available jobs.

Help-Wanted Ads

Many people find out about job openings by reading the "help-wanted" sections of newspapers, trade journals, and professional magazines. Employers and employment agencies often, though not always, use these classified ad sections to publicize available jobs. Classified ads use unique terms to convey basic information. You will find some common abbreviations in the chart in this essay titled "Reading the Classifieds." You can usually decode the abbreviations by using common sense, but if something puzzles you, call the newspaper and ask for a translation. Classified ads usually list the qualifications that are required for a particular job and explain how to contact the employer.

As you find openings that interest you, answer each ad using the method requested. Record the date of your contact, and if you don't hear from the employer within two or three weeks, place another call or send a polite note asking whether the job is still open. Don't forget to include your phone number and address in your initial contact.

Some help-wanted ads are "blind ads." These ads give contact information for replying but provide no name, phone number, or address that would identify the company. Employers and employment agencies may place these ads to avoid having to reply to all of the job applicants or being contacted directly by job-seekers.

Situation-Wanted Ads

Another way to get the attention of potential employers is with a situation-wanted ad. You can place one of these in the classified section of your local newspaper or of a trade journal in your field of interest. Many personnel offices and employment agencies scan these columns when they're looking for new employees. The situation-wanted ad is usually most effective for people who have advanced education, training, or experience, or who are in fields where their unique skills are in great demand.

A situation-wanted ad should be brief, clear, and to the point. Its main purpose is to interest the employer enough so you are contacted for an interview. It should tell exactly what kind of job you want, why you qualify, and whether you are available for full-time or part-time work. Use the same abbreviations that employers use in classified ads.

If you are already employed and do not want it known that you are looking for a new position, you can run a blind ad. A blind ad protects your privacy by listing a box number at the publication to which all replies can be sent. They are then forwarded to you. You do not need to give your name, address, or phone number in the ad.

Networking

A very important source of information about job openings is networking. This means talking with friends and acquaintances about your area of interest. If any of them have friends or relatives in the field, ask if they would be willing to speak with you. There's nothing wrong with telling anyone who will listen that you are looking for a job-family, friends, counsellors, and former employers. This will multiply your sources of information many times over.

You can use the Internet to make contacts, too. You can meet people with similar interests in news groups, which are organized by topic. Then you can correspond individually via e-mail. Many fields have professional organizations that maintain Web sites. These can help you keep current on news affecting your field, including employment opportunities. Sometimes a contact knows about a job vacancy before it is advertised. You may have an advantage, then, when you get in touch with the employer. Don't, however, use the contact's name without permission. Don't assume that a contact will go out on a limb by recommending you, either. Once you have received the inside information, rely on your own ability to get the job.

Placement Services

Most vocational schools, high schools, and colleges have a placement or career service that maintains a list of job openings and schedules visits from companies. If you are a student or recent graduate, you should check there for job leads. Many employers look first in technical or trade schools and colleges for qualified applicants for certain jobs. Recruiters often visit colleges to look for people to fill technical and scientific positions. These recruiters usually represent large companies. Visit your placement office regularly to check the job listings, and watch for scheduled visits by company recruiters.

State Employment Services

Another source of information about job openings is the local office of the state employment service. Many employers automatically list job openings at the local office. Whether you're looking for a job in private industry or with the state, these offices, which are affiliated with the federal employment service, are worth visiting, online or in person, if there are offices locally.

State employment service offices are public agencies that do not charge for their services. They can direct you to special programs run by the government in conjunction with private industry. These programs, such as the Work Incentive Program for families on welfare, are designed to meet special needs. Some, but not all, of these offices offer vocational aptitude and interest tests and can refer interested people to vocational training centers. The state employment service can be a valuable first stop in your search for work, especially if there are special circumstances in your background. For example, if you did not finish high school, if you have had any difficulties with the law, or if you are living in a difficult home environment, your state employment service office is equipped to help you.

PRIVATE EMPLOYMENT AGENCIES

State employment services, though free, are usually very busy. If you are looking for more personal service and want a qualified employment counselor to help you find a job, you might want to approach a private employment agency.

Private employment agencies will help you get a job if they think they can place you. Most of them get paid only if they're successful in finding you a job, so you need to show them that you are a good prospect. These agencies will help you prepare a resume if you need one, and they will contact employers they think might be interested in you.

Private employment agencies are in the business of bringing together people who are looking for jobs and companies that are looking for workers. For some positions, usually mid-and higher-level jobs, the employment agency's fee is paid by the employer. In such cases, the job seeker pays no fee. In other cases, you may be required to pay the fee, which is usually a percentage of your annual salary. Paying a fee can be a worthwhile investment if it leads to a rewarding career.

Some agencies may also ask for a small registration fee whether or not you get a job through them. Some agencies may demand that you pay even if you find one of the jobs they are trying to fill through your other contacts. Be sure to read and understand the fine print of any contract you're expected to sign, and ask for a copy to take home. Since the quality of these agencies varies, check to see if an agency is a certified member of a state or national association. Some employment agencies, called staffing services, operate in a different way. They are usually paid by employers to screen and refer good candidates for job openings. They earn money when they refer a candidate who is hired by the employer. The employee pays no fee. Staffing firms, however, only spend time on candidates they think they may be able to place. Private employment agencies are usually helping many people at one time. They may not have the time to contact you every time they find a job opening. Therefore, you may need to phone them at reasonable intervals after you have registered.

Civil Service

In your search for work, don't forget that the civil service-federal, state, and local-may have many jobs in your field. You may contact the state employment office or apply directly to the appropriate state or federal agency. The armed services also train and employ civilians in many fields. Don't neglect these avenues for finding jobs. Civil service positions usually require you to take a civil service examination. Books are available to help you prepare for these exams, and your local civil service office can also provide information.

Unions

In certain fields, unions can be useful sources of information. If you are a member of a union in your field of interest, you may be able to find out about jobs in the union periodical or through people at the union local. If you do not belong to a union, you may contact a union in the field you are interested in for information about available employment services. You will find addresses for some unions in the job profiles in this book.

Temporary Employment

A good way to get a feel for the job market-what's available and what certain jobs are like-is to work in a temporary job. There are both private and state agencies that can help place people in short-term jobs. Some jobs are seasonal, and extra workers may be needed in the summer or at another busy time.

Temporary employment can increase your job skills, your knowledge of a particular field, and your chances of hearing of permanent positions. In today's tight labour market, many companies are using the services of temporary workers in increasing numbers. In fact, temporary agencies may sign multimillion-dollar contracts to provide businesses with a range of temporary workers. In some cases, temporary workers are in such demand that they may receive benefits, bonuses, and the same hourly wages as equivalent permanent employees. Some temporary agencies are even joining with companies to create long-term career paths for their temporary workers.

Marketing Yourself

An employer's first impression of you is likely to be based on the way you present yourself on print. Whether it is in an application form or on a resume, you will want to make a good impression so that employers will be interested in giving you a personal interview. A potential employer is likely to equate a neat, well-written presentation with good work habits, and a sloppy, poorly written one with bad work habits.

Writing an Effective Resume

When you write to a company to follow up a lead or to ask about job openings, you should send information about yourself. The accepted way of doing this is to send a resume with a cover letter.

MANAGEMENT OF HOTELS

A hotel is an establishment that provides paid lodging, usually on a short-term basis. Hotels often provide a number of additional guest services such as a restaurant, a swimming pool or childcare. Some hotels have conference services and meeting rooms and encourage groups to hold conventions and meetings at their location. Hotels differ from motels in that most motels have drive-up, exterior entrances to the rooms, while hotels tend to have interior entrances to the rooms, which may increase guests' safety and present a more upmarket image.

In Australia, a hotel may also be an establishment that serves alcoholic drinks, and usually meals in a casual setting but which does not necessarily provide accommodation. This type of establishment would more usually be called a pub or bar in other countries. In general use in Australia the terms "'hotel" and *pub* are usually taken to be synonymous.

In India, the word may also refer to a restaurant since the best restaurants were always situated next to a good hotel.

ORIGINS OF THE TERM

The word *hotel* derives from the French *hotel*, which referred to a French version of a townhouse, not a place offering accommodation (in contemporary usage, *hotel* has the meaning of "hotel", and *hotel particulier* is used for the old meaning). The French spelling (with the circumflex) was once also used in English, but is now rare. The circumflex replaces the 's' once preceding the 't' in the earlier *hostel* spelling, which over time received a new, but closely related meaning.

SERVICES AND FACILITIES

Basic accommodation of a room with only a bed, a cupboard, a small table and a washstand has largely been replaced by rooms with en-suite bathrooms and, more commonly in the United States than elsewhere, climate control. Other features found may be a telephone, an alarm clock, a TV, and broadband Internet connectivity. Food and drink may be supplied by a mini-bar (which often includes a small refrigerator) containing snacks and drinks (to be paid for on departure), and tea and coffee making facilities (cups, spoons, an electric kettle and sachets containing instant coffee, tea bags, sugar, and creamer or milk). In the United Kingdom a hotel is required by law to serve food and drinks to all comers within certain stated hours;

to avoid this requirement it is not uncommon to come across "private hotels" which are not subject to this requirement. However, in Japan the capsule hotel supplies minimal facilities and room space.

CLASSIFICATION

The cost and quality of hotels are usually indicative of the range and type of services available. Due to the enormous increase in tourism worldwide during the last decades of the 20th century, standards, especially those of smaller establishments, have improved considerably. For the sake of greater comparability, rating systems have been introduced, with the one to five stars classification being most common.

BOUTIQUE HOTELS

"Boutique Hotel" is a term originating in North America to describe intimate, usually luxurious or quirky hotel environments. Boutique hotels differentiate themselves from larger chain or branded hotels by providing an exceptional and personalized level of accommodation, services and facilities.

Boutique hotels are furnished in a themed, stylish and/or aspirational manner. Although usually considerably smaller than a mainstream hotel (ranging from 3 to 100 guest rooms) boutique hotels are generally fitted with telephone and wi-fi Internet connections, honesty bars and often cable/pay TV. Guest services are attended to by 24 hour hotel staff. Many boutique hotels have on site dining facilities, and the majority offer bars and lounges which may also be open to the general public. Of the total travel market a small percentage are discerning travellers, who place a high importance on privacy, luxury and service delivery. As this market is typically corporate travellers, the market segment is non-seasonal, high-yielding and repeat, and therefore one which boutique hotel operators target as their primary source of income.

Famous Hotels

Some hotels have gained their renown through tradition, by hosting significant events or persons, such as Schloss

Cecilienhof in Potsdam, Germany, which derives its fame from the so-called Potsdam Conference of the World War II allies Winston Churchill, Harry Truman and Joseph Stalin in 1945. Other establishments have given name to a particular meal or beverage, as is the case with the Waldorf Astoria in New York City, USA, known for its *Waldorf Salad* or the Raffles Hotel in Singapore, where the drink *Singapore Sling* was invented. Another example is the Hotel Sacher in Vienna Austria, home of the *Sachertorte*.

There are also hotels which became much more popular through films like the Grand Hotel Europe in Saint Petersburg, Russia when James Bond stayed there in the Blockbuster, Goldeneye. Cannes hotels such as the Carlton or the Martinez become the center of the world during Cannes Film Festival (France). A number of hotels have entered the public consciousness through popular culture, such as the Ritz Hotel in London, UK ('Putting on The Ritz') and Hotel Chelsea in New York City, subject of a number of songs and also the scene of the alleged stabbing of Nancy Spungen by her boyfriend Sid Vicious. Hotels that enter folklore like these two are also often frequented by celebrities, as is the case both with the Ritz and the Chelsea. Other famous hotels include the Beverly Hills Hotel, the Hotel Bel-Air and the Chateau Marmont, in California, Watergate complex in Washington DC, the Hotel Astoria in Saint Petersburg, Russia, the Hotel George V and Hotel Ritz in Paris, Palazzo Versace hotel on the Gold Coast, Queensland, Australia, Hotel Hermitage and Hotel de Paris in Monaco (in the French Riviera), Peninsula Hotel in Hong Kong and Hotel Leningradskaya in Moscow.

Unusual Hotels

Many hotels can be considered destinations in themselves, by dint of unusual features of the lodging and/or its immediate environment:

Treehouse Hotels

Some hotels, such as the Costa Rica Tree House in the Gandoca-Manzanillo Wildlife Refuge, Costa Rica, or Treetops

Hotel in Aberdare National Park, Kenya, are built with living trees as structural elements, making them treehouses. The Ariau Towers near Manaus, Brazil is in the middle of the Amazon, on the Rio Negro. Bill Gates even invested and had a suite built there with satellite internet/phone. Another hotel with treehouse units is Bayram's Tree Houses in Olympos, Turkey.

Cave Hotels

Desert Cave Hotel in Coober Pedy, South Australia and the Cuevas Pedro Antonio de Alarcon (named after the author) in Guadix, Spain, as well as several hotels in Cappadocia, Turkey, are notable for being built into natural cave formations, some with rooms underground.

Capsule Hotels

Capsule hotels are a type of economical hotels that are quite common in Japan.

Ice Hotels

Ice hotels, such as the Ice Hotel in Jukkasjarvi, Sweden, melt every spring and are rebuilt out of ice and snow each winter.

Snow Hotels

The Mammut Snow Hotel in Finland is located within the walls of the Kemi snow castle, which is the biggest in the world. It includes The Mammut Snow Hotel, The Castle Courtyard, The Snow Restaurant and a chapel for weddings, etc. Its furnishings and its decorations, such as sculptures, are made of snow and ice.

There is snow accommodation also in Lainio Snow Hotel in Lapland (near Yllas), Finland.

Garden Hotels

Garden hotels, famous for their gardens before they became hotels, includes Gravetye Manor, the home of William Robinson and Cliveden, designed by Charles Barry with a rose garden by Geoffrey Jellicoe.

Underwater Hotels

As of 2005, the only hotel with an underwater room that can be reached without Scuba diving is Utter Inn in Lake Malaren, Sweden. It only has one room, however, and Jules' Undersea Lodge in Key Largo, Florida, which requires scuba diving, is not much bigger.

Hydropolis is an ambitious project to build a luxury hotel in Dubai, UAE, with 220 suites, all on the bottom of the Persian Gulf, 20 meters (66 feet) below the surface. Its architecture will feature two domes that break the surface and an underwater train tunnel, all made of transparent materials such as glass and acrylic.

Other unusual Hotels

The Library Hotel in New York City is unique in that its ten floors are arranged according to the Dewey Decimal System.

The Rogers Centre, formerly SkyDome, in Toronto, Canada is the only stadium to have a hotel connected to it, with 70 rooms overlooking the field.

The Burj al-Arab hotel in Dubai, United Arab Emirates, built on an artificial island, is structured in the shape of a sail of a boat.

The RMS Queen Mary in Long Beach, California is the only 1930s ocean liner still in existence. Its elegant first-class staterooms are now used as a hotel.

The Oriental Pearl Tower in Shanghai houses an extremely expensive hotel with only 20 rooms.

WORLD-RECORD SETTING HOTELS

Tallest

The tallest hotel in the world is the Burj al-Arab in Dubai, United Arab Emirates, at 321 metres, which however will soon be surpassed by the nearby Rose Rotana Suites at 333 meters (1,091 feet). The Ryugyong Hotel in Pyongyang was intended to reach 330 meters (1,083 feet), but is unlikely to be completed; it has been under construction since 1987 and was abandoned in 1992.

The highest hotel rooms are in the *Grand Hyatt* in the Jin Mao Building in Shanghai, the highest floor being at around 350 m.

Largest

The largest hotel in the world is the MGM Grand Las Vegas in Las Vegas, Nevada, USA with a total of 6,276 rooms as of December 20, 2006. On December 18, 2006 Guinness World Records listed the First World Hotel in Genting Highlands, Malaysia as the worlds largest hotel. It has a total of 6,118 rooms and is part of the Genting Highlands Resort and Casino. The First World Plaza which is joined to the two hotel towers boasts 500,000 square feet of indoor theme park, shopping centres, casino gaming areas, and eateries. Previously, Guinness had listed the MGM Grand Las Vegas in Las Vegas, Nevada, USA with 5,005 rooms as the largest hotel in the world.

Oldest

According to the Guinness Book of World Records, the oldest hotel still in operation is the Hoshi Ryokan, in Awazu, Japan. It opened in 717, and features hot springs.

HOTEL OCCUPATIONS

The owner, chairman, or CEO of a hotel or hotel group is known as a *hotelier*.

Living in Hotels

The American billionaire Howard Hughes lived much of his life in hotels. He moved with his entourage from hotel to hotel and from Beverly Hills to Boston before deciding to move to Las Vegas and become a casino baron. Less than a month after his November 27, 1966 arrival, Hughes made a public offer to buy the Desert Inn.

The hotel's 8th floor became the nerve center of his empire and the 9th floor penthouse became Hughes's personal residence. Hughes moved to the Bahamas, Vancouver, London and several other locations — always taking up residence in the top floor penthouse of the hotel. Between 1966 and 1968, he also purchased several other hotel-casinos from the Mafia: Castaways, New Frontier, The Landmark Hotel and Casino, Sands and Silver Slipper.

Coco Chanel made the Hotel Ritz in Paris her home for more than thirty years, until the day of her death, at 87, in a suite now named "Coco Chanel Suite".

King Peter II of Yugoslavia spent much of the Second World War at Claridge's, a hotel in London. His son, Aleksandar Karadordevis, was born in the hotel.

Prince Felix Yusupov lived in the Hotel Vendome in Paris.

Alois Brunner, Austrian Nazi war criminal, is believed to have lived in the Meridian Hotel in Damascus, Syria, under the name Georg Fischer.

Sultan Said Bin Taimur of Muscat lived at Dorchester Hotel in London after he was deposed by Qaboos of Oman in 1970, He died in the hotel in 1972.

Eleftherios Venizelos, Greek statesman and diplomat, lived in the Hotel Ritz Paris while he was in exile in France from 1935-1936.

HOTELS IN FICTION

Hotels have been chosen by authors as settings for crime fiction, farce and mystery works. A hotel is perfect as a mysterious, anonymous setting where various characters may gather. Hotels also feature in films, television series, songs and even theme park rides.

Taj Hotels

Taj Hotels Resorts and Palaces is the largest Indian luxury hotel chain. A wholly owned subsidiary of the Tata Group, Taj Hotels Resort and Palaces comprises 57 hotels in 39 locations across India with an additional 18 international hotels in the Maldives, Mauritius, Malaysia, Seychelles, United Kingdom, United States of America, Bhutan, Sri Lanka, Africa, the Middle East and Australia.

Their first and most well known property is the Taj Mahal Palace & Tower in Colaba, Mumbai. The Taj Mahal Palace &

Tower, Mumbai was opened on December 16, 1903, by the founder of the Tata Group, Jamshetji Nusserwanji Tata. Taj President-a business hotel and Taj Land's End-an ultimate luxury boarding are also located in Mumbai.

It operates TajAir, a luxury private jet operation with state-of-the-art Falcon 2000 aircraft designed by Dassault Aviation, France; and Taj Yachts, two 3-bedroom luxury yachts which can be used by guests in Mumbai and Kochi.

Falaknuma Palace

Falaknuma Palace is situated on a hill 650 meters in height, in the Old City of Hyderabad, India. It was built by Nawab Vikar-ul-Umra. It was purchased by the then Nizam VI during 1897 for use as a royal guest house. The palace provides a good view of Hyderabad.

The palace is spread out in a scorpion shape with two pincers spread out as wings on the north. The middle part occupies the main building. The Harem quarters and the kitchen stretch towards the south.

The palace was designed by an Italian architect. The palace boasts of lavishly decorated interiors made of the Italian marble, and follows a western architectural style. It took almost nine years to complete. This famous palace houses a large collection of rare treasures, paintings, statues, furniture, manuscripts and books collected by the Nizam. The jade collection displayed here is considered to be unique in the world. Some old models of artillery are also exhibited in the front. The Palace is being converted into a heritage hotel by the Taj Hotels group.

OPERATIONS OF THE HOTELS

No hotel company operating today can be unaware of the swift pace of global change and its impact on every facet of the hospitality industry. With just five years left in this century, we can expect change to be the only constant. New business practices are evolving virtually as fast as our technologies, while resistance to change has become one of the primary causes of business failure.

The specter of constant change raises fundamental questions as to the creation of shareholder wealth in a capital-constrained, highly competitive environment. How will hotel organizations build shareholder wealth, and what key drivers will result in success? What future products and services will be essential in a technology-driven, global environment marked by rising customer expectations? Moreover, what alternative approaches and skills must organizations develop to ensure market success?

The future success of hotel organizations will be driven in large part by the ability to foresee--and capitalize--on change. Beyond this truism, however, there is an urgent need to identify what will be required in the competitive environment of the future with its intense focus on serving customer needs.

The hospitality industry--as is the case with business generally--is subject to deep currents of change set in motion as economic and social systems shaped in the industrial era evolve to a knowledge-based era driven by technology advances.

In this period of global transition, it behooves hotel organizations to examine the key factors that will not only define success, but the ability to survive in coming years. Many of these issues were spotlighted in a global study undertaken by the Economist Intelligence Unit and co-sponsored by Arthur Andersen. The Successful Corporation of the Year 2000 surveyed more than 600 senior executives around the world. Its mission was to identify the characteristics needed to lead successful businesses in the next century. These executives offer a number of compelling messages regarding the key success factors of the future. Customers will have the strongest influence on the corporation in the year 2000. Indeed, these executives believe that the customer will be "king" in the new century. Exceptional leadership was by far the attribute most frequently cited by CEOs and senior executives; the consensus appears to be that successful companies in the year 2000 will be led by corporate visionaries.

A strategic planning focus is not only essential, but must embody a concept of planning for the future that anticipates change, rather than being based exclusively on historical models.

In structuring organizations for the future, companies must build management capabilities to deal with one of the most critical challenges--diversity in the marketplace. Employing information technology to drive business success in this information-driven era is not only the path of least resistance, but vital to virtually every aspect of operations.

The study's top-line results create an excellent backdrop to address key issues confronting the hotel industry, and what factors will lead to membership--rather than rejection--in the elite club of the world's corporate success stories in the year 2000.

FROM AN ASSET TO CUSTOMER FOCUS

Recognizing that the hotel industry has a somewhat split personality reflecting the inherent conflicts between its real estate and operational aspects, it is important to understand the industry's real estate origins and how they are shaping the challenges ahead.

The origins of the industry's real estate persona are embodied in the classic theory of location-"if we build it, they will come." As a result of this "building" complex, the industry has tended to have a real estate and asset orientation, rather than a customer focus. From the hotel company perspective--especially that of the brand-oriented "chain"--the varied interests of a diffused property ownership group can be quite different than the singular interest of the chain that operates and markets the properties.

Even when the ownership of geographically dispersed hotel properties is controlled by a single hotel organization, the financial structuring tends to be property-specific. Corporate financial strategies are frequently subjugated to the needs of the last property deal brought into the company's fold.

Each property in a so-called "chain," is frequently the subject of a unique and distinctive ownership and financial structure. This phenomenon--quite common in the real estate sector, but unusual for business enterprises generally--makes for elusive economies of scale in the structuring and financing of property-driven expansion. Collectively, these factors have produced low comparative returns in real estate, although criticism leveled at commercial real estate returns is somewhat less germane to the hotel industry, where management and franchise fees can produce high returns for those companies where property ownership is held by third parties. Nevertheless, average returns in the real estate industry in the United States, for example, are just over 10 percent, compared to small company stock returns at almost 20 percent and large company stocks at an average of about 15 percent.

While hotel chains have adopted traditional corporate frameworks, there are a number of predominantly real estate-driven, family-owned businesses in the hotel sector that continue to operate as relatively unstructured organizations. In meeting the future, these businesses will need plans, people and processes in order to establish viable corporate forms that can compete in tomorrow's marketplace and capitalize upon its opportunities.

In today's changed environment, the hotel organization must deal with a number of new realities. Investors in our industry are no longer satisfied with long-term capital appreciation and psychic income that heretofore were often the justification for otherwise seemingly uneconomic investments in hotel property or, indeed, hotel chains.

The first reality is that there is a very specific and identifiable relationship between bottom line performance and value. Improvements in business operations raises values. It is not surprising, therefore, that the new owners attracted to this industry in recent years have new sets of demands. This transformation from an old-guard group of investors and owners to income and return-driven newcomers has meant that the once "quiet enjoyment" of operators in their management of hotels for third parties is being disturbed, interrupted and overturned.

These challenges all take place in an environment where capital has become extremely selective in markets that have little stability. A global shortage of capital will not remain a short-term problem, and future hotel organizations must have a stronger alignment to capital providers--a critical "customer" group. Hotel companies will need to compete by offering better returns and performance than in the past. Hotel chains have found their development timetables quashed in recent years, making it difficult to achieve goals of critical mass often required to improve performance. These factors are driving consolidation in the brand "sweepstakes." Capital markets, therefore, continue to favour well-established companies, a reality that must drive entrepreneurial organizations to meet the future now by planning for an evolving corporate context in which to operate.

KEY SUCCESS FACTORS

Within this broad context, hotel developers, owners and management companies will all need to develop new strategies, skills and processes that look forward to the competitive demands of the future. These ultimately must address issues related to vision and planning, as well as organizational skill sets and processes to attract and retain customers. To stake a claim in the future, current business practices should be examined in light of what can be expected to be the key success factors in the year 2000.

Embrace a global change orientation. As the information age produces greater worldwide integration of business activities, a global knowledge base will become invaluable. Success in local and regional hotel markets will be shaped decisively by a global business environment that defines capital movement, customer expectations and applications of new technologies.

Focus on the Customer. If the customer is "king" in the 21st century, hotel organizations will be best served by focusing less on their hotel assets as measures of success, and more on their customers.

This involves a fundamental shift in viewing the real estate asset as the wealth creator--to the customer as the key to building shareholder wealth. A customer focus must imbue business decisions at all levels of developing and operating a hotel organization. Pursuing such a course will inevitably impact shareholder wealth. To accomplish this, however, customers need to participate in the product development process.

Fully realizing a customer focus in the industry poses a significant challenge. The hotel industry must confront problems due to conflicts between operational needs and real estate goals. Quite simply, an operator must remain customer-focused, but the short-term strategies to meet these needs may be inconsistent with the long-term objectives of property owners. Balancing those goals will be essential. A customer focus implies a significant shift in what drives hotel development--placing primary emphasis on the customer with the locations to follow. Nevertheless, a hotel organization with its large investment in fixed assets--the real estate--can never be as nimble as a consumer products company in adjusting products and services to match rapid shifts in the marketplace.

The Japanese taught us that the concept of "zero defects" in products and services can yield tremendous benefits. But today an even more rigorous standard dominates--quality that surprises. In practical terms, the hotel industry finds it extremely difficult to meet the standard of zero defects in service. Hotel services are based primarily on people, not computers or other equipment. Quality that surprises takes the concept of zero defects a step further. Yesterday's surprising product or service is today's status quo.

Twenty years ago, a business executive did not expect a consistent and predictable level of service wherever he or she travelled in the world. Today that is a standard--not the exception--as is the expectation for sophisticated technology in hotel rooms to support business needs. With customer discrimination so acute, it is not surprising that brand loyalty is a diminishing "commodity" in the hotel industry.

Find the ingredients for visionary leadership. Today's hotel organizations need to recognize the need for visionary leadership. The ability to forecast the future--to anticipate change rather than react to it--will be one of the single greatest determinants of market dominance in the years ahead. The old "command and control" model of leadership is giving way to a focus on leadership in ideas, information, inspiration, vision and teamwork. Warren Bennis, an authority on leadership in the U.S., puts it this way--"For the most part, failing organizations tend to be over-managed and under-led. The leader sets the tone for the moral character, the vision, the corporate culture and the fiber of the institution."

While visionary leadership is essential, it must be linked to business operations and foster a risk bias, rather than a procedural bias. This will allow the organization to stretch and, in turn, change. And it must be shared by empowered professionals and staff throughout the organization, including those who meet the customer. Overcoming the resistance to change can be a daunting task, particularly in large hotel organizations in which diversions from the status quo may threaten established management lines. It suggests that a culture based on conformance may need to be replaced by an emphasis on flexibility, learning and cooperation. Management competencies will need to be aligned in order to achieve the desired result. For many organizations, this may mean a shift from traditional hierarchies typical of companies in an industrial era to a flatter organization with a more transparent interface between leadership, organizational functions and employees.

Create a defensible position through corporate strategy. For many of the industry's leaders, vision is driven by the strategic planning process, a function which has become critical for success.

Strategic planning, however, has at times been a step-child in the hotel industry, and it is often the first to be cut when organizations are downsized. It is clearly in transition. There also has been a tendency to decentralize and simplify this function--both actions of potential benefit. Strategic planning must be led by the top people in the organization--the CEO and COO. On the other hand, it should be close enough to the customer to ensure that planners can "listen" to and be influenced by customer needs.

Empower Management: Beyond the ability to envision the future, core management capabilities will make the difference--they are essential. A clear vision without the management skills to support it cannot be a recipe for success. First and foremost, hotel management must have strategic development skills and the ability to integrate complex factors affecting success. Market volatility has become the norm, in part caused by the rapidly changing tastes of customers. Customers are increasingly approaching the hotel industry with widely different social, economic and political backgrounds, to say nothing of employees. Being able to deal with these diversities in a positive and constructive fashion that capitalizes on the differences, rather than working to find ways to mitigate them, is the clear path for successful management in the future.

The organization will also need to be imbued with a sense of entrepreneurship that reacts proactively to the market's diversity. Traditional organizations that follow well-documented rules must give way to leaders who can balance a sense of discipline with that of flexibility. Talent and resources must be marshalled and leveraged. In an industry with high fixed costs and labour intensity, the concept of leverage in the hotel business is an all-important one. Improving labour productivity through technology must be a goal for today's forward-looking hotel organization. Management must also be able to narrow the gap between the employer and the employee, forcing a flatter organization in the process. This will put management closer to the customer and speed the two-way communication process up and down the organization.

Be in the Information Fast Lane: The traditional role of information technology (IT) as a back office support for accounting and bookkeeping has clearly moved front and center stage. IT today influences all aspects of business from corporate strategies to organizational structure--and from the very business processes it is designed to support to performance measurement. In a world where the customer is "king," IT must also deliver in two critical areas: sales and marketing and customer service.

Technology was once viewed as a way to reduce costs by replacing people. That attitude has been firmly supplanted by one that seeks IT support for the creative work that all organizations must pursue. IT must allow organizations to react more speedily to market needs and, of course, produce the fulfilment of customer demands both quickly and accurately. To do this IT must operate on a decentralized basis. IT delivers but it has to be the right information to the right people, and it needs to be done on a timely basis.

IMPROVING MANAGEMENT (GEF) PROJECT

Improving Management of NGO and Privately Owned Nature Reserves and High Biodiversity Islands in Seychelles Project funded by the Global Environment Facility through the World Bank

The Seychelles is known world wide as a storehouse of rare biodiversity. Historically, most of the islands and ecosystems have been severely impacted by human activities. Nevertheless, a few examples of whole island ecosystems have been protected and restored. These islands are Cousin, Cousine, Aride, Fregate and Aldabra, all managed, surprisingly, by civil society organisations. Nevertheless, there are significant barriers to sustainability of conservation efforts by these organisations.

The focus of the project is two islands, Cousin and Cousine, which are host to numerous rare and endemic species, and immense biodiversity. These include shared resources such as 10 species of breeding seabirds, 5 species of endemic land birds, rare floral species, 8 species of reptiles and hundreds species of invertebrates, the most important population of hawksbill turtles in the Western Indian Ocean and the highest biomass of reef fish in the granitic islands of Seychelles.

The project is to ensure the islands' function as a reserve for the preservation of globally important biodiversity through understanding processes and changes in sites, species and habitats in the islands for better management and decision-making on activities to preserve this globally important biodiversity.

Cousin and Cousine are adjacent to Praslin-the second most populous island of the Seychelles. Cousin was purchased in the 1960's through a world wide appeal at a time when unique biodiversity in Seychelles was in jeopardy. An international NGO held the title to the island because land tenureship was the only method of securing the island for perpetuity and thereby restoring the ecosystems. This NGOs also assisted the previous owners of Cousine in the early years to conserve its biodiversity. This proved to be a very wise move because the islands are remarkable in that unlike other granitic islands of Seychelles, endemic and globally important fauna and flora have been saved.

They have been protected by NGO/private resources and management, and at least for Cousin, through national legislation and policy.

The ownership and management regimes by civil society organisations and the relative remoteness, which are the main reasons why biodiversity has been saved, are now proving to be constraints for not only continuing with established activities but also for initiating new programs; the civil society organisations cannot source adequate resources from the local private sector, governmental or international sources. In addition, anthropogenic impacts and lack of knowledge of ecosystem-level changes, all mean that science and conservation action on each of them cannot move beyond present capacity and limits. The project assumption is that conservation of island biodiversity can be sustained and at the same time greatly improved through an inter-island integrated and collaborative approach geared to clear management outcomes and also to the development of public education and community buy-in.

The project recognises the importance of developing financial sustainability to maintain these conservation programs. The project intends to build long-term capacity for sustainable conservation and use of island biodiversity through program and capacity building, infrastructure acquisition and installation, co-management, and education and advocacy.

The two islands are small, close to each other, and share similar and sensitive ecosystems, associated conservation activities and problems. They are both focused on biodiversity conservation, chiefly concerning globally threatened endemic land birds and internationally important colonies of breeding seabirds. Each island also hosts similar important reptile, botanical and invertebrate species. Both islands have a distinguished conservation history and offer a slightly different model and philosophy for biodiversity conservation. Cousin Island is owned by an international NGO but managed by an independent, locally registered, not-for-profit Association. Cousine Island is owned and managed by a private limited company registered in Seychelles. Management of the islands are supposed to be undertaken with in-country resources.

PROJECT VISION

The project will remove barriers that currently prevent civil society organisations from augmenting and enhancing their capacity to conserve and restore species, sites and habitats.

The project will aims to create partnerships between neighbouring islands which have shared globally important biodiversity and similar environmental issues. This will be done through a substantial number of new and improved linked programs, the creation of a common resource and management center, institutional strengthening and capacity building, and public education and advocacy.

The ultimate aim of this model partnership is to catalyze further collaboration and public buy-in, to remove other barriers and to mitigate negative ecosystem changes. The process set in motion by the project will improve the management of high biodiversity islands as well as increase the number of managed conservation sites in Seychelles. This project will thus have global biodiversity benefits, lead to greater sustainability of biodiversity and permit the sharing of these benefits to be directed principally at local levels. The vision mirrors the three principal objectives of the 1992 Convention of Biological Diversity.

OVERALL GOAL OF THE PROJECT

The Goal of the project is to improve management of biodiversity-rich islands by installing a shared multi-pronged programme framework and infrastructure for enhanced and sustainable conservation, financing and use of biodiversity. The project vision and overall goal will be delivered through two principal components namely Small Island Ecosystem Management, and Public Education and Advocacy.:.

Component 1: Small Island Ecosystem Management

A. Improved management of terrestrial and marine habitats and important species.

B. Establish collaborative management and resource center on Praslin

C. Institutional strengthening

D. Capacity building and training

Component 2: Public Education and Advocacy

A. Develop biodiversity awareness and advocacy programs

B. Establish community outreach, partnerships and stakeholder participation programs

PROJECT PARTNERS

Nature Seychelles, formerly known as Bird Life Seychelles, is a local not-for-profit association registered in Seychelles.

It is currently the largest independent environment organisation in Seychelles. The association is involved in a suite of activities including species and habit conservation, monitoring, research, island restoration, eco-tourism, education and awareness and advocacy.

Nature Seychelles manages Cousin Island Special Reserve and has a presence on several other islands. It has a multi-stakeholder and result-oriented approach through its programs such as the Seychelles Magpie-robin Recovery Team (SMART) and the Seychelles Seabird Group (SSG) as well with other organisations such as the Wild Life Clubs of Seychelles, Ministry of Environment and Ministry of Education.

Its donors and partners include the World Bank/GEF and the Royal Society for Protection of Birds. It is a member of the Bird Life International network, WIOMSA, the African Bird Club and IUCN, works in close collaboration with WWF, the Mauritian WildLife Foundation and many others.

Cousine Island LTD (Owner and Manger of Cousine Island): is a private limited company registered in the Seychelles. The company has built a very small and ecologically friendly luxury hotel. The island is not legally protected and the owner is not obliged to conserve its biodiversity. The company has voluntarily put in a system for biodiversity conservation using its own resources. It delegates management responsibility for the island to a Conservation Warden.

The Warden works in close collaboration with the hotel manager. The purpose of setting up the small hotel is to bring in sufficient revenues to maintain the conservation and research programs on the island and to maintain it as a high biodiversity area. The company supports other conservation programs in Seychelles, for example the Magpie Robin Recovery Program and the Seychelles Rare Birds Committee.

LANDMARKS ACHIEVEMENTS

Hotel Association of India, established on 24th October 1996, within a short span of less than a decade of its inception, has successfully provided an integrated hospitality platform produced ground breaking results and recorded several notable 'firsts' for the hospitality industry described in the ensuing pages:

Export House Status for Tourism and Hospitality Industry

Among the path breaking industry 'first' initiatives of Hotel Association of India is the unique recognition secured for tourism and hospitality sectors in India as 'export industries'. This was an unparelled achievement of the Association which undertook the entire groundwork and created consensus in support of according export status for hospitality industries. HAI organized series of inter-active meetings with the concerned Ministries of the Government of India, culminating in a high level Conclave presided over by Shri Ramakrishna Hegde, then Hon'ble Minister of Commerce, Government of India, on 16th July 1998 at the Oberoi Hotel, New Delhi which cleared the decks for the action plan blue-printed by HAI receiving the official seal of approval of the Government of India manifested in the a Gazette Notification of November 26th, 1998 declaring Hotels and Tourism Units eligible for the benefits of Service

Export House/International Service Export House/International Star Service Export House/International Super Star Service Export House categories on the basis of their quantum of foreign exchange earnings.

This extraordinary recognition placed hotels and tourism units on par with industries engaged in export of products for imports of projects and products against their foreign exchange entitlements and facilitated hotels in acquiring competitive edge vis-a-vis hotels overseas in providing world class facilities.

Tourism Export Promotion Council

Another notable first for hospitality and tourism industries, synchronizing with the grant of Export House Status, was notched by the Hotel Association of India by formulating the Constitution of the Tourism Export Promotion Council (TEPC) on 20th November 1998. The approval of the Company Law Board was also secured for the new body under Section 25 of the Companies Act 1956. TEPC represented an unique experiment in bringing together for the first time all constituents of the tourism sector-hotels, travel agents, tour operators, transporters, airlines, tourism finance companies-under a single umbrella on a common platform.

Establishment of SAARC Hotel Association

HAI reached beyond the national boundaries to provide regional co-operation aiming hotels in South Asia and became the prime mover in the formation of the SAARC Hotel Association. This was achieved by developing close synergy between the hospitality industry organizations of Bangladesh, Bhutan, India, Maldives, Nepal, Pakistan and Sri Lanka. The SAARC Hotel Association was formally launched at Mumbai on 7th April 1999 with Nepal being assigned the responsibility of hosting the SAARC body for its initial two years and later by rotation by other member countries.

International Code of Conduct to Govern Relations Between Hoteliers, Travel Agents and Tour Operators

For the first time in the history of travel trade in India on 28.4.2000, HAI successfully evolved consensus among the

Travel Agents Association of India (TAAI) and the Indian Association of Tour Operators (IATO) and the Hotel Association of India (HAI) resulting in the signing of the International Code of Practice governing the relations between Hoteliers, Travel Agents and Tour Operators.

The code represents a watershed for the tourism and travel industry in India, as protracted negotiations for adopting a code of practice for over three decades had not yielded any results till HAI took the lead and crafted consensus in favour of adopting the global practice. It's signing by the three national bodies signalled to the international travel fraternity and business travellers that India had opted for internationally approved policies of hotel bookings, cancellations, refunds, claims etc.

Legal 'First' for Hotel Industry

The Hotel Association of India took the lead in invoking the intervention of the High Court of Delhi in protecting the interests of hospitality industry in India on a matter of vital importance to the hotels as well as to the foreign and domestic tourist staying in hotels. Hotel Association of India filed a writ in the High Court Delhi against an arbitrary and ad hoc administrative directive requiring the hotels in approved categories, classified by the Ministry of Tourism, to follow a Single Tariff system. The directive would have proved detrimental and counter productive to national tourism interests. The industry perspective presented by HAI was accepted by the High Court of Delhi which granted a Stay in favour of hotel industry, signifying an unique legal validation of hospitality industry system of operation across the country.

Seeking Repeal of Anti-women Legislation

The Punjab Excise Act enacted during the British rule in India in 1914 contains an archaic and anti-women provision prohibiting the employment of women in licenced premises, i.e., bars and restaurants in hotels. The Hotel Association of India challenged the validity of this ancient legislation before the Hon'ble High Court to protect the interest of women. The

HAI's Writ against the constitutional validity of the provisions of the Punjab Excise Act, 1914

Media Centric Initiatives

The large number of foreign correspondents stationed in India, representing powerful and popular foreign publications, newspapers, journals, T. V. Channels, Broadcasters play a major role in making or marring the image of India as a peaceful tourists destination country through their news reports and dispatches. HAI took the lead in organizing the first ever hospitality industry meeting with the foreign correspondent stationed in New Delhi.

The event was organized with the objective to discuss adverse the impact of Travel Advisories issued by foreign Governments on the State of Indian hospitality and tourism industry and correct their perspective to restore consumer confidence in travel, tourism and hospitality sectors adversely affected by global events of preceding years. Because of the unique nature of the special event and its potential for future tourists arrivals in India, the Ministry of Tourism fully associated with HAI.

Survey on the Impact of Travel Advisories in Hospitality Industry

Foreign Embassies and Missions are often instrumental in advising their respective countries to issue "Travel Advisories" to caution their citizens from undertaking visits to specific countries owing to adverse conditions of safety and security. Travel Advisories against visiting India were issued by several countries following global events like the terrorist attacks on 9/11 in USA and 13/12 in New Delhi, War in Afghanistan and tension on Indo-Pak borders etc. The adverse travel advisories affected tourists arrivals to India over a prolonged period.

The Hotel Association of India stepped in by organizing an innovative Survey among foreign tourists staying in hotels to obtain their reactions to such advisories issued by the foreign governments. The HAI Survey brought out that a preponderant majority of tourists declared India as a safe and peaceful destination and foreign travellers viewed the travel advisories and warnings as "coloured by political considerations" and based on "inadequate knowledge of ground realities". Some of them opined that they found New Delhi "safer than Manhattan". HAI Survey facilitated the Governments of the respective countries in reviewing and withdrawing the adverse travel advisories and re-assured tourists of their safety and security in India.

Setting Up of Confederation of Indian Travel and Tourism Industry

Another first initiative mooted by the Association related to the need for creating a Confederation of Indian Travel and Tourism Industry (CITTI) as an umbrella organization to represent all components of the Travel & Travel industry in India. Unlike other industries, there has never been an umbrella organization in the tourism industry. To fill this gap, HAI proposed the setting up of CITTI which would address the policy issues and concerns of the industry. The Constitution of the proposed new body has been drawn up and made available to all sectoral associations to facilitate its establishment in the future.

Study of Tariff System in Hotels

The first ever 'While Paper' on Tariff Systems in Hotels in India, produced by a Central Government Autonomous Organisation the National Institute of Public Finance and Policy (NIPFP), was undertaken at the behest of the Hotel Association of India. The NIPFP headed by eminent economists of the standing of Dr. Raja J Chelliah, former Chief Economic Advisor of the Government of India and Dr. C. Rangarajan, former Governor of the Reserve Bank of India, provided the Indian hospitality industry with its most appropriate perspective and authentic study of tariff systems.

First Afro-Asian Infotech Hotels Expo

HAI-led initiative resulted in Afro-Asian Region's first Conference-cum-Exposition on Information Technology being institutionalized as 'an annual event in New Delhi for countries in the South Asian Region. The first Conference-cum-Expo organized by HAl on April 10-11, 2000 at the ITC Maurya Sheraton Hotel, New Delhi received support from the United Nations Economic and Social Commission for Asia and the Pacific, and the SAARC Tourism Council. The Ministries of Tourism and Information Technology, Government of India, extended official support to HAl as Co-sponsors of the event.

Second Afro-Asian Infotech-hotels Expo

The Second Conference-cum-Exposition on Information Technology in Hotels was organized on March 15-16, 2001 at the Taj Palace Hotel, New Delhi. This Afro-Asian conference was supported by United Nation Economic and Social Commission for Asia and like the front conference the Pacific (UN-ESCAP); Ministry of Tourism, Ministry of Information Technology, Government of India, SAARC Tourism Council and SAARC Hotel Association, Pacific Asia Travel Association (PATA) and International Hotel & Restaurant Association (IH&RA).

Creating a National Network of HAI Chapters

The Hotel Association of India, established in April 1997, enlisted co-operation on a voluntary basis of professional hoteliers in twenty five State and fifty three cities to monitor hospitality related developments to enable the Association to address the concerns of the hospitality industry at the grass-roots level.

Going Global with Knowledge Exchange Partners

Knowledge Exchange partnerships were formed with international organization such as the World Travel and Tourism Council (WTTC); the Pacific Asia Travel Association (PATA); World Tourism Organisation (WTO); the International Hotel and Restaurant Association (IH&RA); the United Nation Economic and Social Commission for Asia and the Pacific (UN-ESCAP); the South Asia Association of Regional Countries (SAARC), the World Health Organisation (WHO) and the European Union's South Asia Integrated Tourism Human Resource Development Programme (EU-SAITHRDP).

Inter-sectoral Linkages With Apex National Fora

At the National level working partnerships were established with apex industry for a like the Federation of Indian Chamber of Commerce and Industry (FICCI); Associated Chamber of Commerce and Industry of India (ASSOCHAM); Confederation of Indian Industry (CII); to provide hospitality industry perspective in the formation of national industrial policies and development.

Affiliation with World Health Organisation (WHO)

HAI's pioneered the concept of 'Healthy Hotels' in line with WHO's 'Healthy Cities' campaign by initiating programmes for the hospitality industry on 'Hygiene Management in Hotels' at Agra in 1997. The WHO representative in India delivered the keynote address at the First Hygiene Management Seminar.

Innovative-"India Quiz Contest" at ITB Berlin 2002

A new promotional first was scored by the HAI at ITB Berlin, held from 16th to 20th March 2002.

This was the first time 25 leading Indian hotels were brought together by HAI on the industry net to sponsor prizes of FAM Holiday Tours to Travel Trade visitors at the ITB. The India Quiz Contest brochure of HAI provided a high visibility to the Indian hospitality industry products among visitor to the ITB, Berlin.

The participating hotels received excellent marketing exposure of their properties in the Quiz brochure. This also offered unique opportunities for prospective agents and operator for the familiarization and experience of the hotels.

Guidelines for Provision of Disabled Friendly Facilities in Hotels

The Association undertook a pioneering role in formulating a comprehensive set of Guidelines for provision of Disabled Friendly facilities in Hotels, especially in parking and Approach Areas, Lobbies, Public Areas, Lifts, Rooms, Bathrooms and to install special Fire Prevention measures for the disabled.

Promoting Public-Private Partnership

The Association in a step towards promoting the public-private partnership called upon its members to extend their full corporation to the Archeological Survey of India in the maintenance of the National monuments, which has translated into following public-private sector partnership:-

(i) Illumination of Humayun's Tomb at Delhi by the Oberoi Group of Hotels.

(ii) Development of facilities for visitors at the Agra Fort by the ITC Hotels Ltd.

(iii) Main entrance of the Jantar Mantar observatory at New Delhi by the Apeejay Surrendra Park Hotels Pvt. Ltd.

(iv) Illumination of the Safdarjung Tomb, New Delhi by the Grand Group of

62 Special Promotional Packages in Hotels

A major initiative undertaken by HAI galvanized the entire Indian hospitality industry to come together under the Association's banner to offer for the first time in the history of the industry as many as 62 special promotional packages in hotels for marketing averages in association with Air India.

Memorandum of Undertakings Signed with the Hotel Association of Nepal and the Uganda Investment Authority

The Hotel Association of India signed two Memorandum of Understanding which aimed at fostering and promoting tourism in their respective countries by inter alia agreeing to exchange information in respect to development and trend in the fields of tourism, hospitality and hotel sectors and encourage interaction between their respective hotels and Hospitality Association of India for Tourism Promotion and exploring investment opportunities in these sectors.

India Quiz Contest Brochure at 51st PATA Annual Conference

Encouraged by the overwhelming response received from the ITB Berlin, HAI launched its exclusive India Quiz Contest at the 51st PATA Annual Conference held in New Delhi from 14.04.2002 to 18.04.2002 offering opportunities of FAM Holiday in 14 leading Hotels.

Study Project on Management of Cross-cultural Tourists Movements in Hospitality Sector

HAI initiated a study project on Management of cross-cultural tourism movements in hospitality sector to assess and promote awareness among staff in smaller hotel and upgrade their knowledge and skills for handling of foreign tourists.

Grant of Fiscal Benefits to the Hospitality Industry

For the first time the tourism industry's aspirations elaborated in the Hotel Association of India's various memoranda to the Central Government were translated into "tourism-friendly", measures in the Union Budget of 2003-04. These measures were aimed at making India more affordable destination, fuelling growth of hospitality infrastructure, facilitating business re-organisation, re-structuring hospitality industry and motivating State Governments to rationalize tourism tax regime. The major incentives extended to hospitality industries included and exemption of Service tax in hotels relating to Conference and Banquet business, which have been excluded from the service tax net.

Encouraging Investments

Hotel Association of India orchestrated the strategy leading to announcement in the Union Budget 2003 of benefits under Section 10(23) (g) on loans to hotels (3 star and above categories) for increasing the availability of funds for the hotel industry.

This provision has allowed lending institutions to make available funds to hotel projects at reduced rates of interest. The financial institutions will get a tax break on the interest income they earn on loans extended to such borrowers.

Inclusion of finance to the hotel projects of three star category and above for the first time under Section 10 (23)(g) of the Income Tax Act "signals" the positioning of hotels on the threshold of securing full infrastructure status as granted to other industries. HAI is now carrying this agenda forward to securing the wider benefits of infrastructure under Section 84 I/A of Income Tax Act.

Restructuring Hospitality Business

Amalgamation and Merger

It is at the behest of HAI that the Finance Ministry constituted a Working group under Chief Commissioner of Income Tax Mumbai which recommended the grant of benefits under Section 72 A of the Income Tax Act (which relates to the set-off of accumulated losses and depreciation on amalgamation), for the hotel industry to help loss-making hotel companies in re-organising their business. The facility of mergers and acquisitions was hitherto available only to industrial undertakings and manufacturing units. With its extension to hotel companies, it has facilitated moves towards consolidation with the hospitality industry and releasing of resources blocked in non-performing assets. This measure has now enabled smaller hotel units to enter into franchisee arrangements with established hotel groups/chains which in turn has led to improvements in occupancy levels and service standards.

Zero Duty Facility for Imports by Hotels

HAI pursued with the Ministry of Commerce, Government of India for grant of the zero duty import facility to hotels and standalone restaurants. The Industry has now been granted under the "Served from India Scheme", the zero duty facility to all hotels including one star, two star hotels for import of food items and alcoholic beverages sell which would make India an affordable destination.

HAI Directory of Hotels Going Global

The exclusive HAI Directory of Hotels is an annual publication promoted with a singular aim of fulfilling the promotional need for tourists and visitor coming to India for an authentic compendium of leading Indian hotels recognized by the Ministry of Tourism. For the first time in 2005 the Directory was utilized by the Ministry of Tourism for distribution among foreign travel agents and tour operators in 12 countries through the Government of India's Tourist Offices abroad.

World Tourism Day Celebration

A new promotional first was scored by HAI for creating awareness about the World Tourism Day on 27th Sept. 2005 amongst not only the member-hotels but also the school children. To encourage and facilitate the member-hotels in celebrating the World Tourism Day on 27th September 2005, HAI outlined a bouquet of activities to be organized by the member-hotels. The member-hotels came forward in large numbers and organized the activities with enthusiasm and excitement. In New Delhi, HAI collaborated with the Sanskriti School to launch a Quiz Contest on Tourism for school children on the World Tourism Day.

Members Services

Variety of professional member-services are provided by HAI to its members these include:-

(i) INFORMATION BULLETINS sent out regularly with updates on latest developments concerning hotel industries, policy changes and pronouncements by Ministry of Tourism, Ministry of Finance, Ministry of Commerce, CBEC, CBDT, State Governments and affiliate international organizations such as WTTC, IH&RA, WTO etc.;

(ii) HAI TODAY-the first hospitality industry magazine of its kind in India;

(iii) HAI DIRECTORY OF HOTELS-an exclusive high quality reference manual of recognized hotels in India;

(iv) HAI PRIVILEGE CARDS which are offered to members in the Gold and Silver Categories entitling them to discounts on hotel room tariffs and restaurants outlets in all member hotels on reciprocal basis;

(v) HAI LEGAL SERVICES which enables members to avail benefits of highest calibre legal advice on issues of concern them and interventions on their behalf in courts.

HAI GREEN WEEKS

HAI has successfully institutionalized the concept of celebrating annual green weeks in hotels to exhibit its commitment to conservation of environment through use of bio-degradable and environment-friendly products by efficient management of waste generated and by adopting measures for efficient utilization of day light to conserve upon electricity etc. HAI has this year celebrated its ninth annual green week, reaching out to large number of tourists, employees, their families, school children and society with its environment message.

Fundamentals of Revenue Management will be Revealed in a Special Report Commissioned by HSMAI Special Interest Group

MCLEAN, VA The Hospitality Sales & Marketing Association International (HSMAI) Revenue Management Special Interest Group has taken on an ambitious project to produce the first-ever comprehensive "Fundamentals of Revenue Management" special report.

The report will be a practitioner-friendly publication that addresses the fundamentals of revenue management for a broad audience of hospitality professionals. With comprehensive content that is both readable and actionable, it will deliver tools and information for revenue management education, incorporating expert advice from interviews with industry executives and educators, case studies, and practical checklists for implementing successful revenue management strategies at the property level.

"Creating relevance for members and the industry at large through groundbreaking initiatives such as this Revenue Management Special Report is in keeping with HSMAI's mission to be the leading source for sales and marketing information, knowledge and business development for professionals in tourism, travel, and hospitality," states Robert A. Gilbert, CHME, CHA, president and CEO of HSMAI.

"We are very excited about this debut project, and expect it will be a springboard for other initiatives including certification and revenue management research," notes Tim Wiersma, vice president of revenue management for Host Marriott and chair of HSMAI's Revenue Management Tangible Resources Committee. The publication will be produced in a manner similar to the recent special report produced by HSMAI and TIG Global entitled DeMystifying Distribution, widely praised by the industry for its insight, accuracy and comprehensive coverage of the topic.

The commissioned report, which will be released at the third annual HSMAI Revenue Management Strategy Conference on June 19, 2005 in Minneapolis, will be co-authored by Caryl Helsel and Kathleen Cullen of the Solutionz Group, a business development and strategic consulting group based in Florida. Helsel heads the hospitality practice and previously held executive positions with Kimpton Hotels, Pegasus Solutions and Mandarin Oriental Hotel Group, and is the former president of the Hotel Electronic Distribution Network Association (HEDNA). Cullen is a lead consultant on the hospitality team and is a hospitality revenue management and distribution veteran, holding executive positions with Swissotel and Raffles Hotels, as well as past vice president of HEDNA.

Delving deep into the fundamentals, nuances and specifics of revenue management, the special report will address the following:

- Ideas and initiatives to maximize revenue opportunities, optimize profits by managing revenues and develop an infrastructure (strategies, policies, procedures, reports, etc.) to make informed decisions about accepting or rejecting business.
- An overview of the external market such as segmentation, demand forecasting, revenue strategy, operational forecast, interdepartmental integration, strategic pricing, inventory control strategies and internal performance analysis.
- Tactics including rate-level maintenance, inventory management and rate offer assessment (for group and negotiated rates).

- The optimal environment, characteristics and descriptors.

The Revenue Management Special Interest Group is made up of a group of HSMAI members who advance the revenue management discipline through education, certification, participation, resources and guidance, enabling leaders to optimize revenue and performance within their own organizations.

The SIG Advisory Board includes corporate revenue management executives from Accor North America, Destination Hotels & Resorts, Host Marriott Corporation, Hilton Hotels, InterContinental Hotels Group, Outrigger Hotels & Resorts, Peabody Hotels, Preferred Hotel Group, and TravelCLICK.

Among the Board's strategic intentions are:

- Provide education on all levels through programs, events, and an annual strategy conference as well as provide education for senior executives through publications, press releases and conference participation.
- Develop and manage a revenue management certification program.
- Develop a sense of community and participation.
- Provide tangible resources through a fundamentals publication that defines the discipline of revenue management and includes a glossary of terms, maintain a website portal, create a self-auditing system and encourage industry internships.

2

Expectations from the Industry

This is a pilot study designed to help in the development of a large-scale research project on the future of work in the hospitality industry. The hospitality industry has experienced a wave of restructuring, consolidation, and new practices to cut costs including lean staffing and greater performance demands on the workforce. The study will explore the impact of these and related changes on the health and quality of life the largest occupational group within the hospitality industry, room cleaners.

Jobs in housekeeping (and food and beverage) operations of the hospitality industry represent the future of work in this growing service sector with jobs characterized by increasing repetitive physical workloads, low income, low skill utilization, low job control, and virtually no prospects for training and career advancement. There is compelling evidence that this kind of low-income jobs result in a disproportionate high burden of illness, injury, and disability.

Unlike other services, businesses in the hospitality industry, cannot be moved across the borders but will remain a fast growing sector in industrialized countries, creating increasing societal costs including disproportionate workers' compensation and health care utilization costs. Working conditions in the hospitality industry are representative for a growing number of workers of colour, working women, and former welfare recipients. The hospitality industry has become a major target for welfare-to-work and job training programs in cities throughout the country. An aging workforce is faced with increasing job demands in a competitive industry constantly upgrading services. Few studies have been done on this growing workforce and little is known about their specific working conditions and health risks and how they could be addressed. This study will take a broad view at physical and psychosocial job factors, health, including general self-rated health, musculoskeletal disorders, work-related injury, and health-related quality of life.

Further, this study will investigate which innovative organizational strategies can help to reduce the burden of illness and disability in the service sector by comparing hotels in different market segments, different degrees of unionization, and hotels with innovative joint labour management health and safety programs, negotiated child care/elder care benefits, and a multi-employer worker training project. San Francisco is expected to provide several union and non-union cases for comparison to similar cases in low union density markets and to a selected number of additional cases in other high union density markets that highlight organizational innovations (such as training and career laddering in Las Vegas or work redesign in New York to avoid sub-contracting).

The pilot study focuses on housekeeping since it is the largest occupational category in the industry and is the central focus of a larger study including hotels in other cities. The study combines qualitative and quantitative research methods and is participatory in design and implementation thereby laying the groundwork for sustainable efforts in understanding and improving health and safety of service workers.

COOPERATIVE SETTING

The pilot study is administered by the director of the Labour and Occupational Health Program (LOHP) at UC Berkeley Robin Baker, in collaboration with Niklas Krause, physician epidemiologist from the School of Public Health at UC Berkeley. Funding is provided by the United Way of the Bay Area and Local 2 of the Hotel Employees and Restaurant Employees International Union (HERE).

The level of union density in San Francisco is among the highest in the country. The largest union is HERE Local 2 which represents 8,000 workers or around 70 % of the industry's non-supervisory workforce. In San Francisco the multi-employer bargaining agreement with about 50 hotels in the city has taken wages and benefits out of competition.

The starting wage for non-tipped jobs is $11 per hour plus comprehensive portable benefits. San Francisco presents a special opportunity for comparisons of work conditions in the industry and for future workplace interventions because of a unique partnership with twelve first class hotels that is designed to improve customer service and job quality in the industry. The San Francisco Hotels Partnership Project has implemented a core-training program throughout much of the industry, and developed pilot projects to resolve conflicts at the lowest possible level within an organization. The parties have also worked to establish joint decision making processes for redesigning work in the food and beverages and housekeeping operations.

OBJECTIVES

The objectives of the proposed study are:

1. To identify key changes in technology and organization in the hospitality industry that affects the future of work for room cleaners.
2. To explore the impact of industry changes on the health, injury rates, and well being of room cleaners.
3. To develop potential strategies for enhancing the future health and well being of room cleaners.
4. To demonstrate the utility of a participatory research methodology that actively involves room cleaners in every aspect of the study, and that results in the ability of participants to effectively advocate for health-promoting changes in their work.
5. To explore the relevance of the findings to similar low wage populations, particularly in the service sector.
6. To widely disseminate study findings and recommendations to encourage further study and action

by academic researchers, labour, management, policy makers, and advocacy groups.

The pilot consists of establishing an advisory group of participants, focus groups with room cleaners, the development and administration of a survey instrument, analysis and discussion of results with participants, and dissemination of results in a final report. Although designed for comparisons with other cities, the pilot will allow for comparisons between high quality and low quality (in terms of labour relations and customer service) hotels in San Francisco. In addition, the use of some standardized instruments will enable comparisons of working conditions of housecleaners with jobs in different industries. Finally, future studies are planned to investigate the effects of changes in work conditions and labour-management collaboration on injury incidence, health and functional/quality of life outcomes.

Progress

A 30-member advisory group of room cleaners participated in the planning and implementation of this pilot study.

Ten focus groups have been conducted with about 20-25 housecleaners at each meeting recruited from different San Francisco hotels.

A survey instrument has been developed and tested in a focus group of 25 roomcleaners. The revised survey has been translated into Spanish and Chinese languages. The survey includes standard instruments such as Karasek's Job Content Questionnaire, Siegrist's effort/reward balance scales including measures of intrinsic and extrinsic effort, SF36 health-related quality of life/functioning, general health status, and specifically developed questions to measure physical workload, musculoskeletal symptoms, work injury, and demographic variables. Depending on reading and language skills it takes 30 to 75 minutes for workers to complete the survey with assistance available from researchers and translators.

139 out of 397 roomcleaners from 4 selected hotels completed the survey during the first wave of data gathering in December 1998.

Plan

A second wave of data gathering among 258 non-responders is planned for February. Intensive efforts of personal recruitment at the workplace and telephone follow-up is planned for a random 50% sample of 130 non-responders.

Data management and basic analyses limited to descriptive statistics and comparisons between four hotels are planned for March and April. A draft report will be prepared for the union by May 15 and will be available for joint labour management focus groups preparing for upcoming bargaining of five-year contracts. Further analyses including comparisons with national survey data, discussions with participants, and a final report will be completed by December 1999. Publications in peer reviewed scientific journals may be prepared simultaneously or thereafter but no funds have been allocated yet for this purpose.

Specific Aims

(1) Establish cooperative relationships between researchers and stakeholders

(2) Select 2-6 hotels (with a total of about 400 employees) representing "good" and "bad" overall work conditions as perceived by union representatives and key senior employees

(3) Conduct a series of focus groups with room cleaners from different hotels which are not selected into the pilot survey, to (a) gain a detailed understanding of their job tasks, workload, working conditions, and work-related health problems, (b) to discuss the scope and goals of the research project, and (c) to invite further participation in design and execution of the study (e.g. development and administration of survey instrument, organization of meetings with roomcleaners at participating hotels)

(4) Develop draft survey instrument

(5) Discuss draft survey instrument with union representatives and other key informants

(6) Pre-test survey instrument in focus group with 25 roomcleaners

(7) Revise survey instrument

(8) Translate survey instrument into Spanish and Chinese languages

(9) Obtain names and addresses of current employees at selected hotels

(10) Invite employees of selected hotels by mail to fill out the survey in off-site meetings

(11) Conduct first wave of survey under supervision of University researchers and with assistance of translators at different times and locations in San Francisco

(12) Create database for data entry using Microsoft Access software

(13) Enter data from questionnaires and check for completeness

(14) Follow-up of workers with incomplete responses by telephone in their first language

(15) Update list of employees and draw random 50% sample from survey non-responders

(16) Obtain contact information including telephone numbers for non-responders

(17) Invite all non-responders by mail to fill out the survey in off-site meetings

(18) Invite 50% random sample of non-responders by telephone and/or personal contact to fill out the survey in off-site meetings

(19) Conduct second wave of survey

(20) Provide follow-up meetings with research team for workers willing to participate but unable to attend the pre-scheduled survey meetings

(21) Enter data into database

(22) Check data for missing information and inconsistencies

(23) Prepare final data set with variable labels for all data fields and create scales for work conditions based on theoretical and/or empirical approaches

(24) Analyze survey data and (a) prepare frequency tables for all questionnaire answers and scales stratified by hotels, (b) compare responses of first wave responders with second wave of responders in 50% sample intensively followed up, (c) compare responses between "good" and "bad" hotels, (d) compare work conditions with reports from studies in other industries, (e) investigate the association between work conditions and self-reported general health, musculoskeletal symptoms, quality of life, and work injury

(25) Gather OSHA 200 logs in selected hotels for 1998 and enter in separate database

(26) Replace employee names by ID code in injury data set and merge with survey data

(27) Analyze merged injury (OSHA 200 log) and survey data, and, specifically (a) compare frequency of self-reported and formally reported work injuries, (b) examine self-reported reasons for not reporting a work-related injury, (c) investigate associations between working conditions and both self-reported and OSHA 200 log based injury frequency

(28) Prepared draft report on May 15, 1999

(29) Present report to stakeholders in joint labour management meetings

(30) Prepare final report by December 1999

(31) Prepare peer-reviewed journal article(s)

(32) Integrate results of pilot study into proposed larger study comparing working conditions and health outcomes across different US cities representing different organizational settings and labour markets in the hotel industry

HOSPITALITY INDUSTRY GROUPS

The hospitality industry group represents hotel developers and owners, equity investors, ground lessors and lessees, operators and others involved in the State of Hawaii's principal industry: tourism. Representative transactions in which the

Firm's attorneys have been involved in Hawaii have included the acquisition, financing and/or development of such well-known hotels as the Kahala Hilton Hotel, Hyatt Regency Hotels-Kaanapali and Waikiki, Ala Moana Hotel, Waikiki Beachcomber, Kona Village Resort, Westin Maui, Kapalua Bay Hotel, Maui Marriott and Kaanapali Embassy Suites Hotel and in the continental U.S., the Boca Raton Hotel & Club (Boca Raton, Florida), Omni Park Central Hotel, and a 27-hotel acquisition (in 15 States).

THE ORGANIZING PROCESS

Supervision

A key issue in accomplishing the goals identified in the planning process is structuring the work of the organization. Organizations are groups of people, with ideas and resources, working toward common goals. The purpose of the organizing function is to make the best use of the organization's resources to achieve organizational goals. Organizational structure is the formal decision-making framework by which job tasks are divided, grouped, and coordinated. Formalization is an important aspect of structure. It is the extent to which the units of the organization are explicitly defined and its policies, procedures, and goals are clearly stated. It is the official organizational structure conceived and built by top management. The formal organization can be seen and represented in chart form. An organization chart displays the organizational structure and shows job titles, lines of authority, and relationships between departments.

The informal organization is the network, unrelated to the firm's formal authority structure, of social interactions among its employees. It is the personal and social relationships that arise spontaneously as people associate with one another in the work environment. The supervisor must realize that the informal organization affects the formal organization. The informal organization can pressure group members to conform to the expectations of the informal group that conflict with those of the formal organization. This can result in the generation of false information or rumors and resistance to change desired by management. The supervisor should recognize the existence of information groups, identify the roles member play within these groups, and use knowledge of the groups to work effectively with them. The informal organization can make the formal organization more effective by providing support to management, stability to the environment, and useful communication channels.

Organizational Structure

Even though the differences among organizations are enormous, there are many similarities that enable them to be classified. One widely used classification is the twofold system (mechanistic versus organic forms of organizational structure) developed by Tom Burns and G. M. Stalker in their study of electronics firms in the United Kingdom. (See Burns, Tom and G. M. Stalker, Management of Innovation, London: Tavistock Publications, 1961, p. 19.)

The mechanistic structure is the traditional or classical design, common in many medium-and large-size organizations. Mechanistic organizations are somewhat rigid in that they consist of very clearly delineated jobs, have a well-defined hierarchical structure, and rely heavily on the formal chain of command for control. Bureaucratic organizations, with their emphasis on formalization, are the primary form of mechanistic structures. According to Max Weber, bureaucracy is a form of organization characterized by a rational, goal-directed hierarchy, impersonal decision making, formal controls, and subdivision into managerial positions and specialization of labour. Bureaucratic organizations are tall consisting of hierarchies with many levels of management.

In a tall structure, people become relatively confined to their own area of specialization. Bureaucracies are driven by a top-down or command and control approach in which managers provide considerable direction and have considerable control over others. Other features of the bureaucratic organization include functional division of labour and work specialization.

On the other hand, the organic structure is more flexible, more adaptable to a participative form of management, and less concerned with a clearly defined structure. The organic organization is open to the environment in order to capitalize upon new opportunities.

Organic organizations have a flat structure with only one or two levels of management. Flat organizations emphasize a decentralized approach to management that encourage high employee involvement in decisions. The purpose of this structure is to create independent small businesses or enterprises that can rapidly respond to customers' needs or changes in the business environment. The supervisor tends to have a more personal relationship with his or her employees.

Rensis Likert has conducted extensive research on a non-bureaucratic organization design referred to as System 4 (participative-democratic). Management and employees interact in a friendly environment characterized by mutual confidence and trust.

Contingency organization means that the most appropriate organization structure for each situation depends upon technology, organizational size, goals and strategy, environmental stability, and characteristics of the employees. Mechanistic organizations are best suited to repetitive operations and stable environments, while organic organizations are best suited to an uncertain task and a changing environment.

Organization Design

Designing an organization involves choosing an organizational structure that will enable the company to most effectively achieve its goals. Organization design is the creation of an organization's structure, traditionally functional, divisional, and/or matrix.

Functions or divisions arrange traditional organizations. In a functional organization, authority is determined by the relationships between group functions and activities. Functional structures group similar or related occupational specialties or processes together under the familiar headings of finance, manufacturing, marketing, accounts receivable, research, surgery, and photo finishing. Economy is achieved through specialization. However, the organization risks losing sight of its overall interests as different departments pursue their own goals.

In a divisional organization, corporate divisions operate as relatively autonomous businesses under the larger corporate umbrella. In a conglomerate organization, divisions may be unrelated. Divisional structures are made up of self-contained strategic business units that each produces a single product. For example, General Motors' divisions include Chevrolet, Oldsmobile, Pontiac, and Cadillac. A central headquarters, focusing or results, coordinates and controls the activities, and provides support services between divisions. Functional departments accomplish division goals. A weakness however, is the tendency to duplicate activities among divisions.

In a matrix organization, teams are formed and team members report to two or more managers. Matrix structures utilize functional and divisional chains of command simultaneously in the same part of the organization, commonly for one-of-a-kind projects. It is used to develop a new product, to ensure the continuing success of a product to which several departments directly contribute, and to solve a difficult problem. By superimposing a project structure upon the functional structure, a matrix organization is formed that allows the organization to take advantage of new opportunities. This structure assigns specialists from different functional departments to work on one or more projects being led by project managers. The matrix concept facilitates working on concurrent projects by creating a dual chain of command, the project (program, systems, or product) manager and the functional manager. Project managers have authority over activities geared toward achieving organizational goals while functional managers have authority over promotion decisions and performance reviews. An example is an aerospace firm with a contract from NASA.

Matrix organizations are particularly appealing to firms that want to speed up the decision-making process. However, the matrix organization may not allow long-term working relationships to develop. Furthermore, using multiple managers for one employee may result in confusion as to manager evaluation and accountability. Thus, the matrix system may elevate the conflict between product and functional interests.

Boundaryless organizations are not defined or limited by horizontal, vertical, or external boundaries imposed by a predetermined structure. They share many of the characteristics of flat organizations, with a strong emphasis on teams. Cross-functional teams dissolve horizontal barriers and enable the organization to respond quickly to environmental changes and to spearhead innovation. Boundaryless organizations can form relationships (joint ventures, intellectual property, distribution channels, or financial resources) with customers, suppliers, and/or competitors. Telecommuting, strategic alliances and customer-organization linkages break down external barriers, streamlining work activities. Jack Welch, former CEO of General Electric, to facilitate interactions with customers and suppliers, first used this un-structure.

A boundaryless environment is required by learning organizations to facilitate team collaboration and the sharing of information. When an organization develops the continuous capacity to adapt and survive in an increasingly competitive environment because all members take an active role in identifying and resolving work-related issues, it has developed a learning culture. A learning organization is one that is able to adapt and respond to change. This design empowers employees because they acquire and share knowledge and apply this learning to decision-making. They are pooling collective intelligence and stimulating creative thought to improve performance. Supervisors facilitate learning by sharing and aligning the organization's vision for the future and sustaining a sense of community and strong culture.

Organizing Function

The organizing function deals with all those activities that result in the formal assignment of tasks and authority and a coordination of effort. The supervisor staffs the work unit, trains employees, secures resources, and empowers the work group into a productive team. The steps in the organizing process include (1) review plans, (2) list all tasks to be accomplished, (3) divide tasks into groups one person can accomplish-a job, (4) group related jobs together in a logical and efficient manner, (5) assign work to individuals, (6) delegate authority to establish relationships between jobs and groups of jobs.

The nature and scope of the work needed to accomplish the organization's objectives is needed to determine work classification and work unit design. Division of labour, or work specialization, is the degree to which tasks in an organization are divided into separate jobs. Work process requirements and employee skill level determine the degree of specialization. Placing capable people in each job ties directly with productivity improvement. In order to maximize productivity, supervisors match employee skill level with task requirements.

Supervisors should perform workflow analysis to examine how work creates or adds value to the ongoing processes in an organization. Workflow analysis looks at how work moves from the customer or the demand source through the organization to the point at which the work leaves the organization as a product or service to meet customer demand. Thus, workflow analysis can be used to tighten the connection between employees' work and customers' needs. Also, it can help to make major performance breakthroughs throughout business process reengineering (BPR), a fundamental rethinking and radical redesign of business processes to achieve dramatic improvements in costs, quality, service, and speed. BPR uses workflow analysis to identify jobs that can be eliminated or recombined to improve company performance.

DEPARTMENTALIZATION

After reviewing the plans, usually the first step in the organizing process is departmentalization. Once jobs have been classified through work specialization, they are grouped so those common tasks can be coordinated. Departmentalization is the basis on which work or individuals are grouped into manageable units. There are five traditional methods for grouping work activities.

— Departmentalization by function organizes by the functions to be performed. The functions reflect the nature of the business. The advantage of this type of grouping is obtaining efficiencies from consolidating similar specialties and people with common skills, knowledge and orientations together in common units.

— Departmentalization by product assembles all functions needed to make and market a particular product are placed under one executive. For instance, major department stores are structured around product groups such as home accessories, appliances, women's clothing, men's clothing, and children's clothing.

— Departmentalization by geographical regions groups jobs on the basis of territory or geography. For example, Merck, a major pharmaceutical company, has its domestic sales departmentalized by regions such as Northeast, Southeast, Midwest, Southwest, and Northwest.

— Departmentalization by process groups jobs on the basis of product or customer flow. Each process requires particular skills and offers a basis for homogeneous categorizing of work activities. A patient preparing for an operation would first engage in preliminary diagnostic tests, then go through the admitting process, undergo a procedure in surgery, receive post operative care, be discharged and perhaps receive out-patient attention. These services are each administered by different departments.

— Departmentalization by customer groups jobs on the basis of a common set of needs or problems of specific customers. For instance, a plumbing firm may group its work according to whether it is serving private sector, public sector, government, or not-for-profit organizations. A current departmentalization trend is to structure work according to customer, using cross-functional teams. This group is chosen from different functions to work together across various departments to interdependently create new products or services. For example, a cross-functional team consisting of managers from accounting, finance, and marketing is created to prepare a technology plan.

POWER AND AUTHORITY

Organizational structure is a means of facilitating the achievement of organizational objectives. Such structures are not static, but dynamic. They reorganize in response to changing conditions that occur in the environment, new technology, or organizational growth. Organization structures are dependent upon the employees whose activities they guide. Supervisors rely upon power and authority to ensure that employees get things done.

Authority

The organizational structure provides the framework for the formal distribution of authority. Formalization is the degree to which tasks are standardized and rules and regulations govern employee behaviour. It influences the amount of discretion an employee has over his or her job. In an organization with high degrees of formalization, job descriptions and policies provide clear direction.

Where formalization is low, employees have a great deal of freedom in deciding how thy conduct their work. Within the same organization, different departments may have different degrees of formalization. For example, in a hospital, doctors have freedom in selecting treatments, drugs, and methods for treating patients. However, the hospital physical plant staff has a strict schedule for cleaning buildings, mowing lawns, and maintaining the facilities.

Authority is the legitimate power of a supervisor to direct subordinates to take action within the scope of the supervisor's position. Formal authority in the organization can be traced all the way back to the U.S. constitutional right to own property. The owner of the organization has the authority to make decisions. For example, entrepreneurial firms have an informal arrangement of employees and centralization of decision-making authority, the owner.

Forms of Authority

Three forms of authority are line authority, staff authority, and team authority.

Line authority is direct supervisory authority from superior to subordinate. Authority flows in a direct chain of command from the top of the company to the bottom. Chain of command is an unbroken line of reporting relationships that extends through the entire organization that defines the formal decision-making structure. It helps employees know to whom they are accountable, and whom to go to with a problem. Line departments are directly linked to the production and sales of specific products. Supervisors--in line departments, such as marketing and production--give direct orders, evaluate performance, and reward or punish those employees who work for them. Unity of command within the chain states that each person in an organization should take orders from and reports to only one person. This helps prevent conflicting demands being placed on employees by more than one boss. However, the trend toward employee empowerment, fuelled by advances in technology and changes in design from downsizing and reengineering have tempered the importance of being accountable to only one superior. Span of control refers to the number of employees that should be placed under the direction of one manager. Spans within effective organizations vary greatly. The actual number depends on the amount of complexity and the level of specialization. In general, a wide span of control is possible with better-trained, more experienced, and committed employees.

Staff authority is more limited authority to advise. It is authority that is based on expertise and which usually involves advising line managers. Staff members are advisers and counsellors who aid line departments in making decisions but do not have the authority to make final decisions. Staff supervisors help line departments decide what to do and how to do it. They coordinate and provide technical assistance or advice to all advisors, such as accounting, human resources, information technology, research, advertising, public relations, and legal services.

Team authority is granted to committees or work teams involved in an organization's daily operations. Work teams are groups of operating employees empowered to plan and organize their own work and to perform that work with a minimum of supervision. Team-Based structures organize separate functions into a group based on one overall objective. Empowered employees create their own schedules, design their own processes, and are held responsible for outcomes. This facilitates efficiencies in work process, and the ability to detect and react to changes in the environment. Employees with the skills and knowledge to manage more than one specialized task are able to promptly provide customers with quality products and services. Cross-functionally training team members allows any member to perform a variety of problem-solving tasks.

Teamwork is an imperative in a flat, boundaryless organizational structure. A team is a small number of people with complementary skills who work toward common goals for which they hold themselves mutually accountable. Self-managed teams are responsible for producing an entire product, a component, or an ongoing service. In most cases, members are cross-trained on the different tasks assigned to the team. Often, these teams are trained in technical, administrative, and interpersonal skills. Problem-solving teams do not affect an organization's structure because they exist for only a limited period. They are often used when organizations decide to make improvements in the quality of a product or service. Special-purpose teams consist of members who span functional or organizational boundaries and whose purpose is to examine complex issues such as introducing new technology, improving the quality of work process, or encouraging cooperation between labour and management in a unionized setting.

Power

In addition to authority, supervisors have more personal sources of power to draw upon for getting things done. Everyone has power in one form or another and it is by exercising this power that organizations get things accomplished. Supervisors who are capable of achieving their objectives independently of others are said to possess strength. When these "strong" supervisors involve and incorporate others into their plans and activities they are making use of power, and in fact increasing the total amount of power available to incorporate into a particular situation or problem. Involving employees in setting objectives and making decisions as it relates to their jobs empowers everyone, and results in greater job satisfaction and commitment, as well as increased productivity. Empowering employees provides them with greater autonomy.

Power is the ability to exert influence in the organization beyond authority, which is derived from position. The supervisor's personal power could include job knowledge, personal influence, interpersonal skills, and ability to get results, empathetic ability, persuasive ability, and physical strength. J.P. French and B. Raven ("The Bases of Social Power" in Studies in Social Power, edited by D. Cartwright, Institute for Social Research, 1959, pp. 150-167) identify six sources of power: legitimate, coercive, reward, expert, referent, and information. Legitimate power is a result of the position a person holds in the organization hierarchy. This position power is broader than the ability to reward and punish, as members need to accept the authority of the position. Coercive power is the threat of sanctions. It is dependent on fear and includes, but is not limited to the ability to dismiss, assign undesirable work, or restriction of movement. Reward power results in people doing what is asked because they desire positive benefits or rewards. Rewards can be anything a person values (praise, raises, and promotions). Expert power comes from expertise, skill, or knowledge. Referent power refers to a person who has desirable resources or personal traits. It results in admiration and the desire to emulate. Information power is based upon the persuasiveness or content of a communication and is independent of the influencing individual.

In most instances, supervisors do not need to offer incentives or threaten retribution to get employees to do what they request. They influence employees because the employees want to follow. This power to influence comes from the employee granting authority to the supervisor.

Centralization versus Decentralization

Centralization is the degree to which decision-making is concentrated in top management's hands. Decentralization is the extent to which decision-making authority is pushed down the organization structure and shared with many lower-level employees. Centralized organizations have more levels of management with narrow spans of control. Employees are not free to make decisions. Decentralized organizations have fewer levels of management with wide spans of control giving employees more freedom of action. All other things being equal, a wide span of control is more efficient because it requires fewer managers. However, it is important to recognize that, at some point, effectiveness will decline.

The current trend is toward broadening decentralization. As competition intensifies, the need for organizations to be responsive increases. This has made employees, usually those at the lower levels, who are closest to customers extremely important. They are an excellent source of knowledge and implement changes that directly impact performance. Giving this group more input into certain decision-making activities can result in increased firm performance.

Teamwork is an imperative in a flat, boundaryless organizational structure. A team is a small number of people with complementary skills who work toward common goals for which they hold themselves mutually accountable. Self-managed teams are responsible for producing an entire product, a component, or an ongoing service. In most cases, members are cross-trained on the different tasks assigned to the team. Often, these teams are trained in technical, administrative, and interpersonal skills. Problem-solving teams do not affect an organization's structure because they exist for only a limited period. They are often used when organizations decide to make improvements in the quality of a product or service. Special-purpose teams consist of members who span functional or organizational boundaries and whose purpose is to examine complex issues such as introducing new technology, improving the quality of work process, or encouraging cooperation between labour and management in a unionized setting.

Power

In addition to authority, supervisors have more personal sources of power to draw upon for getting things done. Everyone has power in one form or another and it is by exercising this power that organizations get things accomplished. Supervisors who are capable of achieving their objectives independently of others are said to possess strength. When these "strong" supervisors involve and incorporate others into their plans and activities they are making use of power, and in fact increasing the total amount of power available to incorporate into a particular situation or problem. Involving employees in setting objectives and making decisions as it relates to their jobs empowers everyone, and results in greater job satisfaction and commitment, as well as increased productivity. Empowering employees provides them with greater autonomy.

Power is the ability to exert influence in the organization beyond authority, which is derived from position. The supervisor's personal power could include job knowledge, personal influence, interpersonal skills, and ability to get results, empathetic ability, persuasive ability, and physical strength. J.P. French and B. Raven ("The Bases of Social Power" in Studies in Social Power, edited by D. Cartwright, Institute for Social Research, 1959, pp. 150-167) identify six sources of power: legitimate, coercive, reward, expert, referent, and information. Legitimate power is a result of the position a person holds in the organization hierarchy. This position power is broader than the ability to reward and punish, as members need to accept the authority of the position. Coercive power is the threat of sanctions. It is dependent on fear and includes, but is not limited to the ability to dismiss, assign undesirable work, or restriction of movement. Reward power results in people doing what is asked because they desire positive benefits or rewards. Rewards can be anything a person values (praise, raises, and promotions). Expert power comes from expertise, skill, or knowledge. Referent power refers to a person who has desirable resources or personal traits. It results in admiration and the desire to emulate. Information power is based upon the persuasiveness or content of a communication and is independent of the influencing individual. In most instances, supervisors do not need to offer incentives or threaten retribution to get employees to do what they request. They influence employees because the employees want to follow. This power to influence comes from the employee granting authority to the supervisor.

Centralization versus Decentralization

Centralization is the degree to which decision-making is concentrated in top management's hands. Decentralization is the extent to which decision-making authority is pushed down the organization structure and shared with many lower-level employees. Centralized organizations have more levels of management with narrow spans of control. Employees are not free to make decisions. Decentralized organizations have fewer levels of management with wide spans of control giving employees more freedom of action. All other things being equal, a wide span of control is more efficient because it requires fewer managers. However, it is important to recognize that, at some point, effectiveness will decline.

The current trend is toward broadening decentralization. As competition intensifies, the need for organizations to be responsive increases. This has made employees, usually those at the lower levels, who are closest to customers extremely important. They are an excellent source of knowledge and implement changes that directly impact performance. Giving this group more input into certain decision-making activities can result in increased firm performance.

It is impractical for the supervisor to handle all of the work of the department directly. In order to meet the organization's goals, focus on objectives, and ensure that all work is accomplished, supervisors must delegate authority. Authority is the legitimate power of a supervisor to direct subordinates to take action within the scope of the supervisor's position. By extension, this power, or a part thereof, is delegated and used in the name of a supervisor. Delegation is the downward transfer of formal authority from superior to subordinate. The employee is empowered to act for the supervisor, while the supervisor remains accountable for the outcome. Delegation of authority is a person-to-person relationship requiring trust, commitment, and contracting between the supervisor and the employee.

The supervisor assists in developing employees in order to strengthen the organization. He or she gives up the authority to make decisions that are best made by subordinates. This means that the supervisor allows subordinates the freedom to make mistakes and learn from them. He or she does not supervise subordinates' decision-making, but allows them the opportunity to develop their own skills. The supervisor lets subordinates know that he or she is willing to help, but not willing to do their jobs for them. The supervisor is not convinced that the best way for employees to learn is by telling them how to solve a problem. This results in those subordinates becoming dependent on the supervisor. The supervisor allows employees the opportunity to achieve and be credited for it.

An organization's most valuable resource is its people. By empowering employees who perform delegated jobs with the authority to manage those jobs, supervisors free themselves to manage more effectively. Successfully training future supervisors means delegating authority. This gives employees the concrete skills, experience, and the resulting confidence to develop themselves for higher positions. Delegation provides better managers and a higher degree of efficiency. Thus, collective effort, resulting in the organization's growth, is dependent on delegation of authority.

Responsibility and Accountability

Equally important to authority is the idea that when an employee is given responsibility for a job, he or she must also be given the degree of authority necessary to carry it out. Thus, for effective delegation, the authority granted to an employee must equal the assigned responsibility. Upon accepting the delegated task, the employee has incurred an obligation to perform the assigned work and to properly utilize the granted authority. Responsibility is the obligation to do assigned tasks. The individual employee is responsible for being proficient at his or her job. The supervisor is responsible for what employees do or fail to do, as well as for the resources under their control. Thus, responsibility is an integral part of a supervisor's authority.

Responsibilities fall into two categories: individual and organizational. Employees have individual responsibilities to be proficient in their job. They are responsible for their actions. Nobody gives or delegates individual responsibilities. Employees assume them when they accept a position in the organization. Organizational responsibilities refer to collective organizational accountability and include how well departments perform their work. For example, the supervisor is responsible for all the tasks assigned to his or her department, as directed by the manager.

When someone is responsible for something, he or she is liable, or accountable to a superior, for the outcome. Thus, accountability flows upward in the organization. All are held accountable for their personal, individual conduct. Accountability is answering for the result of one's actions or omissions. It is the reckoning, wherein one answers for his or her actions and accepts the consequences, good or bad. Accountability establishes reasons, motives and importance for actions in the eyes of managers and employees alike. Accountability is the final act in the establishment of one's credibility. It is important to remember that accountability results in rewards for good performance, as well as discipline for poor performance.

The Delegation Process

The delegation process has five phases: (1) preparing, (2) planning, (3) discussing, (4) auditing, and (5) appreciating. The first step in delegating is to identify what should and should not be delegated. The supervisor should delegate any task that a subordinate performs better. Tasks least critical to the performance of the supervisor's job can be delegated. Any task that provides valuable experience for subordinates should be delegated. Also, the supervisor can delegate the tasks that he or she dislikes the most. But, the supervisor should not delegate any task that would violate a confidence.

— Preparing includes establishing the objectives of the delegation, specifying the task that needs to be accomplished, and deciding who should accomplish it.

— Planning is meeting with the chosen subordinate to describe the task and to ask the subordinate to devise a plan of action. As Andrew Carnegie once said, "The secret of success is not in doing your own work but in recognizing the right man to do it." Trust between the supervisor and employee-that both will fulfill the commitment-is most important.

— Discussing includes reviewing the objectives of the task as well as the subordinate's plan of action, any potential obstacles, and ways to avoid or deal with these obstacles. The supervisor should clarify and solicit feedback as to the employee's understanding. Clarifications needed for delegation include the desired results (what not how), guidelines, resources available, and consequences (good and bad). Delegation is similar to contracting between the supervisor and employee regarding how and when the work will be completed. The standards and time frames are discussed and agreed upon. The employee should know exactly what is expected and how the task will be evaluated.

— Auditing is monitoring the progress of the delegation and making adjustments in response to unforeseen problems.

— Appreciating is accepting the completed task and acknowledging the subordinate's efforts.

Since motivation influences productivity, supervisors need to understand what motivates employees to reach peak performance. It is not an easy task to increase employee motivation because employees respond in different ways to their jobs and their organization's practices. Motivation is the set of processes that moves a person toward a goal. Thus, motivated behaviours are voluntary choices controlled by the individual employee. The supervisor (motivator) wants to influence the factors that motivate employees to higher levels of productivity.

Factors that affect work motivation include individual differences, job characteristics, and organizational practices. Individual differences are the personal needs, values, and attitudes, interests and abilities that people bring to their jobs. Job characteristics are the aspects of the position that determine its limitations and challenges. Organizational practices are the rules, human resources policies, managerial practices, and rewards systems of an organization. Supervisors must consider how these factors interact to affect employee job performance.

Simple Model of Motivation

The purpose of behaviour is to satisfy needs. A need is anything that is required, desired, or useful. A want is a conscious recognition of a need. A need arises when there is a difference in self-concept (the way I see myself) and perception (the way I see the world around me). The presence of an active need is expressed as an inner state of tension from which the individual seeks relief.

Theories of Motivation

Many methods of employee motivation have been developed. The study of work motivation has focused on the motivator (supervisor) as well as the motivatee (employee). Motivation theories are important to supervisors attempting to be effective leaders. Two primary approaches to motivation are content and process. The content approach to motivation focuses on the assumption that individuals are motivated by the desire to fulfill inner needs. Content theories focus on the needs that motivate people.

Maslow's Hierarchy of Needs identifies five levels of needs, which are best seen as a hierarchy with the most basic need emerging first and the most sophisticated need last. People move up the hierarchy one level at a time. Gratified needs lose their strength and the next level of needs is activated. As basic or lower-level needs are satisfied, higher-level needs become operative. A satisfied need is not a motivator. The most powerful employee need is the one that has not been satisfied. Abraham Maslow first presented the five-tier hierarchy in 1942 to a psychoanalytic society and published it in 1954 in Motivation and Personality (New York: Harper and Row).

Level I-Physiological needs are the most basic human needs. They include food, water, and comfort. The organization helps to satisfy employees' physiological needs by a paycheck.

Level II-Safety needs are the desires for security and stability, to feel safe from harm. The organization helps to satisfy employees' safety needs by benefits.

Level III-Social needs are the desires for affiliation. They include friendship and belonging. The organization helps to satisfy employees' social needs through sports teams, parties, and celebrations. The supervisor can help fulfill social needs by showing direct care and concern for employees.

Level IV-Esteem needs are the desires for self-respect and respect or recognition from others. The organization helps to satisfy employees' esteem needs by matching the skills and abilities of the employee to the job. The supervisor can help fulfill esteem needs by showing workers that their work is appreciated.

Level V-Self-actualization needs are the desires for self-fulfilment and the realization of the individual's full potential. The supervisor can help fulfill self-actualization needs by assigning tasks that challenge employees' minds while drawing on their aptitude and training.

Alderfer's ERG identified three categories of needs. The most important contribution of the ERG model is the addition of the frustration-regression hypothesis, which holds that when individuals are frustrated in meeting higher level needs, the next lower level needs reemerge.

Existence needs are the desires for material and physical well being. These needs are satisfied with food, water, air, shelter, working conditions, pay, and fringe benefits.

Relatedness needs are the desires to establish and maintain interpersonal relationships. These needs are satisfied with relationships with family, friends, supervisors, subordinates, and co-workers.

Growth needs are the desires to be creative, to make useful and productive contributions and to have opportunities for personal development.

McClelland's Learned Needs divides motivation into needs for power, affiliation, and achievement.

Achievement motivated people thrive on pursuing and attaining goals. They like to be able to control the situations in which they are involved. They take moderate risks. They like to get immediate feedback on how they have done. They tend to be preoccupied with a task-orientation towards the job to be done.

Power motivated individuals see almost every situation as an opportunity to seize control or dominate others. They love to influence others. They like to change situations whether or not it is needed. They are willing to assert themselves when a decision needs to be made.

Affiliation motivated people are usually friendly and like to socialize with others. This may distract them from their performance requirements. They will usually respond to an appeal for cooperation.

Herzberg's Two-Factor Theory describes needs in terms of satisfaction and dissatisfaction. Frederick Herzberg examined motivation in the light of job content and contest. Motivating employees is a two-step process. First provide hygienes and then motivators. One continuum ranges from no satisfaction to satisfaction. The other continuum ranges from dissatisfaction to no dissatisfaction.

Satisfaction comes from motivators that are intrinsic or job content, such as achievement, recognition, advancement, responsibility, the work itself, and growth possibilities. Herzberg uses the term motivators for job satisfiers since they involve job content and the satisfaction that results from them. Motivators are considered job turn-ons. They are necessary for substantial improvements in work performance and move the employee beyond satisfaction to superior performance. Motivators correspond to Maslow's higher-level needs of esteem and self-actualization.

Dissatisfaction occurs when the following hygiene factors, extrinsic or job context, are not present on the job: pay, status, job security, working conditions, company policy, peer relations, and supervision. Herzberg uses the term hygiene for these factors because they are preventive in nature.

They will not produce motivation, but they can prevent motivation from occurring. Hygiene factors can be considered job stay-ons because they encourage an employee to stay on a job. Once these factors are provided, they do not necessarily promote motivation; but their absence can create employee dissatisfaction. Hygiene factors correspond to Maslow's physiological, safety, and social needs in that they are extrinsic, or peripheral, to the job. They are present in the work environment of job context.

Motivation comes from the employee's feelings of accomplishment or job content rather than from the environmental factors or job context. Motivators encourage an employee to strive to do his or her best. Job enrichment can be used to meet higher-level needs. To enrich a job, a supervisor can introduce new or more difficult tasks, assign individuals specialized tasks that enable them to become experts, or grant additional authority to employees.

The process approach emphasizes how and why people choose certain behaviours in order to meet their personal goals. Process theories focus on external influences or behaviours that people choose to meet their needs. External influences are often readily accessible to supervisors.

Vroom's Expectancy Model suggests that people choose among alternative behaviours because they anticipate that particular behaviours will lead to one or more desired outcomes and that other behaviours will lead to undesirable outcomes. Expectancy is the belief that effort will lead to first-order outcomes, any work-related behaviour that is the direct result of the effort an employee expends on a job.

Equity is the perception of fairness involved in rewards given. A fair or equitable situation is one in which people with similar inputs experience similar outcomes. Employees will compare their rewards with the rewards received by others for their efforts. If employees perceive that an inequity exists, they are likely to withhold some of their contributions, either consciously or unconsciously, to bring a situation into better balance.

For example, if someone thinks he or she is not getting enough pay (output) for his or her work (input), he or she will try to get that pay increased or reduce the amount of work he or she is doing. On the other hand, when a worker thinks he or she is being paid too much for the work he or she is doing, he or she tends to increase the amount of work. Not only do workers compare their own inputs and outputs; they compare their input/output ratio with the input/output ratio of other workers. If one work team believes they are doing more work than a similar team for the same pay, their sense of fairness will be violated and they will tend to reduce the amount of work they are doing. It is a normal human inclination to want things to be fair.

Bowditch and Buono note (see Bowditch, James L. and Anthony F. Buono, A Primer on Organizational Behaviour, 4th, John Wiley & Sons, 1997) that while equity theory was originally concerned with differences in pay, it may be applied to other forms of tangible and intangible rewards in the workplace. That is, if any input is not balanced with some fair output, the motivation process will be difficult. Supervisors must manage the perception of fairness in the mind of each employee. If subordinates think they are not being treated fairly, it is difficult to motivate them.

Reinforcement involves four types of consequence. Positive reinforcement creates a pleasant consequence by using rewards to increase the likelihood that a behaviour will be repeated. Negative reinforcement occurs when a person engages in behaviour to avoid unpleasant consequences or to escape from existing unpleasant consequences. Punishment is an attempt to discourage a target behaviour by the application of negative outcomes whenever it is possible. Extinction is the absence of any reinforcement, either positive or negative, following the occurrence of a target behaviour. Employees have questions about their jobs. Can I do what management is asking me to do? If I do the job, will I be rewarded? Will the reward I receive be satisfactory to me?

Reinforcement is based primarily on the work of B.F. Skinner, a psychologist, who experimented with the theories of operant conditioning. Skinner's work shows that many behaviours can be controlled through the use of rewards. In fact, a person might be influenced to change his or her behaviour by giving him or her rewards.

Employees who do an exceptionally good job on a particular project should be rewarded for that performance. It will motivate them to try to do an exceptional job on their next project. Employees must associate the reward with the behaviour. In other words, the employee must know for what specifically he or she is being rewarded! The reward should come as quickly as possible after the behaviour. The reward can be almost anything, but it must be something desired by the employee. Some of the most powerful rewards are symbolic; things that cost very little but mean a lot to the people who get them. Examples of symbolic rewards are things like plaques or certificates.

NEW TECHNIQUES OF ORGANISING AND MANAGEMENT

To meet the many demands of performing their functions, managers assume multiple roles. A role is an organized set of behaviours. Henry Mintzberg has identified ten roles common to the work of all managers. The ten roles are divided into three groups: interpersonal, informational, and decisional. The informational roles link all managerial work together. The interpersonal roles ensure that information is provided. The decisional roles make significant use of the information. The performance of managerial roles and the requirements of these roles can be played at different times by the same manager and to different degrees depending on the level and function of management. The ten roles are described individually, but they form an integrated whole.

The three interpersonal roles are primarily concerned with interpersonal relationships. In the figurehead role, the manager represents the organization in all matters of formality. The top level manager represents the company legally and socially to those outside of the organization. The supervisor represents the work group to higher management and higher management to the work group. In the liaison role, the manger interacts with peers and people outside the organization. The top level manager uses the liaison role to gain favours and information, while the supervisor uses it to maintain the routine flow of work. The leader role defines the relationships between the manger and employees.

The direct relationships with people in the interpersonal roles place the manager in a unique position to get information. Thus, the three informational roles are primarily concerned with the information aspects of managerial work. In the monitor role, the manager receives and collects information. In the role of disseminator, the manager transmits special information into the organization. The top level manager receives and transmits more information from people outside the organization than the supervisor. In the role of spokesperson, the manager disseminates the organization's information into its environment. Thus, the top level manager is seen as an industry expert, while the supervisor is seen as a unit or departmental expert.

The unique access to information places the manager at the center of organizational decision making. There are four decisional roles. In the entrepreneur role, the manager initiates change. In the disturbance handler role, the manger deals with threats to the organization. In the resource allocator role, the manager chooses where the organization will expend its efforts. In the negotiator role, the manager negotiates on behalf of the organization. The top level manager makes the decisions about the organization as a whole, while the supervisor makes decisions about his or her particular work unit.

The supervisor performs these managerial roles but with different emphasis than higher managers. Supervisory management is more focused and short-term in outlook. Thus, the figurehead role becomes less significant and the disturbance handler and negotiator roles increase in importance for the supervisor. Since leadership permeates all activities, the leader role is among the most important of all roles at all levels of management

In order to perform the functions of management and to assume multiple roles, managers must be skilled. Robert Katz identified three managerial skills that are essential to successful management: technical, human, and conceptual. Technical skill involves process or technique knowledge and proficiency. Managers use the processes, techniques and tools of a specific area. Human skill involves the ability to interact effectively with people. Managers interact and cooperate with employees. Conceptual skill involves the formulation of ideas. Managers understand abstract relationships, develop ideas, and solve problems creatively. Thus, technical skill deals with things, human skill concerns people, and conceptual skill has to do with ideas.

A manager's level in the organization determines the relative importance of possessing technical, human, and conceptual skills. Top level managers need conceptual skills in order to view the organization as a whole. Conceptual skills are used in planning and dealing with ideas and abstractions. Supervisors need technical skills to manage their area of specialty. All levels of management need human skills in order to interact and communicate with other people successfully.

As the pace of change accelerates and diverse technologies converge, new global industries are being created (for example, telecommunications). Technological change alters the fundamental structure of firms and calls for new organizational approaches and management skills.

Successful organizations continually innovate and change based upon customer needs and feedback. Values, mission, and vision form the foundation for the execution of the functions of management. They are an organization's guidelines that affect how it will operate. They work only if visible and used in everyday activities and decisions. An organization's values are its beliefs or those qualities that have intrinsic worth and will not be compromised. Its mission is its purpose for existing. The vision is the image of itself in the future.

Values

Each supervisor's approach to management will reflect his or her values, as well as those of the organization. Building trust starts with creating culture based on shared values. Values are traits or qualities having intrinsic worth, such as courage, respect, responsibility, caring, truthfulness, self-discipline, and fairness. Values serve as a baseline for actions and decision-making and guide employees in the organization's intentions and interests. The values driving behaviour define the organizational culture. A strong value system or clearly defined culture turns beliefs into standards such as best quality, best performance, most reliable, most durable, safest, fastest, best value for the money, least expensive, most prestigious, best designed or styled, easiest to use. If asked, "What do we believe in?" or "List our organization's values" all employees in the organization should write down the same values. For example, McDonald's values were captured in its motto of "Q.S.C. & V." which stands for quality, service, cleanliness, and value.

Supervisors need to appreciate the significance of values and value systems. Values affect how a supervisor views other people and groups, thus influencing interpersonal relationships. Values affect how a supervisor perceives situations and solves problems. Values affect how a supervisor determines what is and is not ethical behaviour. Values affect how a supervisor leads and controls employees. Since employees often base behaviour on perceived values it is critical to ensure their perceptions reflect organizational values. Supervisors must communicate, encourage and reinforce the desired values and related behaviours to integrate them into the organizational culture.

Geert Hofstede identified a work-related value framework that has four dimensions: power distance, uncertainty avoidance, individualism, and polarization. Power distance is the attitude to human inequality and relationships to superiors and inferiors in any hierarchy. Uncertainty avoidance is the tolerance for uncertainty that determines choices and rituals to cope with it in social structures and belief systems. Individualism is the relationship between the individual and the collectivity, especially in the way individuals choose to live and work together. Polarization is the extent to which differences such as masculinity or femininity have implications for social organization and the organizations of beliefs. Every person has a different mental program, based on patterns of thinking, feeling, and acting, which are learned throughout a lifetime. The effects of these differences have many practical implications for those who work or are managers in multinational business and for those involved in international negotiations.

Mission

A mission is a broad definition of a business that differentiates it from all other organizations. It is the justification for the organization's existence. The mission statement is the "touchstone" by which all offerings are judged. In addition to the organization's purpose other key elements of the mission statement should include whom it serves, how, and why. The most effective mission statements are easily recalled and provide direction and motivation for the organization.

Since an organization exists to accomplish something in the larger environment, its specific mission or purpose provides employees with a shared sense of opportunity, direction, significance, and achievement. An explicit mission guides employees to work independently and yet collectively toward the realization of the organization's potential. Thus, a good mission statement gets the emotional bonding and commitment needed. It allows the individual employee to say; "I know how I should do my job differently."

For example, many people might think that The Walt Disney Company's mission is to run theme parks. But, Disney's mission is always moving toward an expanded view. Disney provides entertainment. "Disney's overriding objective is to create shareholder value by continuing to be the world's premier entertainment company from a creative, strategic, and financial standpoint."

Also, many people might think that Revlon's mission is to make cosmetics. Yet, Revlon provides glamour, excitement and innovation. Charles Revson, Revlon's founder understood the importance of mission. He said "In the factory, we make cosmetics; in the store, we sell hope."

Vision

Erich Fromm pointed out; "The best way to predict your future is to create it." A vision might be a picture, image, or description of the preferred future. A visionary has the ability to foresee something and sees the need for change first. He or she challenges the status quo and forces honest assessments of where the industry is headed and how the company can best get there. A visionary is ready with solutions before the problems arise.

A study over the period from 1926 to 1990 found visionary companies that set a purpose beyond making money outperformed other companies in the stock market by more than six to one. (See Gilbert Fuchsberg, "Visioning' Mission Becomes Its Own Mission," The Wall Street Journal, January 7, 1994, B1, 3.) Managers require more vision than ever because change is coming faster than ever. Leaders have the ability to make their vision real by engaging the minds, as well as the hearts of others.

Microsoft's early vision statement was "A Computer on Every Desk and In Every Home." (At approximately the same time, President John Akers said IBM's goal was to become a $100 billion company by then end of the century. At that time IBM sales were $50 billion.) Microsoft's vision has evolved [1998 the "Connected PC and the Connected TV"-the idea of integrating the intelligence and interactivity of PCs with the video and sound of TV] to 2002 "to enable people and businesses throughout the world to realize their full potential."

Life consists in what a man is thinking of all day.--Ralph Waldo Emerson.

A goal is an end that the organization strives to attain. However, the supervisor cannot "do" a goal. Supervisors break down processes, analyze them, set objectives and then drive hard to achieve them. Doing the same thing and expecting different results doesn't work. The supervisor must write an objective for what he or she is trying to accomplish. Thus, an objective is the object or aim of an action. It implies an explicit direction for the action to take and a specific quality of work to be accomplished within a given period of time. Objectives reflect the desired outcomes for individuals, groups and organizations. They provide direction for decision-making and a criterion against which outcomes are measured. Thus, objectives are the foundation of planning.

MANAGEMENT BY OBJECTIVES

An effective planning tool to help the supervisor set objectives is Management by Objectives (MBO). MBO gained recognition in 1954 with the publication of Peter Drucker's book The Practice of Management. MBO is a collaborative process whereby the manager and each subordinate jointly determine objectives for that subordinate. To be successful MBO programs should include commitment and participation in the MBO process at all levels, from top management to the lowest position in the organization.

MBO begins when the supervisor explains the goals for the department in a meeting. The subordinate takes the goals and proposes objectives for his or her particular job. The supervisor meets with the subordinate to approve and, if necessary, modify the individual objectives. Modification of the individual's objectives is accomplished through negotiation since the supervisor has resources to help the subordinate commit to the achievement of the objective. Thus, a set of verifiable objectives for each individual are jointly determined, prioritized, and formalized. The supervisor and the subordinate meet periodically to review the latter's progress. Communication is the key factor in determining MBO's success or failure. The supervisor gives feedback and may authorize modifications to the objectives or their timetables as circumstances dictate. Finally, the employee's performance is measured against his or her objectives, and he or she is rewarded accordingly.

Steps in MBO Process

Research has demonstrated that when top management is committed and personally involved in implementing MBO programs, they significantly improve performance. This finding is not surprising when one considers that during the MBO process employees determine what they will accomplish. After all, who knows what a person is capable of doing better than the person does him or herself?

Objectives are the driver of planning processes. It is imperative that top managers safeguard the intention of their goals to facilitate middle and lower management's effective translation and implementation of them. Objectives guide managerial activities such as budgeting, the development of action plans, staffing, and the purchasing of equipment. The organization's success ultimately depends on the combined outcomes of its objectives.

Objectives

Most supervisors set objectives, but not with equal skill. Few, who do not correctly write objectives, will reap MBO's full benefits. An objective is simply a statement of what is to done and should be stated in terms of results. A mnemonic aid to write objectives is SMART (Specific, Measurable, Attainable, Result-oriented, Time-limited).

Specific

An objective must be specific with a single key result. If more than one result is to be accomplished, more than one objective should be written. Just knowing what is to be accomplished is a big step toward achieving it. What is important to you? Once you clarify what you want to achieve, your attention will be focused on the objective that you deliberately set. You will be doing something important to you.

Measurable

An objective must be measurable. Only an objective that affects behaviour in a measurable way can be optimally effective. If possible, state the objective as a quantity. Some objectives are more difficult to measure than others are. However, difficulty does not mean that they cannot be measured. Treatment of salespeople might be measured by looking at the absenteeism and turnover rates among the sales force. Also, salespeople could be asked to fill out a behavioural questionnaire anonymously giving their observations of the supervision they receive.

Customer service could be measured by such indices as the number of complaints received, by the number of customers lost, and by customer interviews or responses to questionnaires. Development of subordinates could be measured by determining the number of tasks the subordinate has mastered. Cooperation with other functions could be measured by length of delay in providing requested information, or by peer ratings of degree of cooperation. Avoid statements of objectives in generalities. Infinitives to avoid include to know, to understand, to enjoy, and to believe. Action verbs are observable and better communicate the intent of what is to be attempted. They include to write, to apply, to recite, to revise, to contrast, to install, to select, to assemble, to compare, to investigate, and to develop.

Scaling the Progress

Attainable

An objective must be attainable with the resources that are available. It must be realistic. Many objectives are realistic. Yet, the time it takes to achieve them may be unrealistic. For example, it is realistic to want to lose ten pounds. However, it is unrealistic to want to lose ten pounds in one week.

What barriers stand between you and your objective? How will each barrier be overcome and within what time frame?

Result-oriented

The objective should be central to the goals of the organization. The successful completion of the objective should make a difference. How will this objective help the organization move ahead? Is the objective aligned with the mission of the organization?

Time-limited

The objective should be traceable. Specific objectives enable time priorities to be set and time to be used on objectives that really matter. Are the time lines you have established realistic? Will other competing demands cause delay? Will you be able to overcome those demands to accomplish the objective you've set in the time frame you've established?

Write Meaningful Objectives

Although the rules are difficult to establish, the following may be useful when writing an objective.

1. Start with an action or accomplishment verb. (Use the infinitive form of the verb. This means to start the with "to.")
2. Identify a single key result for each objective.
3. Give the date of the estimated completion.
4. Be sure the objective is one you can control.
5. To test for validity of SMART objectives, ask yourself the following questions.
   * S = Exactly what is my objective?
   * M = What would a good job look like?
   * A = Is my objective feasible?
   * R = Is my objective meaningful?
   * T = Is my objective traceable?

The following fill-in-the-blank equation may be useful when writing an objective.

Objective: To (+ action verb + single key result + target date)

ORGANIZING PROCESS

In cases of management transfer, the estalishment process focuses on a level of user organization where no organization presently exists, that is, at a level of the irrigation network previously managed by the government irrigation agency. Typically this entails organizing federations of user groups at the tertiary level under a secondary-canal association. The challenge of creating a new organization of users is perhaps the most central feature of the management transfer process. The act of management transfer from the agency to the users depends upon a user organization that is capable of assuming those management responsibilities.

Before any organizing of the users is carried out, there needs to be a package of incentives in place for both the users and the agency staff whose jobs would be affected by the transfer program. Such incentives are needed both to make the program work, and to maintain credibility with farmers whose long-term support will be required. If organizing is attempted before an adequate incentive structure is established, the transfer program could well collapse, thus setting the entire program back by several years, as well as causing short-term hardships to those concerned. Thus, if the incentives are not clear and attractive to farmers, the organizing process should be delayed until the incentives are clarified.

First determine:

Who Will do the Organizing?

The first step is to decide on the type of organizers who will work directly with farmers in helping establish the organization. [We use the term "water user association" (WUA) to refer to this new organization, although the term, "WUA" can also refer to organizations at the tertiary level of the system which have always been outside the management control of the government irrigation agency.] In the Philippines, a special cadre of social organizers was recruited and trained by the National Irrigation Administration in the late1970s and early 80s. These organizers were mostly social workers or social scientists selected for their ability to work easily with farmers in village conditions. They were trained in irrigation management so they could better understand the technical problems of the farmers they were trying to organize.

The work of the Philippines social organizers was effective, yet this approach has not been widely replicated by irrigation agencies in other countries. The investment and bureaucratic difficulties involved in recruiting new temporary staff from a different discipline has led many irrigation agencies to try other approaches. In Mexico's transfer program, the National Water Commission's own staff were used along with staff from a sister agency, the Institute for Water Technology (IMTA). In addition, a few consultants were brought in on a case by case basis. In India, some state irrigation departments have relied on extensionists from the Agriculture Department under the Command Area Development Program.

Also in India, several NGOs have been involved in organizing, at the request of the irrigation departments. But the organizers of choice, for most irrigation agencies, will be their own field staff. These staff are already within the bureaucratic structure of the agency, so the lines of authority are clear, there is little additional expense involved, and these staff are already familiar with the physical systems and with the local farmers.

The problems with using irrigation agency field staff for organizing work, however, are considerable. These staff are not necessarily interested in organizing farmers, They have not received any prior training in social work (in most cases), and their superiors have also no training (nor interest) in these tasks. These would-be organizers must be re-trained for their organizing tasks, and just as importantly, their job assignments need to be re-defined to reflect their new role. In addition, their superiors need to be trained and re-oreinted so they understand and appreciate the new role to be played by their field staff.

What Training do the Organizers Need?

Assuming that agency staff will be used for the organizing, and assuming that their professional training has been in irrigation engineering, they would need to be re-tooled as organizers. First of all they would need a thorough understanding of the rationale for PIM, so that they can present a clear message both to the farmers and to their own colleagues within the irrigation agency. Secondly, they will need training in communcation skills (including listening skills) for effective interaction with the users. Thirdly, they will need training in social analysis, including an understanding of social stratification (by caste, ethnicity, or class), kinship, patron-client relations, labour relations, religious factors, political affiliation, land tenure (tenants, share-croppers, owners), etc.

And fourthly, they would need training in methods for gathering information from farmers (e.g., participatory rural appraisal) and in methods for organizing farmers.

Who will Provide the Training?

Irrigation management training institutes?

Universities?

Administrative staff colleges?

NGOs?

What capacity building do these organizations need?

skills training: TOT course on PIM?

structural change in the organization itself? (IMTI case)

financing?

new or clarified mandate?

Building support for capacity building may require training and consensus building at political levels, just to provide an enabling environment for the PIM program to get started. Then,

Organizing Steps

Note: This assumes there are reasonable incentives for farmers to take over system, and for the government irrigation agency to hand over the system; if not, go back and work on the incentives!

- Organize the organizers: Arrange for supervision/support for the organizers, and clear lines of communication with Departmental staff responsible for the overall project (Ensure that PIM component of program is well integrated with rest of project).
- Meet the farmers and other irrigation stakeholders/ Discuss plans formulated during participatory design phase:
  - — village head
  - — local administrative officials
  - — local political leaders (MLAs/MPs)

  - leaders of other farmer organizations (producer cooperatives)
- Identify key power relations among farmers; develop strategy for organizing
- Establish provisional boundaries of the system (through consultation with key power brokers among the farmers); conduct inventory of potential members; draw map showing command area and irrigation system.
- Arrange series of meetings between farmers and Departmental field staff to discuss improvements that need to be made prior to handover.
  - arrange canal walk-through to discuss specifics of design/infrastructure improvements
  - discuss general terms of WUA contracts
- Arrange farmer visits to other associations to discuss with those farmers (and invite those farmers to visit new association).
- Organizational Assistance:
  - Help prospective WUA leaders arrange farmer meetings to discuss plans
  - Help formulate/revise by-laws
  - Advise on elections/selections
  - Assist with legal registration
  - Arrange management training for WUA leaders
- Arrange meetings between WUA leaders and Department staff to discuss details of WUA contract and terms of transition phase leading to hand-over;
- Advise on staff recruitment(?)
- Assist with formal hand-over
- Visit periodically to monitor WUA's performance

3

Personnel Management

The foundation of recognition and motivation is that people need and want Acceptance, Approval and Appreciation. Almost all positive motivation is based on these needs. People want to know that what they do makes a difference. Just recognizing the staff is the most important step one can take. You may want to count the number of "we's that are said instead of "I's in order to assess the extent to which your staff feels part of the team and part of the business' future. One saying is, "Powerlessness corrupts, absolute powerlessness corrupts absolutely."

These nine actions will help immensely to give your staff what they need: Communicate, Communicate, Communicate, Recognize, Recognize, Recognize, Thank, Thank, and Thank! From various sources, Vicki developed a list of ideas for ongoing weekly or monthly programs to keep employees connected to the hotel or restaurant emotionally, to create excitement and to make your business unique relative to your nearby competitors for employees.

Remember, the competition for staff may be from other industries such as retail, manufacturing, etc. Pick a few and try them for a while; but, you must give them a chance, one time will not do it. The staff will see right through you.

- Gift certificate for the most challenging question posed to the President
- Money or chocolates or lottery ticket to a spouse with a note thanking for his/her support during overtime
- Thumbs-up certificates redeemable for merchandise

- Soda, fruit, snacks to housekeeping staff all the time
- When anyone makes a negative comment, put $0.25 or $0.50 into a pot and use the money for a Fun Committee
- Bring Polaroid camera to work occasionally and take candids of staff and post pictures on a bulletin board for all to enjoy
- Selection of employee of the month/quarter/year by peers not just management
- When he/she is employee of the month, give him/her a special name tag highlighting that status
- Points given out at any time for anything, good attendance, helping out a guest, etc., and are redeemable for prizes
- When you reach a certain level in revenues, give all staff a reward, being sure to give them the goal in advance
- Spontaneous calls from corporate to line staff saying how they are appreciated
- Allow line workers to participate in all personnel function decisions, hiring, training, evaluating, firing, schedules
- Fine those who arrive late to a meeting and distribute the money to those who were there on time
- Create a symbol of the team, maybe just property logo but put it on T-shirts, mugs, caps
- Certificate of achievement, lunch, and mug for perfect attendance, gift certificate to the one with longest perfect attendance
- Allow those with perfect attendance record to enter a lottery to get a $100 or $200 gift certificate
- Quarterly teleconference with all employees and support staff, especially CEO
- Family orientation for new employees with slide show or video program with refreshments
- Several line staff call new hire to welcome him/her to the team the day before he/she starts

- Toll-free hot line to President where they can leave any question, suggestion, etc. and will get a response
- Hold a regular meeting to tell staff what is going on and how they are doing
- Always hang charts, graphs, etc. to depict regularly how the property is doing
- Full page ad in newspaper once a year thanking employees and name all individually
- Public praising of an individual at a department or hotel meeting
- Make sure all rewards, praise, bonuses, etc. are in public
- Have the General Manager spend at least an hour with every new employee
- Golden Broom Award to all (excluding housekeeping staff) who are seen picking up trash-after two, they can redeem them for a gift
- Pick a trophy that is passed from rewardee to rewardee so it is much desired, it does not matter what it is and actually the odder the better so it is fun
- Pre-printed "you done good" or "a pat on the back" or "bravo" note cards to have management inscribe whenever appropriate spontaneously
- Praise immediately and tell them specifically what they did right and how it helps the company
- Always find ways to get staff's input into the operation-just simple suggestion box works great
- Work hard at finding a way to implement each suggestion and give a clear explanation why it cannot be used if that is the case
- Acknowledge all suggestions, even if not implemented, express appreciation perhaps also a small reward If you implement an idea, give a reward, and widely publicize it
- Pins for uniforms that say "The guest comes first" or "I will do my best" or "We're glad you're here" or something similar

- Periodically hold contests like a TV game show where employees answer questions about the property hotel, perhaps in teams
- Use an 800# service which employees call periodically to be given randomly selected test questions and win a prize if they get them all correct
- Give a small gift on the date of their anniversary
- Hold an annual banquet for those with more than a certain number of years of service
- Give every employee printed business cards
- At Ritz Carlton, all employees throughout the hotel are authorized to spend up to $2,000 each incident to resolve a guest's complaint, but few spend anywhere near that amount
- Ask employees regularly what else we can do for them to enable them to do a good job
- Tell employees regularly what else they can do for management to enable you to do a good job
- Hold weekly meetings with small groups of employees to discuss anything, serve food
- Hold a weekly 20 minute meeting with one employee to discuss anything
- Make it personal, people naturally commit themselves to other people, not to organizations
- Hold monthly employee meetings at which the financial performance of the previous month and other goals are discussed in specific
- Distribute daily reports of revenue performance last night and month-to-date
- Send employees and family to a competitive property and have them write a report
- Send employees and family to your property and have them write a report
- Imprint the hotel's four key business goals on T-shirts
- Include career development discussion in all performance reviews

- Send line staff to schools to do recruiting and interviewing
- Tell staff that if they achieve x,y,z, etc., you will call their mothers and tell them how great their child is and actually do it
- Always make sure their work environment is positive, attractive, and reflective of your goals and values
- Ideas for back-of-the-house areas: plants, framed art (let them choose), clean unworn carpets, adequate ventilation, natural light, meeting space, adequate work-space, well-functioning equipment, attractive break facilities
- Form a recreation committee to plan monthly activities
- Regular employee newsletter
- Ask for input on cost-cutting programs during times of low demand
- Implement management reviews where line staff assess management's performance

These are only a few of the infinite number of ideas to keep good staff members and motivate them to work hard toward common goals. Whatever you choose to do, keep doing it consistently and make sure that you are sincere. Good luck on making your hotel or restaurant a unique and rewarding place to work.

4

Essentials of Hotel and Restaurants

The Uniform Conditions for the Hotel and Catering Industry (UVH) are the terms and conditions on which catering establishments set up in the Netherlands, such as hotels, restaurants, bars and related businesses (including catering firms, party service firms, etc.), provide catering services and enter into catering agreements. The UVH are registered with the District Court and the Chamber of Commerce and Industry in The Hague.

DEFINITIONS

In the UVH and in the offers and agreements to which the UVH applies, the words below shall have the meanings assigned to them in this clause.

Catering Establishment

The natural person or legal entity or partnership which is in the business of providing hotel and/or catering services and is a member of Koninklijk Horeca Nederland (Dutch trade association for hotel and catering industry).

Host

Whoever represents a Catering Establishment in entering into and carrying out catering agreements.

Provision of Catering Services

The provision by a Catering Establishment of accommodation and/or food and/or drink and/or the supplying of halls and/or rooms and/or grounds, all these with all the associated work and services, and all in the broadest sense of the word.

Customer

The natural person or legal entity or partnership which has entered into an agreement with a Catering Establishment.

Guest

The natural person(s) entitled to one or more Catering Services based on a catering agreement entered into with the Customer.

Wherever the UVH speak of Guest, or Customer, this refers to both Guest and Customer, unless it is clear from the content and implication of the clause that only one of the two can be intended.

Catering Agreement

An agreement between a Catering Establishment and a Customer involving one or more Catering Services to be provided by the Catering Establishment at a price to be paid by the Customer. The term Reservation is sometimes used in place of the term Catering Agreement.

Hotel Establishment

The Catering Establishment where the provision of Catering Services consists mainly or exclusively of supplying accommodation.

Restaurant Establishment

The Catering Establishment where the provision of Catering Services consists mainly or exclusively of supplying food and accompanying drink.

Bar Establishment

The Catering Establishment where the provision of Catering Services consists mainly or exclusively of supplying drink.

Room Rental Establishment

The Catering Establishment where the provision of Catering Services consists mainly or exclusively of providing rooms or halls.

Reservation Value (the value of the Catering Agreement)

The total expected turnover of the Catering Establishment including service charges, (tourist tax) and VAT relating to a Catering Agreement concluded with a Customer, which expected turnover is based on the averages applicable to that Catering Establishment.

Koninklijk Horeca Nederland

Het Koninklijk Verbond van Ondernemers in het Horeca- en Aanverwante Bedrijf (The Royal Association of Businesses in the Catering and Related Industries) known as "Horeca Nederland" or any legal successor to this.

Cancellation

The written notice by the Customer to the Catering Establishment that one or more of the agreed Catering Services is no longer required in part or in full, or the written notice by the Catering Establishment to the Customer that one or more of the agreed Catering Services shall no longer be provided in part or in full.

No-show

The failure of a Guest, without prior Cancellation, to make use of one of the Catering Services provided on the basis of a Catering Agreement.

Group

A group of 10 or more persons entitled to one or more Catering Services from a Catering Establishment under the terms of a Catering Agreement or more than one agreement regarded as connected.

Individual

Every person that does not form part of a Group as defined above.

Goods

All Goods, including money, valuables and papers of value.

Corkage

The price charged when drink not provided by a Catering Establishment is consumed on the premises of that Catering Establishment.

Food Charge

The price charged when food not provided by a Catering Establishment is consumed on the premises of that Catering Establishment.

Turnover Guarantee

A written declaration from the Customer that the Catering Establishment will realise a certain minimum turnover from one or more Catering Agreements. Clause headings are used exclusively for reference purposes. No rights may be derived from these.

SCOPE

The UVH apply to the making and content of all Catering Agreements, as well as all offers relating to the making of such Catering Agreements, to the exclusion of all other general terms and conditions. If other general terms and conditions besides these are actually in force, the UVH shall prevail where any conflict arises. Departure from the UVH is only possible if set down in writing and on a case by case basis.

The UVH also cover all natural persons and legal entities which the Catering Establishment uses or has used in concluding and/or carrying out a Catering Agreement or a different agreement or in running the Catering Establishment.

Once the UVH have been declared legally applicable to a certain Catering Agreement, then the latest valid version of the UVH is considered to apply to all subsequent Catering Agreements between the same parties, unless agreed otherwise in writing.

THE MAKING OF CATERING AGREEMENTS

A Catering Establishment can at any time and for any reason refuse to enter into a Catering Agreement, except where such a refusal is based purely on one or more of the grounds specified in Clause 429 of the Criminal Code (discrimination).

All offers presented by a Catering Establishment in connection with the making of a Catering Agreement are without obligation and conditional "on the supply (or capacity) being adequate". If the Catering Establishment invokes the said restriction within a period which can be considered reasonable in the circumstances following the Customer's acceptance of the offer then the intended Catering Agreement shall be considered not to be made.

If the Catering Establishment has granted the Customer (option holder) a right of first refusal, this right cannot be revoked, except if and insofar as another potential Customer makes an offer to the Catering Establishment to enter into a Catering Agreement concerning all or part of the Catering Services due in the option. In that case the option holder must be informed of this offer by the Catering Establishment, whereupon the option holder must state whether or not he wishes to take up the right of first refusal.

If the option holder does not give notice that he wishes to take up the right of first refusal then this right shall lapse. A right of first refusal can only be granted in writing.

Catering Agreements for one or more Guests entered into by intermediaries (shipbrokers, travel agencies, other Catering Establishments, etc.), whether or not in the name of their business connection(s), shall be considered to be concluded partly for account and risk of this intermediary. The Catering Establishment shall not owe any commission or percentage, by whatever name, to the intermediary unless specifically agreed otherwise in writing. Payment by the Guest of the whole or part of the amount due shall release the intermediary to the same extent.

GENERAL OBLIGATIONS OF THE CATERING ESTABLISHMENT

The obligations specified in this clause apply to every Catering Establishment. All obligations arising from the special nature of the Catering Establishment and the type of Catering Services to be performed are contained in the following clauses.

Under the terms of the Catering Agreement, the Catering Establishment is, without prejudice to the stipulations in the following clauses, bound to provide the agreed Catering Services at the agreed times in the manner customary in that Catering Establishment.

The Catering Establishment is not obliged to accept and/ or take into safe keeping any property of the Guest.

If the Catering Establishment makes any charge to the Guest for accepting Goods and/or taking Goods into safe keeping, the Catering Establishment is obliged to take reasonable care of those Goods, without prejudice to the stipulations in Clause 12.

The Catering Establishment is never obliged to admit any domestic animal belonging to the Guest and may attach conditions to such admission.

OBLIGATIONS OF THE HOTEL ESTABLISHMENT

The Hotel Establishment is during the agreed period obliged to provide the Guest with accommodation of the standard customary in that hotel, subject to the stipulations in the third subclause.

The Hotel Establishment must also be able to provide the associated Catering Services customary in that hotel and to supply the facilities customary there.

The accommodation should be available to the Guest from 14.00 hours on the day of arrival until 12 noon on the day of departure.

The Hotel Establishment should hang or affix or deposit the house rules in a clearly visible place for the information of the Guest, or hand over the house rules in writing to the Guest. The Guest is obliged to observe the house rules.

The Hotel Establishment is entitled to terminate the provision of Catering Services to a Guest at any time without prior notice if the Guest repeatedly breaks the house rules, or otherwise behaves in such a way that the order and peace and quiet in the Catering Establishment and/or the normal running of the place may be or is disturbed. In that case the Guest must leave the hotel at the first request. The Hotel Establishment may only exercise this right if the nature and seriousness of the breaches of the house rules by the guest give sufficient cause, in the reasonable opinion of the Hotel Establishment.

Unless otherwise agreed, the Hotel Establishment is entitled to regard the reservation as cancelled if the Guest has not checked in on the first day of the reservation by 18.00 hours, without prejudice to the stipulations.

The Hotel Establishment is entitled to ask the Guest to accept accommodation that differs from what is described in the Catering Agreement, except if such a request is clearly unreasonable and must be considered obviously too inconvenient for the Guest. In the latter case, the Guest/Customer has the right to cancel the Catering Agreement to which the aforementioned request of the Catering Establishment applies, with immediate effect, without prejudice to his obligations based on other Catering Agreements. If the Catering Establishment saves money in the above circumstances by providing accommodation that differs from what is described in the Catering Agreement, the Guest and/or Customer is entitled to the amount that is saved. Beyond that the Catering Establishment shall never be obliged to pay any compensation.

OBLIGATIONS OF THE RESTAURANT ESTABLISHMENT

The Restaurant Establishment is obliged to provide the Guest with the agreed facilities at the agreed time and to supply the agreed food and drink in the quantity, quality and in the manner customary in that restaurant.

If no food and drink are agreed in advance then the Restaurant Establishment shall on request provide whatever food and drink is available at that moment, without prejudice to the other stipulations.

The Restaurant Establishment is entitled to refrain from providing Catering Services or to terminate these at any time if the Guest does not behave in a way that is fitting to the class and operation of that restaurant. The Restaurant Establishment may, among other things, lay down rules concerning the outward appearance of the Guest. The Guest must leave the restaurant at the first request.

If the Guest has not arrived by half an hour after the reserved time, the Restaurant Establishment may consider the reservation cancelled, without prejudice to the stipulations.

Obligations of the Bar Establishment

The Bar Establishment is obliged on request to provide the Guest with the drinks which it has in stock. In addition the Bar Establishment must be able to provide the Catering Services customary in that establishment.

The Bar Establishment is entitled to refrain from providing Catering Services or to terminate these at any time if the Guest does not behave in a way that is fitting to the class and operation of that bar. The Bar Establishment may, among other things, lay down rules concerning the outward appearance of the Guest. The Guest must leave the bar at the first request.

Obligations of the Catering Establishment concerning room rental

The Catering Establishment is entitled to provide rooms that differ from what is described in the Catering Agreement, except if such a request is clearly unreasonable and must be considered obviously too inconvenient for the Guest. In the latter case, the Guest/Customer has the right to cancel the Catering Agreement to which the aforementioned request of the Catering Establishment applies, with immediate effect, without prejudice to his obligations based on other Catering Agreements. If the Catering Establishment saves money in the above circumstances by providing rooms that differ from what is described in the Catering Agreement, the Guest and/or Customer is entitled to the amount that is saved. Beyond that the Catering Establishment shall never be obliged to pay any compensation.

The Catering Establishment must in addition be able to provide the Guests with the Catering Services customary in that establishment. The Catering Establishment is entitled to refrain from providing Catering Services or to terminate these at any time if the Guest does not behave in a way that is fitting to the class and operation of that Catering Establishment. The Catering Establishment may, among other things, lay down rules concerning the outward appearance of the Guest. The Guest must leave the Catering Establishment at the first request.

The Catering Establishment is entitled, after consultation with the competent authorities locally, to cancel the Catering Agreement on the grounds of justifiable fear that the public order may be disturbed. If the Catering Establishment makes use of this power, then the Catering Establishment shall not be liable to pay any compensation.

Cancellations

Cancellation by Customers, general

The Customer is not entitled to cancel a Catering Agreement, unless he at the same time makes a binding offer to pay the amounts fixed below. Every Cancellation is considered to include such an offer. Such an offer is considered to be accepted if the Catering Establishment does not reject the offer forthwith. Cancellation should take place in writing and be dated. The Customer cannot derive any rights from a verbal Cancellation.

The Catering Establishment may inform the Customer at the latest one month before the first Catering Service based on the relevant Catering Agreement is due to be provided that it will regard certain Individuals as a Group. In that case all the conditions for Groups apply to those persons.

In the event of No-show, the Customer is in all cases required to pay the Reservation Value.

9.1.5 In the event that not all the agreed Catering Services are cancelled, the conditions below apply pro rata to the Catering Services that are cancelled.

If one or more agreed Catering Services are completely or partly cancelled, the periods in the following clauses shall be increased by 4 months, if the Reservation Value of the cancelled Catering Services amounts to more than the correspondingly calculated value of the other Catering Services that the Catering Establishment could have provided during the period in which the cancelled Catering Services were to have been provided.

Any amounts which the Catering Establishment already owes to third parties at the time of Cancellation based on the cancelled Catering Agreement must at all times be fully reimbursed by the Customer to the Catering Establishment, provided the Catering Establishment has not acted unreasonably in entering into the commitments in question. The amounts involved shall go towards a reduction of the Reservation Value referred to in the following clauses.

Cancellation of hotel accommodation/lodgings

Groups

If a reservation for only hotel accommodation is made, either with or without breakfast, for a Group then the following applies to the Cancellation of this reservation.

1. In case of Cancellation more than 3 months before the time when the first Catering Service should be provided under the terms of the Catering Agreement, hereinafter called "the Commencement Date", the Customer is not obliged to make any payment to the Hotel Establishment.
2. In case of Cancellation more than 2 months before the Commencement Date, the Customer is obliged to pay 15% of the Reservation Value to the Hotel Establishment.
3. In case of Cancellation more than 1 month before the Commencement Date, the Customer is obliged to pay 35% of the Reservation Value to the Hotel Establishment.
4. In case of Cancellation more than 14 days before the Commencement Date, the Customer is obliged to pay 60% of the Reservation Value to the Hotel Establishment.
5. In case of Cancellation more than 7 days before the Commencement Date, the Customer is obliged to pay 85% of the Reservation Value to the Hotel Establishment.

6. In case of Cancellation 7 days or less before the Commencement Date, the Customer is obliged to pay 100% of the Reservation Value to the Hotel Establishment.

Individuals

If a reservation for only hotel accommodation is made, either with or without breakfast, for a one or more Individuals then the following applies to the Cancellation of this reservation.

1. In case of Cancellation more than 1 month before the Commencement Date, the Customer is not obliged to pay any money to Hotel Establishment.
2. In case of Cancellation more than 14 days before the Commencement Date, the Customer is obliged to pay 15% of the Reservation Value to the Hotel Establishment.
3. In case of Cancellation more than 7 days before the Commencement Date, the Customer is obliged to pay 35% of the Reservation Value to the Hotel Establishment.
4. In case of Cancellation more than 3 days before the Commencement Date, the Customer is obliged to pay 60% of the Reservation Value to the Hotel Establishment.
5. In case of Cancellation more than 24 hours before the Commencement Date, the Customer is obliged to pay 85% of the Reservation Value to the Hotel Establishment.
6. In case of Cancellation 24 hours or less before the Commencement Date, the Customer is obliged to pay 100% of the Reservation Value to the Hotel Establishment.

Cancellation of restaurant/table reservation

If a reservation for only a restaurant (table reservation) is made for a Group then the following applies to the Cancellation of that reservation:

1. if a menu has been agreed:
    1. in case of Cancellation more than 14 days before the reserved time no payment is due;

2. in case of Cancellation 14 days or less but more than 7 days before the reserved time the Customer shall pay 25% of the Reservation Value;
3. in case of Cancellation 7 days or less before the reserved time the Customer shall pay 50% of the Reservation Value;
4. in case of Cancellation 3 days or less before the reserved time the Customer shall pay 75% of the Reservation Value.

2. if no menu has been agreed:
   1. in case of Cancellation more than twice 24 hours before the reserved time no payment is due;
   2. in case of Cancellation twice 24 hours or less before the reserved time the Customer shall pay 50% of the Reservation Value.

Individuals

If a reservation for only a restaurant (table reservation) is made for one or more Individuals then the following applies to the Cancellation of that reservation:

1. if a menu has been agreed:
   1. in case of Cancellation more than four times 24 hours before the reserved time no payment is due;
   2. in case of Cancellation four times 24 hours or less before the reserved time the Customer shall pay 50% of the Reservation Value.
2. if no menu has been agreed:
   1. in case of Cancellation more than twice 24 hours before the reserved time no payment is due;
   2. in case of Cancellation twice 24 hours or less before the reserved time the Customer shall pay 50% of the Reservation Value.

Cancellation of other Catering Agreements

The following shall apply to the Cancellation of any reservations not covered by Clauses 9.2 and 9.3.

The Cancellation of a Reservation made for a group shall be subject to the following.

1. In case of Cancellation more than 6 months before the time when under the terms of the Catering Agreement the first Catering Service should be provided, the Customer is not obliged to make any payment to the Catering Establishment.
2. In case of Cancellation more than 3 months before the said time, the Customer is obliged to pay 10% of the Reservation Value to the Catering Establishment.
3. In case of Cancellation more than 2 months before the said time, the Customer is obliged to pay 15% of the Reservation Value to the Catering Establishment.
4. In case of Cancellation more than 1 month before the said time, the Customer is obliged to pay 35% of the Reservation Value to the Catering Establishment.
5. In case of Cancellation more than 14 days before the said time, the Customer is obliged to pay 60% of the Reservation Value to the Catering Establishment.
6. In case of Cancellation more than 7 days before the said time, the Customer is obliged to pay 85% of the Reservation Value to the Catering Establishment.
7. In case of Cancellation 7 days or less before the said time, the Customer is obliged to pay 100% of the Reservation Value to the Catering Establishment.

The Cancellation of a Reservation made for one or more individuals shall be subject to the following.

1. In case of Cancellation more than 1 month before the time when under the terms of the Catering Agreement the first Catering Service should be provided, the Customer is not obliged to make any payment to the Catering Establishment.
2. In case of Cancellation more than 14 days before the said time, the Customer is obliged to pay 15% of the Reservation Value to the Catering Establishment.

3. In case of Cancellation more than 7 days before the said time, the Customer is obliged to pay 35% of the Reservation Value to the Catering Establishment.
4. In case of Cancellation more than 3 days before the said time, the Customer is obliged to pay 60% of the Reservation Value to the Catering Establishment.
5. In case of Cancellation more than 24 hours before the said time, the Customer is obliged to pay 85% of the Reservation Value to the Catering Establishment.
6. In case of Cancellation 24 hours or less before the said time, the Customer is obliged to pay 100% of the Reservation Value to the Catering Establishment.

Cancellation by the Catering Establishment

The Catering Establishment is entitled to cancel a Catering Agreement subject to the following, unless the Customer has given written notice within seven days after the signing of the said Catering Agreement requiring the Catering Establishment to waive its powers to cancel the agreement, provided that the Customer at the same time clearly states that he is also waiving his own powers to cancel the agreement.

The Catering Establishment is at all times entitled to cancel a Catering Agreement, without being obliged to pay the aforementioned amounts, if there are sufficient indications that the gathering to be held in the Catering Establishment on the grounds of the Catering Agreement is of such a different character from what might have been expected on the grounds of the Customer's statement or on the grounds of the capacity of the Customer or Guests, that the Catering Establishment would not have concluded the agreement, if it had been aware of the actual nature of the gathering. If the Catering Establishment exercises this right after the gathering in question has started, the Customer shall be obliged to pay for the Catering Services provided up to that point in time, but the Customer's obligation to pay for the rest shall cease to apply. In such an event, the payment for the Catering Services provided shall be calculated in proportion to the time the gathering was due to last.

If and insofar as the Catering Establishment also acts as a tour operator in the legal sense, the following shall apply with regard to travel agreements in the legal sense. The Catering Establishment may change an essential point in the travel agreement, owing to important circumstances that are immediately reported to the Customer. The Catering Establishment may also change a non-essential point in the travel agreement, owing to important circumstances that are immediately reported to the Customer. Up to twenty days before the commencement of travel, the Catering Establishment may increase the cost of the trip in connection with changes in the cost of transport, including fuel costs, the levies that are due, or the applicable exchange rates. If the traveller refuses to accept any such change, the Catering Establishment may cancel the travel agreement.

Guarantee deposit and interim payment

The Catering Establishment can at any time require the Customer to deposit or arrange to have deposited with the Catering Establishment a guarantee deposit amounting at most to the Reservation Value less any interim payments already made. Guarantee deposits received shall be subject to proper accounting procedures, shall serve exclusively as security for the Catering Establishment and definitely do not count as already realised turnover.

The Catering Establishment can in each case ask for an interim payment for Catering Services already provided.

The Catering Establishment may recover all sums owed by the Customer on any account out of the amount deposited in accordance with the previous clauses. The balance must be repaid to the Customer by the Catering Establishment immediately.

Turnover Guarantee

If a Turnover Guarantee is issued, the Customer is obliged to pay the Catering Establishment at least the sum determined in the Turnover Guarantee in respect of the Catering Agreements concerned.

Liability of the Catering Establishment

The exclusion of liability in this clause does not apply insofar as the Catering Establishment has received a payment from an insurance company or from another third party relating to the risk that has materialised.

Without prejudice to the conditions in Clause 4.6, the Hotel Establishment is not liable for damage or loss of Goods which have been brought into the hotel by a Guest who is staying there. The Customer indemnifies the Hotel Establishment against claims from Guests in this respect. These stipulations do not apply insofar as the damage or loss is caused intentionally or the hotel is grossly at fault.

This liability exclusion also applies in particular to damage resulting from consuming foods prepared or served by the Catering Establishment, and to damage resulting from computer-related problems. If imperative law only permits a less extensive liability restriction, that less extensive restriction shall apply.

In no case is the Catering Establishment obliged to pay a higher sum in compensation than:

1. the Reservation Value or, if that is more,
2. (1) the amount paid out by the Catering Establishment's insurer to the Catering Establishment for the damage, or (2) the compensation for the damage received from another third party.

The Catering Establishment is never liable for damage to or caused by vehicles of the Guest, except if and insofar as the damage is caused intentionally or the Catering Establishment is grossly at fault.

The Catering Establishment is never liable for damage caused directly or indirectly to any persons or property as a direct or indirect result of any defect or any feature or circumstance on or in any moveable or immoveable property which the Catering Establishment is looking after, holding on a long or short lease, hiring or which it owns or which is in any other way at the disposal of the Catering Establishment, except if and insofar as the damage is caused intentionally or the Catering Establishment is grossly at fault.

If the Guest finds there has been any damage to the Goods placed in safe keeping, in exchange for payment, the Catering Establishment is obliged to make good the damage to these Goods resulting from their being damaged or lost. Compensation is never due in connection with other Goods contained inside the Goods which are handed in.

If the Catering Establishment accepts Goods or if Goods are deposited, left in safe keeping and/or left behind in any way, anywhere or by anyone without the Catering Establishment charging any money for this, then the Catering Establishment is never liable for damage to or in connection with those Goods however this may arise unless the Catering Establishment deliberately caused this damage, or the Catering Establishment is grossly to blame for the damage.

The Customer (not being a natural person who is not acting in the exercise of a profession or business) indemnifies the Catering Establishment in full against any claim, by whatever name, which the Guest and/or any third party may lodge against the Catering Establishment, if and insofar as this claim has any connection in the broadest sense with any (Catering) Service to be provided or which has been provided by the Catering Establishment under the terms of any agreement with the Customer or has any connection with the accommodation where such a (Catering) Service was provided or was to be provided.

The liability to indemnify referred to in Clause 12.9 also applies if the Catering Agreement with the Customer and/or the Guest is cancelled in full or in part for any reason.

LIABILITY OF THE GUEST AND/OR CUSTOMER

The Customer and the Guest and anyone accompanying them are severally liable for all damage which has occurred and/or may occur to the Catering Establishment and/or to any third party as a direct or indirect result of any non-fulfilment of obligations (culpable deficiency) and/or wrongful action, including breaking the house rules, committed by the Customer and/or the Guest and/or anyone accompanying them, as well as for all damage caused by any animal and/or any substance and/or any article which is in their possession or which is under their supervision.

SETTLEMENT OF ACCOUNTS AND PAYMENT

The Customer has to pay the price fixed in the Catering Agreement or, insofar as the Catering Agreement was signed more than three months before the time when the Catering Services arising out of that Agreement have to be provided, the prices which apply at the time that the Catering Service(s) has/have to be provided, which are understood to be the prices stated on the lists displayed by the Catering Establishment in a place visible to the Guest or which are included in a list which is handed to the Customer/Guest, if necessary at the request of said Customer/Guest.

A list is considered to be displayed in a place visible to the Guest if the list is visible in rooms which are normally accessible in the Catering Establishment.

An extra charge can be made by the Catering Establishment for special services, such as the use of a cloakroom, garage, safe, laundry, telephone, telex, TV rental, etc.

All accounts, including accounts relating to Cancellation or No-show, are due for payment by the Customer and/or Guest at the time they are presented to him. The Customer is responsible for paying in cash unless otherwise agreed in writing or unless agreed otherwise.

If an invoice is sent out for an account which is below e 150,-according to the conditions in the fourth subclause, then the Catering Establishment may add for administration costs to the account. The stipulations in this clause correspondingly apply to that amount.

The Guest and the Customer are severally liable for all amounts which one or both of them may owe the Catering Establishment on any account. Neither of them may appeal to benefit of excussion. Except where stipulated otherwise,

Catering Agreements are considered to be concluded jointly on behalf of every Guest. By turning up the Guest acknowledges that the Customer was competent to represent him in concluding the relevant Catering Agreement.

As long as the Guest and/or Customer has not entirely fulfilled all his obligations to the Catering Establishment, the Catering Establishment is entitled to take over and keep all Goods which the Guest and/or Customer has brought with him to the Catering Establishment, until the Guest and/or Customer has fulfilled all his obligations to the Catering Establishment to the satisfaction of the Catering Establishment. Should this situation arise, the Catering Establishment has a right of lien as well as a right of retention on the Goods in question.

If payment otherwise than in cash is agreed, all invoices for any amount must be paid by the Customer to the Catering Establishment within fourteen days of the invoice date. If an invoice is sent out, the Catering Establishment is at all times entitled to add an extra 2% to the invoice to cover the restriction of its credit, which is removed if the Customer pays the invoice within fourteen days.

If and insofar as payment is not made in good time, the Customer is in default without any notice of default being necessary.

If the Customer is in default he must reimburse the Catering Establishment for all costs, both judicial and extrajudicial, arising from collection. The set level of extrajudicial collection costs is at least 15% of the principal amount owed, with a minimum of e 100.-all to be increased by the VAT due on that amount.

Over and above this, if the Customer is in default he will be charged interest at 2% above the legal interest rate. When the amount of interest due is calculated, part of a month is counted as a full month.

If the Catering Establishment has in its keeping Goods and if the Customer from whom the Catering Establishment has received the Goods into keeping is in default for three months, the Catering Establishment is entitled to sell these

Goods publicly or privately and to recover the amount owed from the proceeds. The costs associated with the sale are also the responsibility of the Customer, and the Catering Establishment can also recover these costs from the proceeds of the sale. After the Catering Establishment has recovered everything it is owed, any remaining money shall be paid to the Customer.

Every payment shall, regardless of any endorsements or observations made by the Customer at the time of payment, be considered as serving to reduce the debt of the Customer to the Catering Establishment in the following order:

1. the costs of execution
2. the judicial and extrajudicial collection costs
3. the interest
4. the damage
5. the principal amount.

Payment shall take place in Dutch currency. If the Catering Establishment accepts foreign instruments of payment then the market exchange rate in force at the time of payment shall apply. The Catering Establishment may charge administration costs amounting to a maximum of 10% of the amount offered in foreign currency. The Catering Establishment can effectuate this by adjusting the market exchange rate then in force by a maximum of 10%.

The Catering Establishment is never obliged to accept cheques, giro payment cards and other such instruments of payment and may attach conditions to the acceptance of such instruments of payment. The same applies to other instruments of payment not referred to here.

Force majeure

Force majeure for the Catering Establishment, which means that any deficiency caused by this cannot be attributed to the Catering Establishment, shall be defined as every foreseen or unforeseen, foreseeable or unforeseeable circumstance which interferes with the fulfilment of the Catering Agreement by the Catering Establishment to such an extent that the fulfilment of the Catering Agreement becomes impossible or difficult.

Such circumstances are also understood to include such circumstances involving persons and/or services and/or institutions which the Catering Establishment is planning to use in fulfilling the Catering Agreement, as well as everything that applies to the aforementioned in terms of force majeure or reasons for postponement or cancellation, as well as non-fulfilment by the aforementioned.

If one of the parties to a Catering Agreement is not in a position to fulfil any obligation in that Catering Agreement, he is obliged to inform the other party of this as soon as possible.

Lost and found

Any objects which are lost or left behind in the building and appurtenances of the Catering Establishment and which are found by the Guest, must be handed in to the Catering Establishment by the Guest with all convenient speed.

Any objects which the rightful owner has not claimed from the Catering Establishment within a year of their being handed in become the property of the Catering Establishment.

If the Catering Establishment sends the Guest any objects that have been left behind, this shall take place entirely for account and risk of the Guest. The Catering Establishment is never obliged to send on such objects.

Corkage

If the Guest and/or Customer consumes drink that has not been provided by a Catering Establishment on the premises of that Catering Establishment, the Customer has to pay Corkage for each bottle consumed. If the Guest and/or Customer consumes food that has not been provided by a Catering Establishment on the premises of that Catering Establishment, the Customer has to pay a Food Charge.

Applicable law and disputes

Catering Agreements shall be governed exclusively by the laws of the Netherlands.

Any dispute between the Catering Establishment and the Customer (not being a natural person who is not acting in the exercise of a profession or business) shall be exclusively subject to the jurisdiction of the court in the domicile of the Catering Establishment, unless another court is competent under the strictly binding provisions of the law and without prejudice to the authority of the Catering Establishment to settle the dispute through the court which would have jurisdiction in the absence of this condition.

If and as soon as an arbitration committee is established under the auspices of Koninklijk Horeca Nederland and any other organisations which may be involved, the disputes which the arbitration committee is set up to mediate shall be settled in accordance with the regulations drawn up for this purpose.

All claims from the Customer become barred after one year has elapsed from the time of their origination.

The nullity of one or more clauses in these general terms and conditions does not affect the validity of all the other clauses. If a clause in these general terms and conditions turns out to be invalid for any reason, then the parties are assumed to have agreed a valid replacement clause which comes as close as possible to the meaning and scope of the invalid clause.

SAFETY RULES IN THE CATERING INDUSTRY

The hotel and catering industry is both large and diverse in character. It employs over two million full and part-time workers and embraces a wide range and scale of catering activities; from large scale food processing to individual cook to order catering. Accident rates in the catering industry have shown a rising trend since the Reporting of Injuries Diseases and Dangerous Occurrences Regulations (RIDDOR) first came into force in 1986/87. Statistics show that the rate is high when compared with other parts of the services sector. Accidents give rise to unnecessary pain and suffering. They also place an enormous financial burden on the catering industry.

In addition to the worrying news about accident trends, the industry also needs to be aware of a range of health and safety legislation which came into force on 1 January 1993. Health and safety is an issue which the catering industry cannot afford to ignore.

The Costs of Accidents

Every working day in Great Britain two people are killed and over 6000 are injured at work. Every year three-quarters of a million people take time off work because of what they regard as work-related illness. Around 31 million work days are lost as a result; more than 30 times that lost through strikes. The catering industry is a significant contributor to these statistics.

Workplace accidents and ill health cause unnecessary misery to the individuals concerned and to their families. They can also cripple companies because, in addition to the direct costs of personal injuries, they may also incur other far greater costs such as damage to property or equipment and lost production. Only a small proportion of these are recoverable from insurance.

A recent HSE study costed 6000 accidents from a range of companies. All were considered to be preventable by improved management control. The costs were alarming:

— accidents cost one organisation 8.5% of turnover;

— in another, costs represented 37% of profits;

— in a third, costs were 5% of operating costs.

In all cases the losses were between eight and 36 times greater than the insured costs.

A key outcome of the study was the recognition that the investment needed to increase market share and generate extra profits to cover accidental losses could be much greater than the investment needed to reduce the losses.

The Committee

The Health and Safety Executive (HSE) and the catering industry have established the Health and Safety in Catering Industry Liaison Committee as a direct response to these issues. The Committee comprises representatives of HSE and local authorities (LAs), together with employers, employees and trade associations from the catering industry. The committee will act as a network to develop and communicate information and guidance through the industry and will provide a forum where issues can be identified and resolved.

New Regulations

Six sets of Health and Safety at Work Regulations came into force on 1 January 1993 in order to implement six European Community directives. The Regulations are written in such a way as to encourage proper health and safety management. They also require risk assessments to be carried out. It is good practice to ensure that money spent on health and safety matters is directed at the hazards presenting the greatest risk. The assessment requirements in the new Regulations seek to ensure that you identify such risks before moving down the path of providing adequate control. The key will be to make systems efficient and effective: mountains of paper will not impress inspectors, but assessment of risk conducted at a level appropriate to the nature of the business and its work activities, leading to effective risk control, should find favour.

The Regulations cover health and safety management, manual handling, safety in the workplace and with work equipment, personal protective equipment, and display screen equipment (VDUs). The existing Health and Safety at Work etc Act 1974 will remain almost totally unchanged. Most of the duties in the six sets of Regulations are not new: they clarify and make more explicit duties which were already legal requirements. Exceptions to this are new requirements concerning health and safety management, manual handling and the use of display screens. Each of the sets of Regulations are backed up by either an Approved Code of Practice or guidance, giving comprehensive advice on compliance.

The catering industry should be in a particularly strong position to respond to the new Regulations because businesses will be able to draw on experience gained from operating within the requirements of the Food Safety Act. The systems needed to meet customers' quality assurance standards should also tie in well with the systems approach to health and safety management.

Initial action should be concentrated on the areas which experience has shown present the highest levels of risk. In the catering industry these are SLIPS, TRIPS AND FALLS; LIFTING AND MANUAL HANDLING; CONTACT WITH HOT SURFACES, HARMFUL SUBSTANCES ETC; BEING STRUCK BY AN OBJECT; DERMATITIS; AND WORK-RELATED UPPER LIMB DISORDERS.

The following paragraphs give further information on the new Regulations, how they are likely to be enforced and the priorities for the catering industry.

Priorities

The new Regulations introduce a number of requirements which deal specifically with the hazards responsible for most of the deaths, injuries and ill health in the catering industry. Employers will therefore need to concentrate on these high priority areas.

The key requirement to which all businesses will need to give priority is the management of health and safety. The Management of Health and Safety at Work Regulations 1992 ('The Management Regulations') require every employer and self-employed person to make a risk assessment. They also cover the need for health surveillance (which you should already be looking at under The Control of Substances Hazardous to Health Regulations 1994, better known as COSHH) and training. When looking at training needs, new recruits, part-timers and temporary staff will have to be considered. Additional information on managing health and safety and on risk assessment is given later.

The Management Regulations contain two other important items. Firstly, they require employers to appoint competent people to help the company to comply with the legislation. The Approved Code makes it clear that in most cases this can be done using existing staff, provided they are given the facilities to acquaint themselves with best practice etc. Secondly, the more detailed requirements for making arrangements for health and safety may mean it is necessary to revise any existing safety policy to expand on how it is proposed to plan, organise, control, monitor and review the arrangements.

Between them, slips, trips and falls and being struck by an object, account for over half of all reported injuries in the catering sector. The Workplace (Health, Safety and Welfare) Regulations 1992 ('the Workplace Regulations') address these problems. They require floors to be of suitable construction, non-slip where appropriate, and to be kept free from any article or substance which might cause a person to slip.

The Workplace Regulations also require effective measures to be taken to prevent people falling any distance likely to cause injury (unlike the previous legislation, which was concerned with falls of 6 feet or more). Precautions have to be taken to prevent falling objects causing injury, including simple things like pots and pans falling from high shelves. A further specific duty aimed at preventing falls involves the design of windows, which must take account of those who use them normally and those who are required to clean them

Handling, lifting and carrying accidents account for 14% of all accidents in catering. The Manual Handling Operations Regulations 1992 ('the Manual Handling Regulations') require employers to avoid the need for hazardous manual handling operations, so far as is reasonably practicable. Those hazardous operations which can't be avoided have to be assessed and the risk of injury reduced. It should be remembered that manual handling does not just mean lifting: pushing, pulling etc also need to be taken into account. Training in proper lifting techniques is important, but is not an alternative to reducing the risk in the first place.

The catering industry is unique in having a high level of accidents involving contact with hot surfaces and harmful substances. The Workplace Regulations contain a requirement for appropriate protection to be provided wherever there is a risk of contact with equipment or substances that are at high or low temperature. The health problems prevalent in the catering industry are dermatitis and work-related upper limb disorders. Those caused by contact with harmful substances are covered by COSHH so little change may be required to comply with the new Regulations.

Think positively about this new legislation. Look at the work you do and try to foresee the major problem areas, then implement changes to reduce the risks. This approach will help you to meet your legal requirements and may prevent the tragedy of an accident or case of ill health at work.

ENFORCING THE REGULATIONS

Responsibility for the enforcement of health and safety legislation in the industry is divided between HSE and local authorities, (usually through their Environmental Health Department). HSE is the enforcing authority for institutional catering, for example in prisons, hospitals and schools. Local authority enforcement officers have responsibility for retail catering establishments such as pubs, restaurants, hotels, fast food establishments and small catering firms.

HSE inspectors' approach to employers in the period immediately after the coming into force of the new Regulations will be to promote awareness of the Regulations and the duties they place on employers. They will point employers in the direction of sources of advice and guidance as necessary.

Consideration of formal enforcement is not likely unless:

— the risks to health and safety are evident and immediate; or

— what needs to be done is not new (ie existing duties transposed into new legislation); or

— employers appear deliberately obdurate and unwilling to recognise their responsibilities to ensure the long-term health, safety and welfare of employees and others affected by their activities.

Local authorities have yet to develop their own uniform enforcement policy. The joint Chairman and Local Authority Leader of the HSE/Local Authority Enforcement Liaison Committee (HELA) has, however, written to LAs saying that HELA recommendations on enforcement would be unlikely to differ significantly from the HSE approach.

Managing Health and Safety

The most effective way of preventing accidents and ill health at work is to manage the business in such a way as to encourage all staff to develop a positive culture towards health and safety. The aim should be to control all accidental loss, because the mistakes that can cause injuries and illness can also lead to property damage and interrupt production.

Any company health and safety policy should be based on commitment at the very top. Where possible, it should be developed in consultation with staff, to give them a feeling of ownership. The policy should aim to ensure that commitment and accountability are shared by all staff, including supervisors and managers, and that they are aware of their health and safety responsibilities and have the competence and training necessary to carry them out.

Planning is the key to ensuring that your health and safety efforts really work. This means setting objectives; identifying hazards; assessing risks; implementing standards of performance for the protection of people, and safeguards for plant and production; and developing a positive culture. These are all management concepts which the catering industry has used to implement its general move towards improved standards of food safety and quality assurance.

In the catering industry there is a wealth of information on hazard identification and assessment of risk.

Once appropriate measures have been taken to try and reduce risks, you need to consider how to measure performance, just as you would for finance, production or sales. This should involve two types of monitoring. Firstly, regular inspections, which take place before things go wrong and show whether the standards you have set are being met. Secondly, reactive monitoring, after things go wrong. This includes investigating accidents, property damage and near misses.

The monitoring described above provides information to enable you to review your activities and improve performance. However, it is also recommended that health and safety is occasionally subjected to a more comprehensive review (audit), either by your own staff or outsiders. The audit should complement monitoring activities by looking to see if your policy, organisation and systems are achieving the right results. It should tell you about the reliability and effectiveness of your systems and enable you to learn from your experiences. Although not a legal requirement, audits are worthwhile, particularly in larger organisations, to ensure that money spent on health and safety is not being wasted.

Risk Assessment

Risk assessment is a concept which is common to all of the new sets of Regulations. Confusion can arise because the term sounds more complicated than the process it describes. The underlying concept is, in fact, very simple. We all carry out risk assessments every day. When crossing the road the HAZARD of being knocked down by a car is always there. For this reason you assess the RISK of being run over before deciding to cross. If you think the risk is too great because the traffic is particularly heavy, then you may decide to eliminate it by not crossing, or to reduce it to an acceptable level by waiting until there is a gap, or walking to a pedestrian crossing. The new health and safety laws work in a similar way. They require an employer to identify all the hazards in the premises eg mincers, slicers, slippery floors etc. Any associated risks must then be assessed, ie are the hazards likely to cause harm to the employees? If the answer for any hazard is yes, then the employer needs to think of ways of eliminating it or reducing the risk to an acceptable level. Failure to do this can have the most tragic consequences.

The main requirement to carry out a risk assessment is contained in the Management Regulations. The Approved Code of Practice, which gives advice on how to comply with the Regulations, clearly states that for small undertakings presenting few or simple hazards, a suitable and sufficient risk assessment can be a very straightforward process based on judgement and requiring no specialist skills or complicated techniques. In addition to looking at the risks and the people affected by them, it should consider existing precautions and how these can be improved. In practice it may be easier to look at risk assessment as a two stage process, the first stage being an initial judgement which screens out those activities where a risk assessment is not needed.

Employers with five or more employees need to record the SIGNIFICANT findings of the risk assessment. For the catering industry this will most probably include those associated with slips, trips and falls, manual handling, contact with hot surfaces or harmful substances, dermatitis, and upper limb disorders.

Where risk assessments have already been done to meet the requirements of Regulations covering specific aspects of work, for example the Manual Handling Regulations, there is no need to duplicate the work when conducting the overall assessment required by the Management Regulations, but care should be taken to ensure that all significant risks are covered.

The requirement for a risk assessment should be regarded as a means of identifying the likely safety and health problems in a premise, and of putting them in some order of priority, so that the activities presenting the greatest risk can be dealt with first. This Helps To Ensure That You Get Maximum Benefit From Any Money Spent. The process is not meant to be complicated, and in the main it relies far more on common sense and good judgement than any complicated paper analysis.

OCCUPATIONS IN THE CATERING INDUSTRY

There are many different occupations available within the catering industry:

Kitchen Attendant

Kitchen hands assist cooks and chefs in preparing and storing food, washing dishes and utensils, and cleaning work areas. Kitchen hands work in hotels, motels, restaurants, cafes, hospitals, takeaway food bars, boarding schools, and factory or office canteens.

Work

Kitchen hands may perform the following tasks:

- wash and clean utensils and dishes that are returned to the kitchen and make sure they are stored appropriately
- handle, sort, store and distribute food items
- wash, peel, chop, cut and cook foodstuffs and help to prepare salads and desserts
- dispose of rubbish
- organise laundering of linen
- wash dishes
- clean food preparation equipment, floors and other kitchen tools or areas.

The particular duties of a kitchen hand may vary depending upon the type of workplace and their level of experience. Inexperienced kitchen hands or those in larger restaurants or hotels may focus on cleaning and housekeeping tasks such as scrubbing pots, sweeping floors and putting utensils and crockery away. Other kitchen hands may be involved in preparing ingredients: cleaning, chopping, slicing, grating, peeling and trimming. Kitchen hands usually aren't involved in cooking the food, though in smaller establishments there may be opportunities to be more involved in the cooking side of things.

Work Conditions

The role of the kitchen hand tends to involve repetitive work. Commercial kitchens can be very hot and noisy, and working conditions may be uncomfortable. However, the work is varied and working as part of a team in a busy kitchen can be fun. Kitchen hands are often employed on a part-time, casual or seasonal basis and usually work in shifts. They must be prepared to work irregular hours and to stand for long periods. Protective clothing such as overalls or gloves may be provided. Kitchen hands must be able to use knives and other cooking equipment efficiently and safely.

Personal Requirements

- interested in practical work
- good hand-eye coordination

- able to work quickly and safely
- good personal hygiene
- free from skin allergies to foods and detergents
- good communication skills
- able to work as part of a team

Education/Training

You can work as a kitchen hand without formal qualifications. However, there are formal qualifications available, and these may assist you in gaining employment and advancing within the industry.

Certificate I in Hospitality (Kitchen Operations) This certificate will provide you with the basic skills to work as a kitchen hand. Other qualifications are available to help kitchen hands move forward into other cookery positions.

These qualifications can be completed in a number of ways. For more information on the main options, see the following pages:

- New Apprenticeships
- Find training

Employment and career opportunities

Most kitchen hands work on a part-time or casual basis.

It is a very large occupation with high staff turnover and there is usually a steady demand for experienced kitchen hands.

The job provides the opportunity to learn about other kitchen work and can serve as a good introduction to the catering and hospitality industries.

Many people in the industry suggest that people interested in a career in hospitality, especially those intending to be a chef, should get some experience as a kitchen hand.

It's a great way to help decide whether you want to become a chef before committing to an apprenticeship. Many chefs have worked their way through the ranks starting out as the kitchen hand.

Cook

If you like cooking, want to work in an energetic and dynamic environment, are creative, like doing things with your hands and don't mind working hard, you could become a cook. Cooks prepare and cook food in a commercial setting. Cooks may work in restaurants, cafes, hotels, motels, clubs, cafes, hospitals, take-away outlets, function centres, catering firms, flight catering centres and ships. The range of duties carried out by cooks will vary depending on where they work. In hotels, clubs, restaurants and take-away food outlets, cooks often specialise in preparing and cooking a particular type of food (e.g. fried chicken, pizza or barbecued meat). They may also specialise in national cuisine (e.g. Thai, Vietnamese, French, or Italian). Other specialisations include entrees, desserts,international and pastry cooking.

Duties and Tasks

A cook may perform the following tasks:

- check food to make sure of its quality
- regulate temperatures of ovens, grills and other cooking equipment
- prepare food for cooking
- cook food by a range of methods (i.e. baking, braising, frying, roasting or steaming)
- divide food into portions and make sure that the food is well-presented
- clean food preparation areas and equipment
- store food in temperature-controlled facilities
- receive and store supplies
- make sure kitchen is hygienic and functional
- plan menus and estimate food requirements
- prepare food to meet special dietary requirements
- train and supervise other staff.

Work Conditions

Commercial kitchens can be very hot and noisy, and working conditions may be uncomfortable.

Cooks are required to do shift work, including weekends and public holidays. The work can be tiring, and involve long hours, and it may be stressful, particularly at peak hours of the day. Cooks spend a lot of time on their feet. On the other hand, it's a very sociable occupation where you work in a team environment. Cooks work with sharp knives and around hot appliances. Cuts and burns are the most common occupational dangers. High standards of personal hygiene are a must, as a lack of attention to health and hygiene can spread disease and put clients at risk.

It is challenging work as you have to work long hours and nights and weekends, however it is extremely rewarding and offers great career options and job satisfaction.

Personal Requirements

- a high level of personal cleanliness
- able to plan your time and work under pressure
- good communication skills
- punctuality
- flexibility to perform shift work (sometimes on a 24-hour rotating roster)
- able to stay calm in difficult situations
- able to work well in a team

Education and Training

Cooks generally require formal qualifications. There are a number of nationally-recognised qualifications available, depending upon the type of cookery you choose to specialise in.

Certificate II: Kitchen Operations-This certificate will enable you to be a short order cook, a breakfast cook or a cook in a café or bistro. It is also the pathway to Certificates III in Asian Cookery, Patisserie or Catering

Certificate III: Commercial Cookery-is the standard 'trade' qualification required to become a qualified cook

Certificate III: Asian Cookery-is the trade qualification for those specialising in Asian cookery

Certificate III: Commercial Catering-will enable you to work as a caterer in a catering firm

Certificate III: Patisserie-will enable you to work as a patissier, specialising in fine pastries, cakes and desserts

These qualifications can be completed in a number of ways. For more information on the main options, see the following pages:

- New Apprenticeships
- Find training

Other qualifications are available to help cooks move forward into chef and management roles.

Career and Employment Opportunities

There are excellent job opportunities for cooks, and good cooks are always in demand. Continued growth in the tourist industry has generated a strong demand for cooks, and there is currently a shortage of cooks in all States and Territories.

Cooks can work in a variety of locations and can become a chef or catering manager, or can own their own restaurant or catering company. They can also be specialists in areas such as ethnic cooking, Asian cookery, baking and patisserie or dietary catering. They can even be TV chefs! There is lots of variety and good travel opportunities. Many young cooks get experience overseas before progressing in their chosen career area.

With experience and further training, qualified cooks may be promoted to supervisory positions. Movement between employers within the industry may be required in order to gain experience and promotion.

Chef

Chefs may work in restaurants, cafes, hotels, motels, clubs, cafes, function centres, catering firms, flight catering centres and ships.

Chefs (Heads of kitchens) are in charge of the kitchen and the staff working there as well as responsible for designing the menu and selecting and ordering the food. They are often responsible for planning and organising of the food for a special event such as a wedding, dinner or conference.

Chefs and cooks, particularly those working in larger establishments, often specialise in a particular cuisine or the preparation of a particular food. These range from Asian to African cuisines, to sauces (chef saucier) and to salads. And with confidence, creativity and experience, the possibilities are endless for creating new styles of cooking or combining different ingredients.

Duties and Tasks

Chefs can take on any of a wide range of tasks or specialities depending upon their skills and where they work. They are responsible for managing kitchens, purchasing foodstuffs, preparing and cooking food and presenting it. They are also responsible for keeping kitchens clean and hygienic. They are supported by people working as kitchen hands and fast food cooks.

Chefs perform the following tasks:

- Plan menus and estimate food requirements
- Prepare and cook different kinds of foods
- Portion, present and serve food
- Monitor food quality at all stages
- Store food safely and hygienically
- Prepare food to meet different requirements such as dietary or cultural needs
- Discuss food preparation issues with managers, dieticians and other staff
- Demonstrate techniques and advise on cooking procedures
- Plan staff rosters and supervise the activities of cooks and assistants
- Work out food and labour costs together with the head chef
- Discuss food preparation issues with managers, dieticians and other staff members

- Order food, kitchen supplies and equipment
- Explain and enforce hygiene regulations
- Select and train staff
- Freeze and preserve foods.

The particular duties will depend upon the specific role and the type of kitchen. There are four main 'levels' of chef:

A commis chef: a commis chef is a qualified cook, who works under the direct supervision of other chefs in the kitchen. Commis chefs have often just completed their qualification. Commis chefs are generally the least experienced chefs in the kitchen.

A chef de partie controls a particular section of the kitchen. Chefs de partie can include chefs specialising as larder cooks, butchers, pastry cooks, sauce cooks, roast cooks, relief cooks, side-dish cooks, breakfast cooks, canteen cooks or fish cooks.

A sous chef (also known as second chef) is the second-in-charge in the kitchen.

A chef de cuisine (also known as head chef or executive chef) is in charge of the kitchen. They plan menus, oversee all staff, and supervise the overall operation of the kitchen. In larger establishments, the chef de cuisine or head chef generally does more supervision than cooking. Senior chefs have to attend staff meetings, where they discuss problems related to their areas and receive or issue instructions to other managerial staff. In small restaurants, the head chef may prepare food, assisted by other cooks or apprentices. As well as expert cooking knowledge, chefs involved in supervision need a general knowledge of the skills and activities of all their workers.

Work Conditions

Commercial kitchens can be very hot and noisy, and working conditions may be uncomfortable. Chefs are required to do shift work, including weekends and public holidays. The work can be tiring, and involve long hours, and it may be stressful, particularly at peak hours of the day. Chefs work with sharp knives and around hot appliances. Cuts and burns are the most common occupational dangers. High standards of personal hygiene are a must, as a lack of attention to health and hygiene can spread disease and put clients at risk.

It is challenging work as you have to work long hours and nights and weekends, however it is extremely rewarding and offers great career options and job satisfaction.

Personal Requirements

- a high level of personal cleanliness
- enjoy cooking
- able to organise efficient work schedules
- good communication skills
- punctuality
- flexibility to perform shift work on a 24-hour rotating roster as required
- able to work under pressure and stay calm in difficult situations

What Training do you Need?

A commis chef:

Certificate III: Commercial Cookery-is the standard 'trade' qualification required to become a qualified cook

Certificate III: Asian Cookery-is the trade qualification for those specialising in Asian cookery

Certificate III: Commercial Catering-will enable you to work as a caterer in a catering firm

A chef de partie or sous chef:

Certificate IV: Commercial Cookery-is designed for qualified cooks who want to develop their skills in kitchen supervision

Certificate IV: Asian Cookery-is designed for qualified cooks who want to develop their skills in kitchen supervision in an Asian kitchen

Certificate IV: Patisserie-is designed to give you high level patisserie skills as well as supervisory skills required for running a café or cake shop

Certificate IV: Catering Operations-will enable you to develop more catering skills such as managing functions or catering for hospitals, as well as supervisory skills

A Chef de Cuisine (Head Chef or Executive Chef)

The Diploma of Hospitality Management or Advanced Diploma of Hospitality Management are the qualifications for chefs who wish to acquire skills in management to manage a kitchen or their own restaurant.

These qualifications can be completed in a number of ways. For more information on the main options, see the following pages:

- New Apprenticeships
- Find training

Career and Employment Opportunities

There are excellent job opportunities for chefs. It is a large occupation and employment prospects are good, with relatively strong job growth predicted nationally. Expanded tourism has increased demand for highly skilled chefs, particularly in establishments of international standard. The majority of chefs work in capital cities and in large country centres, particularly in areas where there are tourist resorts.

In large kitchens the progression is usually from commis chef, to chef de partie, to sous chef, to head chef, to executive chef or food manager. Movement between employers within the industry may be required in order to gain experience and promotion. Chefs with sufficient capital may become the owners of restaurants.

Food Service Manager

Food service managers plan, organise and control the operation of establishments where food and beverages are served, such as restaurants, cafes, cafeterias and canteens.

Duties and Tasks

A food service manager may perform the following tasks:

- talk with the chef to plan the menu

- supervise the purchase and storage of food
- supervise provision of all crockery, cutlery, detergents and kitchenware
- make sure there is adequate security for food and equipment
- keep records of payments and expenses
- plan, coordinate and supervise the activities of workers in dining rooms, kitchens, bars and other areas
- manage staff hiring and rostering
- provide some staff training
- discuss catering arrangements with clients
- make sure that the dining rooms, kitchen, storage facilities and other work areas are kept clean and conform to the sanitary regulations
- attend to complaints concerning food and service.

Work Conditions

Food service managers spend most of their time in the dining area and in the kitchen. Most of the time is spent on their feet. They often work in the evenings and on weekends and on public holidays.

The work can be tiring, and involve long hours, and it may be stressful, particularly at peak hours of the day.

There is a high level of customer contact involved, and the job may involve dealing with difficult customers and complaints.

Personal Requirements

- willing and able to work for long hours, on shifts, and on public holidays and weekends
- good communication and organisation skills
- able to remain calm and in control in difficult situations
- able to work as part of a team

Education/Training

There is no specific requirement to have formal qualifications to work as a food service manager. However, there are formal qualifications available, and these may assist you in gaining employment and advancing within the industry.

Diploma of Hospitality Management provides the skills required to work as a manager in the hospitality industry. Advanced Diploma of Hospitality Management provides the skills required to work as a senior manager in the hospitality industry. Most restaurant/catering managers are also expected to have a significant level of experience in the hospitality industry, and many people work their way up through the industry. These qualifications can be completed in a number of ways. For more information on the main options, see the following pages:

- New Apprenticeships
- Find training

Employment Opportunities

It is a large occupation with good job prospects. Growth in the tourism and hospitality industries indicate that there will probably be increased demand for good staff. Positions tend to be filled by promoting an experienced person from within the organisation. Self-employment is possible. People who intend to run their own business are advised to gain several years of experience, both on the job and by completing an appropriate qualification. The costs to purchase or establish your own business are high, so you will need a significant amount of capital.

Waiter (Food and Beverage Service)

Waiters serve food and drinks to guests in hotels, restaurants, clubs and similar establishments. Waiters greet patrons, present them with menus, make recommendations on available food and beverage choices and answer any questions they might have.

Duties and Tasks

A waiter may perform the following tasks:

- set tables with clean linen or place mats, cutlery, crockery and glasses

- welcome and seat customers and hand menus to them
- tell guests about the menu and drinks and appropriate combinations of food and drinks
- in some cases promote local produce and attractions to visitors from interstate and overseas
- take customers' orders and pass them to kitchen staff or bar attendants
- serve food and drinks
- carve meat
- make up bills and present them to customers
- handle money or credit cards
- take restaurant reservations
- clear tables and return dishes and cutlery to kitchens.

Work Conditions

It is busy, exciting work and requires someone with lots of energy and good communication and customer service skills. You will have to work nights and weekends, however, it gives you lots of opportunities to meet people and even to travel. Imagine the fun of working on a cruise ship or in a ski resort!

Waiters often work split shifts and in the evenings, weekends and public holidays. Uniforms may be supplied by employers. Waiters must be a minimum age of 18 years to serve alcohol.

Waiters spend long periods on their feet, and may have to deal with difficult or dissatisfied customers.

Personal Requirements

- well presented
- good communication skills
- good memory
- polite and patient
- friendly, efficient and speedy
- enjoy working with people
- able to work as part of a team

- prepared to work weekends and evenings
- able to handle money
- stamina

Education/Training

You can work as a waiter without formal qualifications. You will probably get some informal training on the job. However, there are formal qualifications available, and these may assist you in gaining employment and advancing within the industry. To be a qualified food and beverage attendant, you should have a Certificate II in Hospitality (Operations) as a minimum, although some places will let you start with no training as they offer training on the job. A Certificate III in Hospitality (Operations) is the qualification for a waiter or bar attendant. You can specialise through electives in whatever best meets your job needs.

The Certificate II: Operations-is the entry-level qualification which provides the basic skills to work as a food and beverage attendant

The Certificate III: Operations-is the certificate for a qualified waiter, in both food and beverage

Other qualifications are available to help waiters to move into supervisory or more specialised roles:

The Certificate IV: Supervision-is designed to provide the supervisory skills to be a head waiter, sommelier or supervisor

The Diploma of Hospitality Management is designed to provide the management skills as well as the operational skills and knowledge needed to be a food and beverage manager

The Advanced Diploma of Hospitality Management provides the advanced management skills for those who are interested in managing a restaurant, heading up a large department or owning their own business.

These qualifications can be completed in a number of ways. For more information on the main options, see the following pages:

- New Apprenticeships
- Find training.

Employment and Career Opportunities

There are many opportunities in a huge variety of places including hotels, motels, cafes, restaurants, clubs, recreation and convention centres and other entertainment venues. Most waiters are employed in cities, although many work in larger country centres, particularly those which are tourist resorts.

There are good job prospects. As turnover is high in this occupation there is usually a steady demand for replacement staff. As the tourism and hospitality industry continues to grow, with a growing number of hotels, cafes and restaurants, there are likely to be increased employment opportunities for skilled waiters.

Waiters who have undertaken appropriate training or who have suitable experience are highly regarded by employers. You can start as a waiter or bar attendant, and with experience and further training, progress to head waiter (maitre d'), supervisor or Food and Beverage Manager. If you are interested in wine, you can become a sommelier. Some waiters also specialise in silver service (serving food, using a fork and spoon, directly from platters on a the guest's plate at the table).

Career paths are flexible and there are many associated jobs in areas such as training, marketing and events management.

Bar Attendant

Bar attendants prepare, mix and serve drinks to customers in hotels, bars, cafes, restaurants and clubs.

Duties and Tasks

A bar attendant may perform the following tasks:

- serve alcoholic and non-alcoholic drinks
- draw beer from the tap or pour from bottles
- mix ingredients to make cocktails and slice fruit to garnish drinks

- prepare and serve a variety of coffees
- refill drink and cigarette dispensers
- collect glasses from tables and place them in glasswashing machines
- wipe down tables and empty ashtrays
- collect payment, operate cash registers and give change
- arrange bottles and glasses on shelves
- clean bar service area and polish glasses
- operate TAB and Keno or gaming machine terminals
- assist in the cellar
- assist in stock control
- make coffee using an espresso coffee machine or filter system
- observe workplace hygiene, occupational health and safety, and security procedures.

Bar attendants may also provide drinks to waiters or serve them to tables, depending on the type of business.

Work Conditions

Bar attendants generally do shift work, often in the evenings, weekends and public holidays. Many bar attendants are employed on a part-time or casual basis. Uniforms may be supplied by employers.

The work environment can be busy and noisy, and may be hot and stuffy, especially during peak periods. While legislation can vary between states, many licensed premises permit smoking, so it can also be smoky.

Bar attendants must be at least 18 years of age, and are required to comply with legislation on the responsible service of alcohol.

Bar attendants spend long periods on their feet, and may have to deal with difficult or intoxicated customers.

Personal Requirements

- good interpersonal skills

- good memory
- efficient and speedy
- enjoy working with people
- prepared to work weekends and evenings
- good cash-handling skills
- able to stand for long periods

Education/Training

You can work as a bar attendant without formal qualifications. You will probably get some informal training on the job. However, there are formal qualifications available, and these may assist you in gaining employment and advancing within the industry.

To be a qualified bar attendant, you should have a Certificate II in Hospitality (Operations) as a minimum, although some places will let you start with no training as they offer training on the job. A Certificate III in Hospitality (Operations) is the qualification for a waiter or bar attendant. You can specialise through electives in whatever best meets your job needs.

The Certificate II in Hospitality (Operations) is the entry-level qualification which provides the basic skills to work as a bar attendant

The Certificate III in Hospitality (Operations) is the certificate for a qualified waiter, in both food and beverage

Other qualifications are available to help bar attendants to move into supervisory or more specialised roles:

The Certificate IV in Hospitality (Supervision) is designed to provide the supervisory skills to be a head waiter, sommelier or supervisor

The Diploma of Hospitality Management is designed to provide the management skills as well as the operational skills and knowledge needed to be a food and beverage manager

The Advanced Diploma of Hospitality Management provides the advanced management skills for those who are interested in managing a restaurant, heading up a large department or owning their own business. These qualifications can be completed in a number of ways. For more information on the main options, see the following pages:

- New Apprenticeships
- Find training

Career and Employment Opportunities

Bar attendants can work in hotels, bars, restaurants, cafes, clubs, recreation and convention centres, and other licensed entertainment venues. There are good job prospects. Most bar attendants are employed on a part-time or casual basis. As turnover is relatively high, there is generally a constant demand to replace those leaving the job. As the tourism and hospitality industry continues to grow, with a growing number of hotels, cafes and restaurants, there are likely to be increased employment opportunities for skilled bar staff. Bar attendants who have undertaken training or are experienced are highly regarded and sought by employers. Bar attendants with experience and additional training may progress to supervisory or management positions. Career paths are flexible and there are many associated jobs in other areas of the hospitality industry, as well as related areas such as training, marketing and events management.

Concierge/porter

Luggage porters carry luggage for guests in hotels and passengers in transport terminals, show them to their rooms, berths or cabins, and provide other guest services.

Concierges provide additional services to guests, such as organising and booking tickets for tours and entertainment for guests, and advising them on the services and attractions available in the local area.

Duties and Tasks

A luggage porter may perform the following tasks:

- take baggage, tag it and give identification slips to guests or passengers
- load or unload luggage and take it to the receiving area

- carry luggage and show incoming guests to rooms
- explain details of hotel room services and facilities to guests as they arrive
- carry the luggage of departing guests to cars, buses or taxis
- talk with transport carriers to make travel arrangements and retrieve lost luggage
- page guests and run errands
- park guests' vehicles.

A concierge may perform the following additional tasks:

- provide guests with information on the local area, attractions and events
- organise and book tours, transport and entertainment for guests
- assist guests and staff with safety and emergency procedures

Personal Requirements

- interested in working with people
- well-presented, alert and perceptive
- interpersonal skills
- physically fit
- good communication skills
- good knowledge of the local area

Work Conditions

Porters and concierges are required to do shift work, including nights, weekends and public holidays. These jobs have a high level of contact with the public. Uniforms are generally provided by the employer. They need to be physically fit to handle luggage, and may be required to stand for long periods of time.

Education/Training

You can work as a porter or concierge without formal qualifications. You will probably get some informal training on the job. However, there are formal qualifications available, and these may assist you in gaining employment and advancing within the industry. Luggage porters should have a good command of the English language, and the ability to speak a second language may be an advantage. A current driver's licence is often required. To be a qualified porter, you should have a Certificate II in Hospitality (Operations) as a minimum, although some places will let you start with no training. A Certificate III in Hospitality (Operations) is the qualification for a concierge. You can specialise through electives in whatever best meets your job needs. The Certificate II in Hospitality (Operations) is the entry-level qualification which provides the basic skills to work as a porter.

Concierge

These qualifications can be completed in a number of ways. For more information on the main options, see the following pages:

Career and Employment Opportunities

Porters and concierges are mainly employed in the larger international standard hotels, so available jobs tend to be in capital cities and regional centres that cater to large numbers of tourists. There are only a limited number of job openings in this occupation, although once you gain a position there are good career opportunities in the tourism and hospitality industries. Experienced porters and concierges may eventually be promoted to duty managers or front office managers.

Housekeeping Attendant

Housekeeping attendants (room attendants) clean and maintain rooms in hotels, motels and other lodging places.

Duties and Tasks

A housekeeping attendant may perform the following tasks:

- check that rooms have been vacated before cleaning
- make beds daily and change bed linen
- vacuum carpets, floors and upholstery

- clean bathrooms and supply with fresh towels and toiletries
- check and re-stock tea, coffee, sugar, milk and mini bar supplies
- make sure that televisions, radios, lights and air-conditioning equipment are working
- report to a supervisor articles left behind by guests, damage to rooms and any items which appear to have been stolen
- take laundry and dry cleaning orders from guests.

Work Conditions

Working conditions and hours vary greatly, depending on where room attendants work. The work is not usually heavy, but lifting, carrying and bending are involved.

Personal Requirements

- interested in practical work
- neat personal appearance
- good personal hygiene
- honest and reliable
- physically fit
- able to stay calm in difficult situations

Education/Training

You can work as a housekeeping attendant without formal qualifications. You will probably get some informal training on the job. However, there are formal qualifications available, and these may assist you in gaining employment and advancing within the industry.

To be a qualified housekeeping attendant, you should have a Certificate II in Hospitality (Operations) as a minimum, although some places will let you start with no training. You can specialise through electives in whatever best meets your job needs.

The Certificate I in Hospitality (Operations) is the entry-level qualification which provides the basic skills to work as a housekeeping assistant The Certificate II in Hospitality (Operations) is the certificate for a qualified housekeeping attendant

Other qualifications are available to help housekeeping attendants move forward into supervisory positions.

These qualifications can be completed in a number of ways. For more information on the main options, see the following pages:

Employment and Career Opportunities

Housekeeping attendants are employed by individual hotels, motels or guest houses, or by companies that operate a chain of establishments. Most housekeeping attendants work in capital cities and surrounding suburbs and in those country centres where there are tourist resorts. Demand for housekeeping attendants depends on growth in the tourism and travel industries and on the general level of economic activity. As turnover is relatively high, there is generally a constant demand to replace those leaving the job. With experience and training, housekeeping attendants may be promoted to supervisory levels and to the position of executive housekeeper.

Hotel/motel Front Office Clerk

Hotel and motel front office clerks look after the needs of guests on arrival and during their stay in the hotel or motel.

Duties and Tasks

A front office clerk may perform the following tasks:

- receive reservations for accommodation from clients either in person or by telephone, fax or email
- take guests' details as they arrive and allocate them a room
- talk to transport carriers (e.g. airlines, bus companies, rental car agencies) to make travel arrangements for guests and to find lost luggage
- inform guests about the hotel/motel's facilities, policies and procedures

- provide tourist information to guests
- make reservations for sight-seeing tours, restaurants, the cinema and live entertainment
- deal with enquiries and requests from guests
- take messages for guests
- calculate guests' bills and issue receipts upon payment
- arrange accommodation for guests travelling to other destinations
- perform cashier duties, cash travellers' cheques and exchange foreign currency
- place guests' possessions in a safe if requested
- coordinate the cleaning of guests' personal laundry, shoe shining and room service deliveries
- follow in-house procedures to help make sure of the security of guests and employees
- perform general secretarial duties such as preparing correspondence and attending to a switchboard.

In a small or medium-sized hotel all of the above duties may be carried out by one person. However, in an international standard hotel several clerks may be employed. Each clerk is allocated a set of specific duties to perform (e.g. one may attend to guest reception, another may be responsible for the switchboard, while another works as an information officer).

Work Conditions

Hotel and motel front office clerks usually work shifts including evenings, weekends and public holidays.

The role involves a high level of public contact, and may involve dealing with difficult customers and solving problems.

Personal Requirements

- enjoy working with people
- friendly, helpful and patient
- able to assist guests with a limited understanding of English

- good communication skills
- able to record information accurately
- able to work as part of a team
- able to project a professional manner at all times
- good interpersonal skills
- flexible
- able to stay calm in difficult situations

Education and Training

You can work as a front office clerk without formal qualifications. You will probably get some informal training on the job. Experience in word processing and operating office machinery such as switchboards is desirable. The ability to speak a second language is an advantage if working in an international hotel. However, there are formal qualifications available, and these may assist you in gaining employment and advancing within the industry.

To be a qualified front office clerk, you should have a Certificate II or Certificate III in Hospitality (Operations) as a minimum, although some places will let you start with no training. You can specialise through electives in whatever best meets your job needs.

The Certificate II in Hospitality (Operations) is the entry-level qualification which provides the basic skills to work as a front office clerk

The Certificate III in Hospitality (Operations) provides additional training to develop a broader range of skills

Other qualifications are also available to help front office clerks move forward into supervisory positions.

These qualifications can be completed in a number of ways. For more information on the main options, see the following pages:

Employment and Career Opportunities

Hotel and motel front office clerks are employed by hotels, motels, guesthouses and hostels throughout the country. They may work in privately-owned hotels or motels, or in companies that operate a chain of establishments. It is a large occupation and employment prospects are good. With experience and training, front office clerks may be promoted to supervisory or managerial levels.

Hotel Service Supervisor

Hotel service supervisors coordinate and supervise the activities of hotel service workers including domestic staff, luggage porters and doorpersons.

Duties and Tasks

Hotel service supervisors may perform the following tasks:

- determine work requirements and allocate duties to domestic housekeepers, luggage porters and doorpersons
- talk to managers to coordinate activities with other organisational units
- maintain attendance records and rosters
- explain and enforce safety regulations
- oversee the work of the unit and suggest improvements and changes
- talk to workers to resolve problems
- perform front office and reception duties
- perform the tasks of a domestic housekeeper, luggage porter or doorperson.

Work Conditions

Hotel service supervisors often work evenings, weekends and public holidays. In some hotels and motels, the hotel service supervisor may work mostly behind the scenes. In an international standard hotel, however, they are likely to have a high level of contact with the public and may have to deal with difficult guests and be on call if major problems arise.

Personal Requirements

- interested in working with people
- friendly, helpful and patient

- able to assist guests with a limited understanding of English
- good communication skills
- good interpersonal skills
- good organisational skills
- able to record information accurately
- able to work as part of a team
- able to project a professional manner at all times
- able to stay calm in difficult situations.

Education and Training

Hotel service supervisors would generally be expected to be experienced employees with a strong background in front office operations.

There is no specific requirement to have formal qualifications to work as a service supervisor, but there are formal qualifications available, and these may assist you in gaining employment and advancing within the industry.

To be a qualified service supervisor, you should have a minimum of a Certificate IV in Hospitality (Supervision). You can specialise through electives in whatever best meets your job needs. The Certificate IV in Hospitality (Supervision) provides the skills required to work as a service supervisor.

The Diploma of Hospitality Management provides the advanced skills required to supervise a large department or the services of a small hotel, motel or restaurant. Other qualifications are available to help service supervisors move forward into further management positions:

The Advanced Diploma of Hospitality Management provides the advanced management skills for those who are interested in managing a hotel, heading up a large department or owning their own business.

These qualifications can be completed through a training program plus some on-the-job experience, or through a New Apprenticeship.

Career and Employment Opportunities

Hotel service supervisors are employed by hotels and motels throughout the country. They may work in privately-owned hotels or motels, or in companies that operate a chain of establishments.

Job prospects depend on the level of tourism and economic activity. It is a small occupation, but high turnover may provide additional job openings.

However, there is very strong competition for available jobs.

Hotel/Motel Manager

Hotel and motel managers plan, supervise and control the operations of a hotel or motel, including food and beverage, front office, housekeeping, budgeting, marketing/advertising and recruiting and managing staff.

Hotel and motel managers may work in privately-owned hotels, motels or resorts, or they may be employed by companies that operate a chain of businesses.

Duties and Tasks

Hotel and motel managers may perform the following tasks:

- plan, direct and coordinate the services of accounting, food and beverages, guest services, maintenance, staff development, and sales and marketing
- allocate tasks and priorities, coordinate resources, develop business plans and marketing strategies
- undertake management tasks such as looking after building costs, rents, maintenance, lighting, power, heating, air conditioning, floorings and furniture
- control capital and operational expenditure
- make sure government health, occupational safety and licensing regulations are followed
- carry out marketing and sales activities for rooms, conventions, banquets and conferences

- supervise arrangement and re-arrangement of furnishings
- prepare reports
- manage the security of the hotel and its staff
- publicise the hotel/motel through public relations activities in the local business community.

The specific duties of the manager will vary with the size and nature of the workplace. In larger hotels/motels, the manager's role is often more administrative, with many of their responsibilities being delegated to others, such as food and beverage managers and function coordinators. In hotel or motel chains, the purchasing and advertising functions are usually centralised.

Work Conditions

Hotel and motel managers often work evenings, weekends and public holidays.

Whether in a small or medium-sized hotel or motel or an international standard hotel, most hotel and motel managers are very 'hands-on'. They have a high level of contact with the public and may have to deal with difficult guests and be on call if major problems arise.

Personal Requirements

- interested in working with people
- friendly, helpful and patient
- able to assist guests with a limited understanding of English
- good communication and organisational skills
- able to record information accurately
- able to work as part of a team
- able to project a professional manner at all times
- good interpersonal skills
- able to maintain control and composure in difficult situations

Education/Training

There is no specific requirement to have formal qualifications to work as a hotel or motel manager. However, there are formal qualifications available, and these may assist you in gaining employment and advancing within the industry.

The Diploma of Hospitality Management provides the skills required to work as a manager in the hospitality industry

The Advanced Diploma of Hospitality Management provides the skills required to work as a senior manager in the hospitality industry

These qualifications are generally completed through a full-time or part-time training course. For more information on accessing these courses, see the Find training page.

Most hotel/motel managers are also expected to have a significant amount of experience in the hospitality industry, and many people work their way up through the industry.

University degrees in related areas, such as business or marketing, may also be an advantage.

The ability to speak a second language is an advantage if working in an international hotel.

Employment and Career Opportunities

Hotel and motel managers are employed by hotels and motels throughout the country. They may work in privately-owned hotels or motels, or in companies that operate a chain of establishments.

Job prospects depend on the level of tourism and economic activity. Growth in the tourism and hospitality industry and the opening of new establishments may increase the number of jobs, but the job prospects are considered to be average.

There is relatively little movement among the people currently employed in these positions, and competition for available jobs is intense. Some managers do get the opportunity for interstate and overseas postings.

Self employment opportunities are possible, but you will typically need substantial funds.

5

Managers and Assistants

NATURE

A comfortable room, good food, and a helpful hotel staff can make being away from home an enjoyable experience for both vacationing families and business travelers. Hotel managers and assistant managers help their guests have a pleasant stay by providing many of the comforts of home, including cable television, fitness equipment, and voice mail. Additionally, some hotels have health spas and other specialized services that the hotel manager and assistant help keep running smoothly. For business travelers, hotel managers often schedule available meeting rooms and electronic equipment, including slide projectors and fax machines. Hotel managers are responsible for keeping the operation of their establishments efficient and profitable. In a small hotel, motel, or inn with a limited staff, the manager may oversee all aspects of operations. However, large hotels may employ hundreds of workers, and the general manager is usually aided by a number of assistant managers assigned to the various departments of the operation. In hotels of every size, managerial duties vary significantly by job title.

The general manager, for example, has overall responsibility for the operation of the hotel. Within guidelines established by the owners of the hotel or executives of the hotel chain, the general manager sets room rates, allocates funds to departments, approves expenditures, and establishes standards for service to guests, decor, housekeeping, food quality, and banquet operations. Managers who work for chains may also organize and staff a newly built hotel, refurbish an older hotel, or reorganize a hotel or motel that is not operating successfully. In order to fill some low-paying service and clerical jobs in hotels, some general managers attend career fairs.

Resident managers live in hotels and are on call 24 hours a day to resolve problems or emergencies. In general, though, they typically work an 8-hour day and oversee the day-to-day operations of the hotel. In many hotels, the general manager is also the resident manager.

Executive housekeepers ensure guest rooms, meeting and banquet rooms, and public areas are clean, orderly, and well maintained. They also train, schedule, and supervise the work of housekeepers, inspect rooms, and order cleaning supplies.

Front office managers coordinate reservations and room assignments as well as train and direct the hotel's front desk staff. They ensure that guests are treated courteously, complaints and problems are resolved, and requests for special services are carried out. Front office managers often have authorization to adjust charges posted on a customer's bill.

Food and beverage managers direct the food service operations of hotels. They oversee the hotels' restaurants, cocktail lounges, and banquet facilities. These managers also supervise food and beverage preparation and service workers, plan menus, set schedules, estimate costs, and deal with food suppliers.

Convention services managers coordinate the activities of large hotels' various departments for meetings, conventions, and special events. They meet with representatives of groups or organizations to plan the number of rooms to reserve, the desired configuration of hotel meeting space, and the banquet services. During the meeting or event, they resolve unexpected problems and monitor activities to ensure that hotel operations conform to the expectations of the group.

Assistant managers help run the day-to-day operations of the hotel. In large hotels they may be responsible for activities such as personnel, accounting, office administration, marketing and sales, purchasing, security, maintenance, and pool, spa, or recreational facilities. In smaller hotels, these duties may be combined into one position. Some hotels allow an assistant manager to make decisions regarding hotel guest charges when a manager is unavailable.

Computers are used extensively by hotel managers and their assistants to keep track of the guest's bill, reservations, room assignments, meetings, and special events. In addition, computers are used to order food, beverages, and supplies, as well as to prepare reports for hotel owners and top-level managers. Managers work with computer specialists to ensure that the hotel's computer system functions properly. Should the hotel's computer system fail, managers must continue to meet guests' needs.

WORKING CONDITIONS

Because hotels are open around the clock, night and weekend work is common. Many hotel managers work more than 40 hours per week. Managers who live in the hotel usually have regular work schedules, but they may be called to work at any time. Some employees of resort hotels are managers during the busy season and have other duties during the rest of the year.

Hotel managers sometimes experience the pressures of coordinating a wide range of functions. Conventions and large groups of tourists may present unusual problems. Moreover, dealing with irate guests can be stressful. The job can be particularly hectic for front office managers during check-in and check-out time. Computer failures can further complicate an already busy time.

EMPLOYMENT

Hotel managers and assistant managers held about 76,000 jobs in 1998. Self-employed managers-primarily owners of small hotels and motels-held a significant number of these jobs. Companies that manage hotels and motels under contract employed some managers.

TRAINING

Hotels increasingly emphasize specialized training. Postsecondary training in hotel or restaurant management is preferred for most hotel management positions, although a college liberal arts degree may be sufficient when coupled with related hotel experience. Internships or part-time or summer work is an asset to students seeking a career in hotel management. The experience gained and the contacts made with employers can greatly benefit them after graduation. Most bachelor's degree programs include work-study opportunities.

In the past, many managers were promoted from the ranks of front desk clerks, housekeepers, waiters and chefs, and hotel sales workers. Although some employees still advance to hotel management positions without education beyond high school, postsecondary education is preferred. Restaurant management training or experience is also a good background for entering hotel management because the success of a hotel's food service and beverage operations is often of great importance to the profitability of the entire establishment.

In 1998, nearly 200 community and junior colleges and some universities offered associate, bachelor's, and graduate degree programs in hotel or restaurant management. When combined with technical institutes, vocational and trade schools, and other academic institutions, over 800 educational facilities have programs leading to formal recognition in hotel or restaurant management. Hotel management programs include instruction in hotel administration, accounting, economics, marketing, housekeeping, food service management and catering, and hotel maintenance engineering. Computer training is also an integral part of hotel management training due to the widespread use of computers in reservations, billing, and housekeeping management.

Hotel managers must be able to get along with many different people, even in stressful situations. They must be able to solve problems and concentrate on details. Initiative, self-discipline, effective communication skills, and the ability to organize and direct the work of others are also essential for managers at all levels.

Most hotels promote employees who have proven their ability and completed formal education in hotel management. Graduates of hotel or restaurant management programs usually start as trainee assistant managers. Some large hotels sponsor specialized on-the-job management training programs allowing trainees to rotate among various departments and gain a thorough knowledge of the hotel's operation. Other hotels may help finance formal training in hotel management for outstanding employees. Newly built hotels, particularly those without well-established on-the-job training programs, often prefer experienced personnel for managerial positions.

Large hotel and motel chains may offer better opportunities for advancement than small, independently owned establishments, but relocation every several years often is necessary for advancement. The large chains have more extensive career ladder programs and offer managers the opportunity to transfer to another hotel or motel in the chain or to the central office. Career advancement can be accelerated by completion of certification programs offered by the associations listed below. These programs usually require a combination of course work, examinations, and experience.

OUTLOOK

Employment of hotel managers and assistants is expected to grow more slowly than the average for all occupations through 2008. Long hours and stressful working conditions result in high turnover in this field, so additional job openings are expected to occur as experienced managers transfer to other occupations, retire, or stop working for other reasons. Job opportunities in hotel management are expected to be especially good for persons with college degrees in hotel or restaurant management.

Increasing business travel and domestic and foreign tourism will drive employment growth of hotel managers and assistants. Managerial jobs are not expected to grow as rapidly as the hotel industry overall, however. As the industry consolidates, many chains and franchises will acquire independently owned establishments and increase the number of economy-class rooms to accommodate bargain-conscious guests. Economy hotels offer clean, comfortable rooms and front desk services without costly extras like restaurants and room service. Because there are not as many departments in these hotels, fewer managers will be needed. In addition, front desk clerks are increasingly assuming some responsibilities previously reserved for managers, further limiting the growth of managers and their assistants.

Additional demand for managers, however, is expected in suite hotels as some guests, especially business customers, are willing to pay higher prices for rooms with kitchens and suites that provide the space needed to conduct meetings. In addition to job growth in suite hotels and economy-class hotels, large full-service hotels-offering restaurants, fitness centers, large meeting rooms, and play areas for children, among other amenities-will continue to offer many trainee and managerial opportunities.

EARNINGS

Median annual earnings of hotel managers and assistants were $26,700 in 1998. The middle 50 percent of these workers earned between $19,820 and $34,690. The lowest 10 percent had earnings of less than $14,430, while the top 10 percent earned over $45,520. In 1997, median annual earnings in the hotel and other lodging places industry, where nearly all of these workers are employed, were $28,600.

Salaries of hotel managers and assistants vary greatly according to their responsibilities and the segment of the hotel industry in which they are employed. Managers may earn bonuses up to 25 percent of their basic salary in some hotels and may also be furnished with lodging, meals, parking, laundry, and other services. In addition to typical benefits, some hotels offer profit-sharing plans and educational assistance to their employees.

WEDDING CATERER

This article deals with the basics of planning a tented wedding reception. Before you start thinking about your menu (and with 14 years experience in the events industry) here are some of the most overlooked fundamentals. Often a wedding reception will be in the garden of a private house and you will need to determine what facilities will be required by your chosen wedding caterer-this is partly dependent on the number of guests.

For example a smaller wedding reception of say up to 50 guests, your own kitchen may be quite adequate for the caterer to prepare and clear away.

For larger guest numbers it is certainly advisable to have what is known as a catering tent. This is a smaller tent adjacent to the main marquee exclusively for the use of your wedding caterer. One of the fundamental first questions for both the wedding caterer and the marquee company is 'will I need a catering tent'? Space for this catering tent needs to be including in the site plan.

For wedding receptions of 50 to 150 guests a small catering tent of 3M x 3M to 6M x 3M may be large enough for your wedding caterer. The caterer needs room to work and space must be allocated early to avoid a disaster.

Another factor to consider early is the question of power requirements for your wedding caterer. For a cold buffet or when your own kitchen is adequate the power requirements may well be minimal. For larger guest numbers and / or hot food the question of power needs to be addressed early. Some caterers use gas and some electric for cooking. If your wedding caterer is going to be cooking with 3 phase ovens on site then you will require a mobile generator. Again space has to be allocated and you should budget accordingly. What about coffee afterwards? A simple question, but catering water boilers are around 3kW and 3 of these on the go will consume around 40 Amps of power-more than your household supply can cope with. You can imagine how often the lights go out in the main tent when it's time for coffee!

Cutlery, crockery and glasses will usually be supplied by your chosen wedding caterer and included within the price per head. There are many catering companies hiring crockery and you may wish to allocate some of your budget on some fine quality cutlery, crockery and crystal glasses for that extra sparkle.

Table linen is again usually supplied by your wedding caterer and either included in the price per head or as a separate charge. There are also specialist table linen hire companies, or indeed many marquee companies offer table linen options.

Tables and chairs are usually supplied by the tent company. Some caterers offer tables and chairs but expect to pay extra for the hire. There are also furniture hire companies with a wide choice of styles of chairs.

You are probably best hiring the tables from the marquee company (even if you don't like their chairs). Wedding guests are usually seated at round tables and a 5 foot round table will seat 10 guests and a 6 foot round table will seat 12 guests. The top table is traditionally a long table made up using 6 foot long trestle tables which the bridal party will sit down one side (and the ends) only. Allow one trestle table for the bride and groom and one trestle for every 3 remaining 'top' table guests. Chairs can be covered with fitted linen chair covers from specialist linen hire companies to match or compliment your choice of table linen.

Choosing a caterer for your wedding reception is very much a matter of personal taste. Many brides have never hired a catering service and expect to be given a bottom line price with minimal information supplied. The caterer will need a lot of information to give an accurate quotation, including the often overlooked subjects above; The catering company will not wish to work in the middle of a field with no running water, no power and no cover against the elements. Before you approach any potential wedding caterer make a list of questions to ask and plan as much as you can first. The caterer will be able to supply you with example set menus and he or she will wish to meet 'on site' to discuss your plans. Unfortunately, you can't make a choice over the phone. In the same way any reputable marquee company will need to do a site visit, measure up for the wedding tent(s) and evaluate access to the site, etc before giving a final quotation.

6

Hotels and Catering

DEFINING THE HOTELS AND CATERING SECTOR

The hotels and catering sector referred to in this article is defined following the statistical nomenclature NACE revision 1.1, where hotel and catering services are classified in section H comprising 'the provision to customers of lodging and/or prepared meals, snacks, and beverages for immediate consumption'. The section includes both accommodation and food services because the two activities are often combined at the same unit.

Table 1: Hotels and catering sector based on NACE Rev. 1.1 nomenclature, 2002

Code	Description
H	Hotels and restaurants
55	Hotels and restaurants
55.1	Hotels
55.10	Hotels, motels and inns
55.2	Camping sites and other provision of short-stay accommodation
55.21	Youth hostels and mountain refuges
55.22	Camping sites, including caravan sites
55.23	Other provision of lodging not elsewhere classified
55.3	Restaurants
55.30	Restaurants, including self-service, cafeterias, fast-food outlets, take-away facilities, dining car activities of transport companies

55.4	Bars
55.40	Bars, pubs, nightclubs, beer halls and vending machines
55.5	Canteens and catering
55.51	Canteens
55.52	Catering

Source: Eurostat, 2002

The hotels and catering sector in the EU generated □338 billion in 2001 and employed more than 7.5 million workers. Of the 1.4 million enterprises in the sector in 2001, more than 90% were micro-enterprises employing 10 people or less. Employment growth in the sector has remained healthy in the wake of September 11, but education and skills levels remain comparatively low, and the workforce composition is skewed towards women and younger workers. Trends and drivers with a significant influence on the sector include changing lifestyles, low-cost air travel and information technologies (IT). These and several other factors are having positive and negative effects on the industry and affected agents, raising some uncertainties and issues for the industry and governments. Examples include the impact of technology on operations and labour demand, the current skills gap that exists in the industry and the impact of consumer protection legislation.

MARKET SIZE, STRUCTURE AND EMPLOYMENT

Market Size

In 2001, there were over 1.4 million enterprises in the hotels and catering industry. Together they contributed □338 billion to the EU economy (see Table 2). The difference between the EU15 and the EU25 was around 10 billion, indicating the relative underdevelopment of the sector in the new Member States (NMS) which joined the EU on 1 May 2004.

France, Italy and Spain accounted for more than half (51.5%) of the sector's enterprises in the EU in 2001. The United Kingdom (UK) was home to just 8.5% of the enterprises, but accounted for the greatest shares of employment and turnover: it employed 24% of the workforce and generated 24% of industry turnover in the EU25 in 2001.

MARKET STRUCTURE

Restaurants, bars and catering enterprises (H55.3 to H55.5) dominate the sector. Together, they accounted for almost two-thirds of the sector's gross value added (GVA) and 75% of its employment in 2001.

Table 2: Number of enterprises, employment and turnover in hotels and restaurants, 2001

Country	Enterprises		Employment		Turnover		Persons employed
	Number	%	Number	%	€ million	%	per enterprise
Austria	38,679	2.7	211,670	2.8	10,512	3.1	5.5
Belgium	40,217	2.9	157,699	2.1	8,627	2.5	3.9
Cyprus	7,103	0.5	33,270	0.4	1,592	0.5	4.7
Czech Republic	42,580	3.0	162,653	2.1	2,684	0.8	3.8
Denmark	13,442	1.0	94,597	1.2	4,405	1.3	7.0
Estonia	1,338	0.1	13,268	0.2	215	0.1	9.9
Finland	10,514	0.7	52,939	0.7	4,275	1.3	5.0
France	207,326	14.7	796,433	10.5	51,826	15.3	3.8
Germany	172,999	12.3	1,082,339	14.3	42,001	12.4	6.3
Hungary	32,121	2.3	111,287	1.5	1,766	0.5	3.5
Ireland	13,662	1.0	125,187	1.7	6,592	1.9	9.2
Italy	255,739	18.2	904,973	11.9	47,996	14.2	3.5
Latvia	1,876	0.1	17,018	0.2	212	0.1	9.1
Lituania	2,906	0.2	24,053	0.3	199	0.1	8.3
Luxembourg	2,570	0.2	12,643	0.2	862	0.3	4.9
Malta	2,135	0.2	17,080	0.2	497	0.1	8.0
Netherlands	39,740	2.8	299,340	3.9	14,302	4.2	7.5
Poland	51,645	3.7	200,232	2.6	3,085	0.9	3.9
Portugal	62,083	4.4	239,142	3.2	7,021	2.1	3.9
Slovak Republic	1,161	0.1	20,482	0.3	254	0.1	17.6
Slovenia	6,056	0.4	27,842	0.4	794	0.2	4.6
Spain	261,671	18.6	1,073,666	14.2	41,393	12.2	4.1
Sweden	21,383	1.5	109,436	1.4	7,250	2.1	5.1
United Kingdom	119,195	8.5	1,792,138	23.6	80,244	23.7	15.0
EU15	1,259,220	89.4	6,952,202	91.7	327,306	96.7	5.5
EU25	1,408,141	100.0	7,579,387	100.0	338,604	100.0	5.4

Note: Data for Greece not available. Source: Eurostat, 2004b, p. 4

However, despite the success of big fast-food chains and catering chains such as Compass Group and Sodexho and hotel franchises such as InterContinental Hotels and Hilton Accor, the hotels and catering sector is dominated by small enterprises.

In the European economy, hotels, restraurants and catering represent a major service sector. As part of the service sector, over 90% of firms in the hotels and catering sector can be classed as micro enterprises (fewer than 10 persons employed). On average, each enterprise in the EU employs around 5.4 employees. Micro-enterprises alone generated over 40% of the sector's turnover and employed almost half of the sector's workforce in 2001. At the same time, large enterprises (more than 250 persons employed) only accounted for 0.1% of total enterprises, generated 24.6% of the sector's turnover and employed around 20% of the sector's workforce.

Table 3: Main enterprises in the hotels and catering sector in the EU15, 2002

Main hotel chains

Company	**Country**	**Number of rooms**
InterContinental Hotels	United Kingdom (UK)	514,873
Accor	France (FR)	440,807
Hilton Group plc	United Kingdom (UK)	96,380
Sol Melia	Spain (ES)	81,096
TUI Hotels and resorts	Germany (DE)	75,000

Main restaurant, bar and catering enterprises

Company	**Country**	**Turnover (million)**
Compass Group	UK	7,953
Sodexho Alliance	FR	4,554
Elior	FR	2,036
Whitbread	UK	1,832
Six Continents	UK	1,334

Source: Adapted from Eurostat, 2004a

EMPLOYMENT

Hotels and catering in the EU employed more than 7.5 million workers in 2001. The sector plays an important role in job creation in the EU economy. According to Eurostat figures, during 1995 to 2000, employment in the sector increased on average by 1.6% per year. Despite the economic downturn in the wake of 9/11 in 2001, employment in hotels and catering grew by 2% to 2.5% per year in 2001 and 2002, well above the 1.3% in 2001 and 0.38% in 2002 for the economy as a whole.

The hotels and catering industry is heavily dependent on tourism, so employment levels tend to be seasonal. In addition, the labour force is, on average, much younger and less skilled than in other sectors, and also has a higher percentage of women.

In 2004, women accounted for 55% of the total jobs in the sector, which is about 20% higher than in the EU economy as a whole At a sub-occupational level, the higher female share exists only in core jobs in the sector, such as travel attendants, housekeeping and restaurant workers. Other, often more senior, jobs, such as cooks and managers, are dominated by men.

Part-time work is also relatively more common in the sector: 28% of employment was part time in 2004, compared with only 18% for the whole economy. Qualification levels of workers in hotels and restaurants are relatively low (ISCED 1997 classification). Fewer than one employee in 10 had attained a high level of education (all tertiary education, including university education) and more than 40% of employees were relatively unskilled.

RECENT DEVELOPMENTS IN THE SECTOR

In the wake of the 9/11 attacks, turnover growth in the hotels and catering sector slowed from around 4% to 4.5% per year before the attacks to about 1.5% per year (see Figure 4). Turnover growth started to pick up in 2004 as consumer confidence was restored and US visitor numbers started to recover. Employment growth also slowed following the 9/11 attacks, and despite picking up in 2003 it continued its downward trend in 2004.

In the EU15 in 2000, more than 40% of employees in the sector were relatively unskilled (see Figure 4). In 2004, a small increase in the proportion of those with upper secondary or tertiary education was seen, thus the qualification level of workers had improved slightly and the share of workers with relatively low skills had diminished. It is not clear to what extent EU enlargement will help in raising skills levels in the sector. Certainly, enlargement is likely to provide a pool of more mobile and cost-effective labour. However, as all the NMS are former communist countries where consumer expenditure on hotels and catering was low or non-existent and the tourist industry was comparatively underdeveloped (except Slovenia), there will perhaps be skills lacking in this area among the workforce from some of the new Member States.

While Figure 3 indicates that employment in the sector has grown by around 2% per year during 2000 to 2004, Figures 5 and 6 indicate that most of this expansion has been among older and part-time workers. During 2000 to 2004, the number of part-time workers increased by 10% to 12%, while the number of full-time workers, despite rising temporarily, has not noticeably changed. This reflects, in part, the role of technological advances in increasing demand for more flexible working patterns. At the same time, the number of 15-to 34-year-olds working in the sector remained largely unchanged during 2000 to 2004, while the number of older workers rose significantly. Workers aged over 55 have registered the biggest rise, of around 30%, while those aged 35 to 54 have increased in number by about 10%.

TRENDS AND DRIVERS

The key drivers in the sector are presented below with a brief description. A more detailed assessment of these drivers is presented in the second article of this series.

Sociological

Key sociological drivers include the ageing of populations in many of the EU Member States, combined with changing lifestyles and tastes among workers and consumers across the EU. The ageing of the workforce and the increasing levels of educational attainment among young people can be expected to affect the structure of the workforce and its working conditions. Population ageing is also likely to lead to a change in consumer preferences and, hence, in the services supplied. Changing consumer lifestyles and tastes, brought on by improvements in living and working conditions, evolving social conventions, economic development and new technology, are creating more informed and demanding consumers, who are also becoming more organised as a collective force.

Technological

On the supply side, the prevalence of information technologies over the last 20 years, and in particular the last 10 years, has allowed enterprises to be more flexible by allowing them to manage and monitor both their resources and supply chains better. Information technologies also facilitate the greater customisation of services on offer.

For consumers, it has led to an expansion of choice of information providers and where they spend their money. It is also changing consumers' shopping habits and the way they interact with enterprises. Beyond developments in information and communication technologies (ICT), new kitchen and production technologies are leading to structural changes in catering establishments by allowing the outsourcing of many operations and the simplification of kitchen processes, but with largely negative effects for the workforce.

Economic

Globalisation is one economic driver influencing the hotels and catering sector. Through the free movement of labour and capital as well as economic and political integration, globalisation has opened up new geographical and consumer markets. These present both threats and opportunities. For all companies, there is the prospect of tapping into new consumer and new labour markets. However, for existing workers, this also throws up the potential threat of more efficient and/or better-skilled labour elsewhere and the threat of new destinations, cultures and companies. Another economic driver is the recent, rapid expansion of low-cost air travel. This has made it easier for agents to travel as both tourists and workers, but it also creates further problems. Together, these drivers stimulate other socio-economic and political issues concerning skills levels, migration and working conditions.

Environmental

Adverse weather patterns in recent years have pushed the issue of climate change and energy use into the political mainstream. Adverse weather itself is likely to affect the sector where it forms part of the tourist industry situated in areas at risk from climate change, with coastal and winter sports resorts most at risk. Politically, part of the response is to target air emissions and energy efficiency. In this way, political efforts to improve resource efficiency across the economy, particularly with respect to utility inputs, are likely to lead to cultural and hardware changes within the industry. Another issue affecting the sector as part of the tourist industry is the environmental impact of tourists who use hotel and catering establishments.

Political

While legislation and international relations represent the clearest types of political drivers, EU enlargement and social dialogue are, respectively, partly economic and partly social drivers. International relations appear to have become more confrontational in recent years, spurred on, in part, by the 9/11 attacks. Developments in international relations continue to influence consumer confidence and behaviour, and this is likely to continue to affect demand for the hotels and catering sector as part of the tourist industry. As the EU becomes more attuned to consumer and human rights and standards of living, key pieces of legislation likely to affect the sector relate to working conditions and to the marking, quality and safety of food. This desire to promote higher living and working conditions should also stimulate social dialogue between companies and employees. Within this social dialogue framework, the accession of new Member States is likely to generate new pressures and perspectives. Beyond this framework, the expansion of the EU offers further opportunities in existing and new Member States by opening up new untapped consumer markets and labour forces.

UNCERTAINTIES AND ISSUES

Working conditions in the hotels and catering sector are characterised by low wages, long hours, poor career structures and often weak enforcement of equality policies. As a result, staff turnover is typically high. This, along with absenteeism, low commitment and poor employee performance, acts as a disincentive for employers to train and invest in their staff. The small, often family, nature of firms and tight margins is also likely to work against opportunities for staff development. The prospects for future skills levels and career prospects are therefore likely to remain an issue, and legislation may be needed to force firms to take staff development more seriously and improve their career prospects.

Within the EU, the hotels and catering industry has been identified as a sector where staff are most at risk of physical violence. Staff may have to work in highly stressful conditions, with frequent contact with inebriated clients and customers. Exposure to violence and sexual harassment is sometimes viewed as being a regular occurrence and as being part of the job in this sector. The dominance of small enterprises in the sector means that most employers lack the means to support and protect their staff from these pressures.

Employee and employer representatives in the sector are working together in order to improve the economic environment for enterprises while making working conditions better for workers. Even so, union membership in the sector is low because of its employment structure.

Attracting workers to union membership is therefore one of the European Federation of Food, Agriculture and Tourism Trade Unions' (EFFAT) main priorities in order to increase the intensity of social dialogue, from the ILO-defined 'exchange of information' and 'consultation' to a higher level of involvement ('negotiation'), such as collective bargaining and negotiating in the decision-making process.

While future legislation will likely raise standards of working conditions, it will also probably lead to job cuts and lower wage growth. Because of their generally tighter operating conditions, small businesses are likely to find it hardest to conform to the new legislation. In general, more rules and regulations are likely to hurt small businesses (which account for 90% of total enterprises in the sector) the most, but the impact may be less if the European Commission succeeds in cutting red tape for business.

The impact of migrant labour should also be considered. In theory, low-skilled migrants can be expected to fill low-skill vacancies that are unfilled by native workers and suppress wage inflation in the sector.

However, as recent data show, there has been less labour migration than was expected following EU enlargement. In addition, because the economies of the new Member States are expected to develop with relatively greater speed than was the case with previous accession countries, the reasons for migration from these countries are expected to diminish more rapidly. As a result, migrant workers are less likely to be a significant force in affecting working conditions.

If the scale of migrant labour does become sufficiently large, it may well lead to more legislation to protect workers rights, but there is also the possibility that it may lead to protectionist legislation in countries where unions are, or become, powerful political bodies.

The adoption of technology in the sector carries some uncertainty and raises certain issues. It is not entirely clear to what extent new technology will improve working conditions and job opportunities and to what extent its impact will be negative. It has led, and will continue to lead, to changes in the quantity and structure of labour demand in the sector.

The International Union of Food, Agricultural, Hotel, Restaurant, Catering, Tobacco and Allied Workers' Associations (IUF) argued that new technologies require less-skilled staff and so result in many job losses in the industry.

Moreover, the IUF argues that technology will devalue wages by deskilling the remaining workforce. In contrast, time-saving technology could benefit workers in the sector by reducing the stress and pressure placed on workers, allowing them to work in a more favourable environment. Given the small scale of many of the enterprises in this sector, the adoption of technology is likely to be very sensitive in terms of the cost of implementation and the expected flow of benefits over time. Another influence in the adoption of new technologies is likely to be legislation on working conditions and health and safety standards. Adopting new technologies generally raises working conditions, but its impact on labour demand is unclear. Time-saving technology may lead to reduced labour demand or it may create new work opportunities, and specialist technology may require new skills that demand higher wages.

It is not clear if globalisation, changes in consumer demand and the internet will benefit the sector. It appears to have made consumers more mobile and flexible as shoppers. It may well be that it leads to a dichotomy where some companies successfully adapt to these forces while others fail to adapt and become unable to compete. Furthermore, these forces probably favour larger businesses more than small ones.

Their greater scale and pool of resources makes it easier for them to exploit these new opportunities. At the same time, although current conditions in the hotels and catering sector are forcing small enterprises to find new ways to compete in order to survive, potential benefits from technologies to small enterprises are likely to be limited because their size limits the opportunity to generate economies of scale. As a result, further consolidation and an increasing presence of chains within the sector can be expected.

FEASIBILITY STUDY ON IS APPLICATIONS IN THE TOURISM SECTOR

Information and Communication Technologies (ICTs) have revolutionised the management of contemporary organisations and introduced a paradigm shift in the way businesses operate. This revolution started in the 80s and propelled organisations to re-engineer their business, in order to improve their competitiveness. The use of ICTs is the enabling mechanism which facilitates the processing and flow of information in an organisation, encompassing the information the business creates, uses, and stores, as well as the technologies used in the physical processing to produce a product or provide a service. The telecommunication networks provide the information highways over which new products and services can be offered, thereby redefining concepts of customer service, opening up new arenas of innovation, and altering the economics of distribution. As telecommunication networks are utilised to transfer information and information technology facilitates networks' operations, it becomes increasingly difficult to distinguish between the two concepts.

Therefore, ICTs should be regarded as a 'synthesis of electronics, computing and telecommunications technologies which enable effective data processing and communication. ICTs increase an organisation's ability to co-ordinate activities regionally, nationally and globally while unlocking the power of broader geographical scope to create competitive advantage.

Paradoxically, the more powerful ICTs become, the more accessible and user friendly they appear, enabling more organisations and people to take advantage. As a result, a business process re-engineering prevails in organisations around the world, revolutionising their strategies, competitiveness and operational processes.

The Tourism industry is inevitably affected by this revolution and a critical issue concerns the relationship between technology and business. The way of conceiving the business environment (e.g. the firm, the corporation, the competition and so on) becomes the driver of ICT applications. As "information is the life-blood of the tourism industry", effective use of the computer technology is fundamental to the tourism sector as we approach the 21st century.

Thus, communication and information transmission tools are indispensable to the tourism industry. Essentially, a whole system of ICTs is being rapidly diffused throughout the tourism sector and no player will escape its impacts. Since the beginning of 1995, the World Wide Web (WWW) emerged as the fastest growing area of the INTERNET, enabling the distribution of textual data, graphics, pictures, video and sounds. It soon became the flagship of the ICTs' revolution and instituted an innovation platform for efficient, live and timely exchange of both ideas and products. The INTERNET provides tailor-made information to meet the needs of individual customers, bridging the tourist demand with supply.

This study addresses the distribution problem of Small and Medium Tourism Enterprises (SMTEs) and peripheral destinations, elaborating at the same time the new challenges originated by the revolution of ICTs. Distribution emerges as the most important element of the strategic marketing. This is more apparent in the tourism industry, due to the intangibility of the product.

The study concentrates on the implication of ICTs for the tourism and more specifically for SMTEs section of the market. Tourism destinations are traditionally dominated by small and medium-sized tourism enterprises, which provide a variety of products and services such as accommodation, catering, transportation, attractions and activities.

Further, this study concentrates on the contribution of SMTE to the prosperity of destinations, focused in particular on the region of Epirus which is one of the most isolated and poorer peripheral regions in the European Union. It attempts to develop strategic thinking and to provide innovative strategic tools, in order to empower SMTEs and peripheral destinations. Also, it tries to strengthen their distribution channels in the increasingly globalised, centrally controlled and highly competitive marketplace.

SMTEs are widely recognised as the backbone of the tourism industry. The small size and flexibility of operation provide them with a unique capability of delivering tailor-made tourism products. However, there is a wide range of strategic weaknesses. Similarly, peripheral, remote and insular regions are often unable to compete in industrial and technological sectors, due to their lack of human resources, management and ICTs experts, infrastructure and capital for investment.

In an attempt to reverse the unfavorable situation for SMTEs and peripheral destinations, the realization of the potential emerging through ICTs and its necessity in the tourism industry, forces the proliferation of various destination-oriented computerized systems world-wide, as facilitators of the coordination, promotion, and distribution functions of destinations and SMTEs. Because ideally these systems contain information on all suppliers and facilities in a destination, they will be referred to as Destination Information Systems, which enable the destinations and the SMTEs to co-ordinate their operations and promote their products. Also, they enable the establishment of platforms for the enhancement of tourism benefits at the destination level.

As a result, the ideal strategy for the development of the region of Epirus and its tourism industry, would be the formation of a broad destination information system which would use the most recent technologies that will be taken over by a non-profit organization. This will be the Supporting Agent for Small and Medium Tourism Enterprises (SASMTE). A great number of benefits can be achieved by the co-operation of SMTEs through a SASMTE. The five main benefit areas may be management, marketing, technology, business support and co-operation with other agents. This integrated system is proposed to assist information provision and reservations for the entire range of tourism products for the region of Epirus.

This study takes this combined concept and formulates an ideal and perhaps near utopian system, the Destination Integrated Computer Information Reservation Management Systems (DICIRMS), which supports the multi-integration and management of destinations and SMTEs, as well as their competitiveness and profitability. These systems provide a strategic tool that enables remote, peripheral and insular destinations and SMTEs to take advantage of the emerging ICTs, in order to overcome some of their strategic weaknesses and enhance their competitiveness. In particular, the DICIRMS concept can be considered the strategic tool for local collaboration, promotion and distribution.

Thus, ICTs developments provide the means to overcome some of strategic weaknesses of SMTEs and peripheral regions. Not only do DICIRMS facilitate the diffusion of the understanding and utilization of ICTs, but they also provide the vehicle for the representation of the small and peripheral tourism sector in the global economic tourism marketplace.

This study introduces the DICIRMS concept as a strategic tool and mechanism for the distribution, promotion and management of the destinations and the SMTEs. These systems revolutionize tourism product promotion and distribution by diffusing information and empowering the reservation procedures for destinations' amenities, transportation and activities, while they support the distribution of ready-made packages.

A close collaboration between the public and the private sectors at destinations is regarded as essential for the successful development and operation of DICIRMSs. The public sector has to provide a certain degree of financial support from its tourism promotion budget, and to ensure that the infrastructure required as well as the telecommunication networks are available.

The private sector, on the other hand, needs to use its technological capability in order to facilitate local networking. Neither the public nor the private sector can operate a DICIRMS alone. Also, each individual SMTE needs to be provided with a disciplined planning framework to identify its position in the destination and to formulate its strategic direction and objectives for the next years. Only in this way can SMTEs and peripheral regions hope to compete with larger enterprises and take full advantage of the emerging technology.

DICIRMSs introduce a great opportunity and a great mechanism for the management of tourism impacts at destinations. It becomes increasingly evident that the SMTEs of the region of Epirus, which fail to utilize the emerging strategic marketing tools, will be unable to attract their target markets.

A closer co-operation between the SMTEs of Epirus, as well as with other regions, will enable the establishment of DICIRMSs as platforms for tourism product efficiency and distribution. They can also provide a major contribution to the improvement of socio-cultural and environmental impacts at the destination level. They would enable consumers to develop realistic expectations for both SMTEs and destinations. This would not only increase their satisfaction, but also enhance their respect for the socio-cultural and environmental resources of the destinations.

This study attempts to contribute towards empowering the competitiveness of SMTEs and remote, peripheral and insular destinations. It proposes a DICIRMS as a strategic tool to strengthen the promotion and distribution elements of SMTEs and destinations, after it has explained their strategic weaknesses.

It is hoped that the peripheral region of Epirus and its SMTEs will realize their vulnerability, will stimulate their strategic thinking and undertake a strategic action. It is believed therefore, that ICTs and DICIRMS in particular, hold a great opportunity for the enhancement of the competitiveness and prosperity of SMTEs and destinations of the region of Epirus for the new century.

Dieticians or nutritionists help to promote good health through corrective eating habits, thus improving the quality of life. They assist people in planning meals depending upon their age, sickness or work routine, counsel and educate them about healthy eating-selection and preparation of food items according to the principles of nutrition and evaluate and make changes in their clients diet periodically.

Dietitians promote nutritious eating habits through education and research, as well as through overseeing the selection and preparation of food services for many different institutions and groups. They fix nutritional regimens for patients in a hospital, athletes in physical training camps, mountaineers on an expedition and so on.

They do research on nutritive value of food which help to understand the various components of food we eat and the right type of food which provides a balanced mix of the essentials like vitamins, minerals etc needed for the human body. They study the digestive process, the various reactions of food stuffs in the body and find out what is harmful and thus help to prevent diseases through a proper diet program. Some of them specialize in areas such as obesity, pediatrics or diabetes. They form a vital part of the health team. Organisations involved in food product manufacture use the services of the nutritionist or dietician to plan and research new products. The nutritionists also has excellent prospects in the mass media where top of priority is given to disseminating vital information on healthy living. They could find employment in hospitals, research labs of food manufacturers, catering departments of star hotels, health departments and recreation clubs, teach the science of nutrition and dietetics in colleges and universities. They can also work as consultants or do private practice.

The trends today show a increasing interest in health and fitness. So future prospects in this women dominated field are bright.

Eligibility: People opting for a career in Dietetics and Nutrition should study home science or dietetics and nutrition, food science/technology courses at the graduate and postgraduate levels. Click here for more details

Job Prospects: Nutrition and Dietetics is a vital, growing field and the opportunities and possibilities in this field are endless. Click here for more Details

Remuneration: Remuneration for Nutrition & Dietetics professionals is depended on the job and the area of work.

HOSPITALITY INDUSTRY

The hospitality industry is growing at a faster rate than ever envisaged and today it has no boundaries.

So high is the confidence in this industry that the only restriction is ambition. Over 250 million people around the world are estimated to be employed in this sector alone and the statistics indicate that one job is created in every two and a half seconds by the hospitality industry.

Being a trade that encompasses industries like aviation, shipping, entertainment, catering, multiplexes, shopping malls, call centers and of course hotels and restaurants, the opportunities are pouring in with exciting career, assured job, handsome pay packets and above all international recognition and job satisfaction.

Why Hotel Management?

For a professional this is a very lucrative segment capable of offering a long growth oriented career. The hotel sector itself requires a large amount of well trained manpower with excellent skill in housekeeping, food & beverage service and production, marketing, accounting, security, engineering, fire fighting, public relations and so on. A hospitality professional can find job opportunity in customer relations, sales and marketing and event management. They can look forward to career opportunities to start with:-

Management Trainee in Hotel and allied industry

Hospitality Executive

Kitchen Management Trainee

House Keeping Management Trainee

Hospital and institutional catering supervisor

Faculty in Hotel Management Institutes

Cabin Crew in Airlines

Catering Officer in Shipping and Cruise lines

In this fast changing world, the hospitality industry has become the ideal place for those having an inborn talent to mingle with people, work with them and serve them. The young entrants have to come up with an open mind to explore the challenging world of hospitality business. They shall need to be multi skilled, talented and proactive not only to stay afloat but also to stay in demand in the challenging times that lie ahead.

ROYAL GROUP AND HOSPITALITY INDUSTRY

Hotel Division

The entry of Royal Group into the hospitality industry was by opening an ethnic village resort namely Royal Village in close harmony with the nature in the suburbs of Cochin. The century old traditional Farm House which stands as a testimony of ancient Kerala lifestyle attracting domestic and international tourists alike symbolizes the desire of the group to preserve and protect the culture and heritage of our country. The flagship hotel of the group, Fort Munnar conceived under the concept of eco friendly holidaying stands tall with its exquisite colonial architecture blending with the picturesque surroundings of Munnar is best known for its personalized and intimate services offered. This luxury hotel with its exceptional five star facilities may be perhaps the only one of its kind in the state with state of the art Discotheque, star gaze gallery and many more making once stay highly enjoyable. All the above properties and their upcoming new proprieties in prime tourist locations in the state are together known as Royal Group of Hotels-for the rich and famous-which is well known in the fields of hotel, travel and tourism all over India and abroad.

HOTELS AND CATERING SECTOR-VISIONS OF THE FUTURE

This second article in the Sector Futures series on the hotels and catering sector looks at the trends and drivers affecting the sector, presents a framework to link them together and assesses their impact. The article also reviews some scenario work relating to the sector before concluding with an examination of the implications on the sector of the drivers and scenarios. Examples of the implications include better working conditions, consolidation and more consumer protection. Following the overview of the sector and initial look at trends and drivers in the first article of this series, this article now examines these trends and drivers in more detail and reviews existing foresight research on the hotels and catering sector.

Trends and Drivers of Change

The first article identified and introduced several trends and drivers that are shaping the sector. In a STEEP (social, technological, economic, environmental and political) breakdown, the key social drivers were identified as ageing populations and changing lifestyles and tastes. Information technologies, along with new production and kitchen technologies, were identified as the key technological drivers. Economic drivers included globalisation and low-cost travel, which in part raise issues about skill levels, migration and competition. Regarding environmental drivers, the main issues were identified as the direct impact of climate change on the sector as part of the tourist industry and the political desire to improve energy and resource efficiency across the economy. The key political drivers are likely to be legislation to improve consumer and worker rights, along with the quality and labelling of food.

Beyond that, the sector, as part of the tourist industry, remains sensitive to the impact of international relations on consumer behaviour. The links and interactions between these forces are shown in the schematic diagram below.

STEEP Analysis

The following table summarises the STEEP factors affecting, or expected to affect, the industry along with their possible impacts.

Table 1: STEEP analysis and possible future of hotels and catering industry

Trends and drivers	Possible future of hotels and catering industry
Social	
Ageing population	Ageing consumers create a new type of demand. Older workers push harder for better conditions and better-qualified young workers choose other careers. These pressures lead to more social dialogue and an improvement in working conditions.
Change in tastes and demands	More informed and flexible consumers demand more value and more personal service. Increase in niche markets, e.g. organic/ethical restaurants, health hotels, etc.; expansion of budget hotels.
Technological	
Information technologies	Leads to better resource management and more flexible service delivery. Consequently, creates demand for new IT skills and less demand for traditional skills. This may shift gender balance in the workforce.

New kitchen technology	Outsourcing and simplification of kitchen operations expected to turn kitchens into assembly lines, deskill staff and bring about lower wages. This may lead to higher margins for companies.
Internet	Expands the range of information providers and establishments on offer to consumers and leads to changes in shopping behaviour. For firms, it expands the customer base and creates new competition, raises the importance of presentation and quality of service and demands new marketing strategies.
Economic	
Low-cost air travel	More tourists and more trips taken, but expenditure patterns are unclear; expansion of services in new destinations. Long-term growth may be curbed by environmental concerns.
Globalisation	New geographic and consumer markets pose threats and opportunities to the sector. Likely to favour large enterprises and promote consolidation. Likely to stimulate debate on skill levels and migration.
Environmental	
Climate change	Negative impact on the industry in affected tourist areas. Policy on use of energy resources might bring about cultural and hardware changes.
Environmental awareness	Increased focus on dealing with pollution and waste management results in more environmentally friendly resource use, which may raise costs.
Political	
Legislation	Improvements in working conditions, consumer protection and product information increase costs for businesses. Small businesses are the most affected, because the improvements encourage consolidation. Effects filter down the supply chain and could alter the products on offer.
EU enlargement	Within the EU, increased tourist demand, migration and competition.
Social dialogue	Better industrial relations and working conditions, with higher skill levels. Potential to reduce labour turnover.

ASSESSMENT OF THE TRENDS AND DRIVERS

Sociological Drivers

Sociological changes, such as changes in lifestyles, are driven by and affect consumers, and directly affect businesses. The temporal impact varies, but some changes, such as the increased use of the Internet for shopping, have had a profound impact on the industry. Such drivers require businesses to adapt in order to survive, for example, by reviewing their relationship with the customer and their marketing strategy. An ageing population will affect the composition of the workforce (as outlined in the first article) and may help improve working conditions; it is also likely to lead to a change in the composition of consumer demand.

In addition, growing interest from consumers in the production and health aspects of food is increasing pressure on caterers to supply better-quality food, produced in socially responsible ways, and with information on its origins. Reluctance by the industry to act on these issues is leading to increased governmental involvement. Changes to the supply chain in response to these trends are likely to be long-lasting.

Technological Drivers

Technology has been a primary driving force of change among consumers and in the sector, thereby helping to globalise it. While it creates opportunities, technology is also a major threat to small enterprises in the sector. Because of their small size, it is much harder for them to generate economies of scale and recover the cost of investment in new technologies. However, if they do not invest in new technologies, they are likely to lose out to those who have.

The increasing use of technology has led to a need to retrain existing staff. Some industry bodies have argued that technology poses a threat to employment by reducing staff hours (as seen in the fall in full-time employment) and thus will exert downward pressure on wages. The initial boom in the use of information technologies appears to be slowing, and while its use will continue to increase, it is likely to be at a more gradual pace.

Economic Drivers

Globalisation has affected all parties. It has pushed governments to cooperate and integrate more, and in doing so has made the world more accessible to all parties. Economically, it has reduced restrictions on the movement of capital, labour and resources. For the consumer, it has opened up new parts of the world, thus the hotels and restaurants most dependent on tourism face stiffer competition for their services, but they may also benefit from tourist visits from newly accessible regions. For companies, it opens up a larger market and offers the possibility of greater economies of scale that benefit larger chain groups and encourage consolidation. Recent trends show that many companies in the sector have chosen to expand by means of mergers or acquisitions as they become more aware of the need to pool resources in order to compete effectively in an expanding market.

The rise in low-cost air travel has above all benefited consumers, offering them more choice, flexibility and pricing options. While establishments are receiving increased numbers of visitors, it is not clear that the increase in visitor spending has been commensurate with the increase in numbers. Many tourists have become far more cost conscious, leading to a growing demand for budget, no-frills hotels. The EU market for low-cost travel still has some way to go before it reaches maturity, so the effects have probably not yet reached a plateau. However, with governments looking increasingly set to levy environmental taxes on air travel and with oil prices rising and staying high, ticket prices can be expected to rise also. The impact of this on consumer demand is uncertain, as it is not yet clear how sensitive consumers are to the pricing of budget air travel.

Environmental Drivers

In general, environmental drivers are likely to have a less immediate impact on the sector than the other drivers discussed. The most direct impact is likely to be felt by establishments that form part of the tourist industry in areas affected by climate change (coastal and ski resorts) and areas of environmental interest. However, the timeframe for such effects is likely to be further in the future than for other drivers. Although freak changes or storms may wreak havoc, the resultant damage they cause is often temporary, but the permanent damage, as from rising sea levels, is taking place as a slow, gradual process. Nevertheless, the net impact on businesses in affected areas can be expected to be negative as the features that made them attractive in the first place are eroded. While some may be able to adapt to the new environment, their success is likely to depend on how consumers react.

In other respects the impact of environmental changes is likely to be felt through policies to reduce emissions, to improve the use of all resources, especially energy resources, and to reduce pollution by improving waste management. Although much of the focus has been on power generation plants, all companies are under pressure to be more energy efficient and such pressures are likely to increase in the medium term. Furthermore, the timeframe for these drivers may be longer than for others, as environmental concerns are often low on the political agenda, and it is not easy to reach political consensus on environment-energy policies when these are believed to curb growth. Any costs created by environmental policy can be expected to affect enterprises in the first place, and it will be up to them how to deal with this. The obvious choice is to pass it on to customers, but regardless of whether this is done or not, any additional costs are likely to favour larger enterprises that enjoy greater economies of scale and have more flexibility in absorbing costs.

Political Drivers

New legislation, such as smoking bans, changes to licensing laws and new regulations governing food safety, is partly a response to changes in people's tastes and lifestyles. However, new laws can bring great costs to businesses. The smoking ban, for example, has improved conditions for workers and customers, but at the same time there is evidence that it has reduced turnover and that this has translated into job losses. Over the medium term, firms are likely to face increased demands from consumers for more informative marking and higher-quality standards for food. How governments will respond to such pressure from consumers is unclear. In the UK, for example, the quality of catered school meals became a hot topic in 2005 after the poor quality of such meals was highlighted by a high-profile chef on TV.

One company supplying such meals (Compass) has suffered as a result, and the UK government is taking action to improve the quality of school meals. On the other hand, among the proposed EU laws recently scrapped by the EC president, José Barroso, there was one on food labelling. Nevertheless, governments may still be willing to take initiatives independently of EU legislation in order to satisfy their electorates.

The enlargement of the EU has positively impacted on the hotels and catering sector because the new Member States provide a new source of demand. However, migration from the new to the old Member States in pursuit of higher wages and a better standard of living is turning out to be lower than had been expected before accession. Moreover, because economic growth in the new Member States is expected to accelerate now that they are in the EU, rising wage levels and improved standards of living will probably make migration to EU15 countries less attractive.

New policies are helping to expand the scope of social dialogue within the hotels and catering sector. Social dialogue is becoming a major part of good governance because it allows all stakeholders to be part of policymaking within the firm and industry. On the other hand, union membership in this sector is comparatively low, making it difficult for workers to agree on objectives and to present a united front.

SCENARIOS FOR THE HOTELS AND CATERING SECTOR

In contrast to STEEP analysis, scenario work allows us to look beyond the familiar environment. It helps the industry to prepare for the consequences of unexpected events by asking the following questions:

- What if (X) happens?
- What would be the effects on the industry if (X) were to happen?
- What are the best ways of counteracting adverse effects?

The search for scenario work on hotels and restaurants failed to discover work related solely to hotels and restaurants. It was only as part of the tourist industry that hotels and catering received attention, and so the scenario analysis here is based primarily on foresight work related to tourism. Although hotels and restaurants are part of and rely on the tourist industry, their market is not confined just to tourists. Furthermore, the published scenario work was reactive, in that it was based on dramatic events in their immediate aftermath. It did not analyse the possible effects of hypothetical events or look at observable and more prosaic trends.

In recent years, there have been several unexpected events that have affected the hotels and catering industry, such as the 9/11 terrorist attacks, the outbreak of SARS, the foot and mouth epidemic in the UK and the bombings in Madrid and London. Such shocks have a low probability of occurrence, but their impact is high.

Recently, however, such shocks have become more frequent and hence people are more inclined to believe that they will happen again. It is extremely difficult to predict these shocks, but good policies at all levels (European, national or firm) or any foresight work must not ignore their possible reoccurrence. Petersen (1997) refers to these shocks as 'wild cards'. He suggests that some shocks are imaginable, and if agents are well prepared, they could be turned into manageable events:

> There is a general assumption that there is nothing to do about these huge surprises. However, not all wild cards are unimaginable and by identifying wild card events that may possibly occur in the future on a proactive rather than reactive matter, these can sometimes be converted into anticipated manageable events.

The chance alone of averting a future catastrophe or at least preparing strategies to handle it may be reason enough to examine wild card possibilities. If not dealt with wild cards can trigger a chain of events much worse than the initial happening. A major natural disaster can for instance cause a global epidemic, which may lead to nations closing their borders in turn leading to a collapse of the airline industry and so forth. (1997, pp. 43-47)

Post-9/11 Scenarios

One topic that scenario work could not ignore was the impact of 9/11 on the travel and tourism industry. Two major scenarios were published shortly after the attack on New York. The World Travel and Tourism Council (WTTC) estimated at that time that there were 207 million people employed worldwide in the travel and tourism economy. Its 'best guess' was that the attacks would lead to 8.8 million job losses worldwide, of which 1.2 million would be in the EU.

Within six weeks of 11 September 2001, the International Labour Organisation (ILO) published the report The social impact on the hotel and tourism sector of events subsequent to 11 September 2001 (136kb), which outlined two possible scenarios:

THE BEST-CASE SCENARIO

Assumptions:

- 9/11 is a one-off;
- there are no other attacks in the United States (US);
- there are no other attacks in other parts of the world.

Travel to Europe, which before the attack was showing recovery from recession, would not be badly affected. Europeans would continue to travel within the continent, while travel to the Middle East was unlikely to revive in the short term. The European tourism industry would benefit as a substitute destination choice. However, US tourists, who account for a significant part of the demand in the industry, would not return to Europe for some time. The reduction in US tourists, who are recognised as big spenders, would affect upmarket restaurants and hotels the most.

The Worst-case Scenario

Assumptions:

- there are other major terrorist attacks in the US;
- there are outbreaks of terrorism in other countries;
- the ongoing war in Afghanistan spreads to other regions.

In this scenario, the tourist demand from Asia and North America would plummet. Within Europe, the travel pattern would also change depending on the scale and location of any attacks. Domestic travel would probably benefit, with demand shifting from the location of an attack to an alternative location. In the extreme position, personal or business holidays would come to a halt. In the ILO's best-case scenario, the WTTC predictions were pessimistic. In the ILO's worst-case scenario, the consequences are far worse than the WTTC's predictions.

Iraq War Scenarios

When the US and the UK decided to invade Iraq in 2003, WTTC looked at the possible outcomes of the Iraq war and their consequences for the US tourist industry in its 2003 research on the United States-Travel and tourism, a world of opportunity (526kb, pp.18-21). The WTTC's scenario was informed by the experience of the 1991 Gulf war, the effects of which, according to the WTTC, were to limit economic growth through three main channels: higher oil prices, shattered consumer and business confidence and lower equity prices.

The base scenario: diplomatic solution or victory after a short, contained war

In the base case, the war is assumed to be short, contained and successful, and to remove global uncertainty. The effects on oil prices, confidence and equity prices are assumed to be very similar to what they would have been had there been a diplomatic solution to the crisis. In the short term, economic growth is assumed to be higher due to increased government spending. The difference in the effects on travel and tourism between no war and a speedy, contained war is therefore predicted to be small. However, the threat of war was assumed to undermine confidence and to reduce international travel, and this would affect the travel and tourism industry more than the rest of the economy.

Assumptions:

- quick, decisive victory or diplomatic solution;
- no use of weapons of mass destruction (WMD) against US troops, Israel or region;
- no reduction in OPEC oil production and exports;
- no challenges to Arab governments in region;
- new Iraqi government installed and in control;
- no damage to oil-producing capacity in Iraq or elsewhere.

The war scenario: victory with regional disruption.

Under this scenario, a longer-lasting war results in persistently higher oil prices, with a deeper and longer fall in confidence and equity markets. The effects on the travel and tourism industry are expected to be more severe.

Assumptions:

- Iraq attacks oil facilities in region, with limited damage but political and economic knock-on effects;
- Iraq attacks Israel and US troops but not with WMD effective enough to trigger a major response or to have highly lethal effects;
- unexpected protracted Iraqi military resistance;
- limited Israeli intervention in war; rising political unrest in region;
- low-level civil tensions and clashes in Iraq after military conflict is over;
- some terrorist attacks on US interests.

These pressures were predicted to lead to a slowing of between 1% and 2% in GDP growth in the US and UK. The effects on the travel and tourism industry are more severe under the war scenario. In the US, under this scenario, in 2003 the travel and tourism industry would experience:

- 0.9% fall in industry demand;
- 3.7% fall in industry GDP;

- 8.9% fall in exports;
- loss of 449,100 jobs.

Climate Change Scenarios

Although the global climate has been changing for some time, there is uncertainty about its future path and patterns as well as the consequences. Research commissioned by the World Tourism Organisation (WTO) suggests two possible scenarios on global climate change, relating specifically to the tourist industry in Hungary, The responses of Lake Balaton to global cliamte change (299kb, Rátz, 2003).

Climate Zone Shift Scenario

Assumptions:

- The temperate climate zone covering Hungary shifts northward and is replaced by a warmer climate.

This would be expected to lead to a longer summer season with much higher temperatures. This could have benefits for the tourist industry, assuming the temperatures are not too high and droughts are infrequent. In contrast, winter sports tourism is likely to disappear under such a scenario.

Ice Caps Melt Scenario

Assumptions:

- Ice caps melt due to global warming.

Under this scenario, the Gulf Stream cools down and changes the climate in Europe. The Hungarian climate becomes colder and wetter. This would have a mainly negative impact on the tourism industry, as the summer season becomes shorter and wetter. However, it could lead to the further development of winter sports tourism.

Scenario Summary

Some scenario work relevant to the hotels and catering industry tends to focus on dramatic events. In some cases, the work is done after the shocks have occurred, with a best-case scenario assuming that these shocks are unique and the worst-case scenario assuming that they are not. In hindsight, it is easy to say that it is a pity such analysis was not conducted before the events occurred and that there were no plans to deal with the consequences of such events. Regarding the climate change scenario, it should be emphasised that it related to Hungary only. Furthermore, the study's primary focus was not the effect of climate change on the hotels and catering sector; instead, it formed part of a wider discussion on the overall impact of climate change on the region. Since the concern here is the European hotels and catering sector, the major drawback of the Iraq war scenario is its focus on the US tourist industry.

Moreover, to date there appears to have been little work done on exploring the future of the industry through scenario planning in the light of the various current influences identified in the first two articles of this series. It may be more useful to project these current trends and drivers and identify possible outcomes and responses.

Possible scenarios to consider are:

- What if the current weakness of the EU economy persists for much longer than expected?
- What if there is a collapse in the world financial market?
- What if there are more outbreaks of deadly viruses?
- What are the implications of developing countries becoming developed over the next 10 years?
- What would happen if the Internet ceased to exist, e.g. because of political censorship?
- What if the current skills gaps remain in 10 or 15 years' time?
- What will the role of information technologies be in the industry in the future, and how will this affect labour demand?
- What are the implications if the European Union breaks up?
- What are the implications of a Europe-wide zero immigration policy?
- What are the implications for labour supply if there are no government pensions?

IMPLICATIONS

As younger workers increasingly become more qualified, they are less likely to consider the hotels and catering industry, with its poorer working conditions, as a career option. This and the ageing of the population are likely to persuade businesses to employ older workers. Because of their circumstances, older workers are often less mobile and have other commitments. Consequently, they are likely to be more demanding about working conditions, to be more favourable to union membership and to become more involved in social dialogue.

Changing lifestyles and more demanding consumers are likely to promote the development of more specialised enterprises and broaden competition among hotels and restaurants. The more specialised nature of services should allow firms to charge a premium. These niche markets are likely to attract multinationals as other parts of the hotels and catering industry become commoditised and less profitable. Commoditisation exerts downward pressure on premiums and profits. In order to survive and make a profit, firms offering commoditised services can be expected to cut costs and homogenise the service/experience on offer.

On the supply side, the increasing use of technology will continue to help establishments better manage their resources and reduce spare capacity. A better knowledge of future demands has implications for staff, in that establishments are likely to seek more flexible working patterns to match demands. This in turn has implications for lifestyle and for where the savings go. On the demand side, the Internet, wireless computing and 3G mobile telephony all make it easier for consumers to obtain information, compare prices and value for money and shop around. This trend and the increasing use of the Internet as a marketing device by businesses will lead to more intense competition and make it harder to close a sale. Firms are increasingly likely to respond by seeking staff with skills in information and communication technologies (ICT), including marketing, sales and web design.

Any increase in outsourcing in the catering industry further separates the consumer from food producers, making it harder to check the origin of food. This implies a possible widening of the information gap and is likely to increase pressure on catering companies to provide information about the food they serve. Businesses can be expected to resist this because of the cost implications, so governments may intervene.

The use of technology in the kitchen can be expected to raise productivity and lower labour demand. This again has implications for where the savings go. Increased productivity should see wages rise, but lower reliance on chefs' food preparation skills would have the opposite effect.

In the context of globalisation, EU enlargement offers a larger labour pool and facilitates migration. It is unclear to what extent this will help to fill the skills gap, as the tourist industry in most new Member States is small in comparison to that in France or the UK, for example. However, as long as relative wage differentials between regions are large enough, workers in poorer regions can be expected to move to richer regions for work. This can be expected to lower employment costs in the hotels and catering industry in richer regions.

Furthermore, this is likely to attract the most skilled from the poorer regions, thus hindering the development of the industry there. At the same time, in enlarging the EU hotel and catering market and making it more accessible, globalisation has created an opportunity for companies to exploit substantial economies of scale. To what extent this could approach the scale seen in the US, for example, is unclear given the much wider cultural and language differences that exist in the EU. Nevertheless, it is still likely to lead to the increased presence of larger multinational hotel and catering chains, which is likely to fuel the demand for migrant labour in order to reduce employment costs. Customers may suffer if this leads to a homogenisation of service on offer, but brand names and reputations should ensure a higher-quality product. In order to maintain this, companies can be expected to recruit the best-skilled staff and improve working conditions in order to retain them. The skills gap in the industry adversely affects the quality of service in the industry and damages the industry's reputation among travellers. This lessens establishments' pricing power and makes it harder to attract customers. This implies handsome rewards for companies that fill the gap (with good practice putting firms on a virtuous cycle) and premium wages for those with the necessary skills.

The existence of the gap suggests that firms are unwilling to undertake training themselves and that working conditions need to be improved in order to attract and retain skilled staff. Establishments therefore have to take a more proactive and united approach. Although low-cost airlines have increased the frequency of trips made by travellers, they often stay for a shorter duration and tend to be more cost-conscious. Furthermore, as profit-maximising companies independent of political or national influence, low-cost carriers will not hesitate to scrap unprofitable services.

This has implications for policy as well as the hotels and catering industry's marketing strategy at a local level. In some regions, the rapid growth in the tourism and leisure industry is likely to work against raising levels of education or skills, while its effect on wages will depend on the industrial structure of the locality.

Legislation to improve the working environment, e.g. smoking bans in bars and restaurants and working time regulations, has negative implications for firms' margins and labour demand. In response, firms are likely to push for productivity gains and seek more cost-effective labour and a greater application of technology.

Political concern over consumer health and the content of food is increasing pressure on catering firms to reduce sugar and salt levels, for example, in prepared food. If catering firms respond to such concerns, this could create new demands for new tastes in food. If health problems such as diabetes and obesity become greater public health issues, then the prospect of health-related taxes on food must surely draw closer. Growing concern among consumers about the origin of their food and the production methods involved is largely a social trend, but it, too, is generating political pressure for more information and increased food labelling.

This raises the prospect of legislation forcing the industry to inform consumers. The disclosure of more information and the demand for food produced in more socially responsible ways is likely to promote good practice in the food supply chain, and may lead to a shift away from low-end food establishments. In the wake of the 9/11 attacks, the EU hotels and catering sector saw turnover growth slow dramatically. US visitor numbers to the EU are only now returning to the pre-9/11 levels. International relations remain fractured because of the US-led 'war on terror' and the Iraq war. The continuation of political and military hostilities and the continued involvement of EU nations mean that some EU Member States remain targets for terrorism, as seen in the Madrid and London bombings. US tourist confidence is therefore likely to remain fragile.

High-profile marketing campaigns may be needed in the US to bolster confidence. That US visitor levels are recovering suggests terrorism has not inflicted long-lasting damage on the industry. Such damage could be caused, however, if one location were to suffer multiple attacks within a space of two or three years. While the industry is likely to be able to recover from this on an EU level, the impact on the affected region is likely to last longer. Heavy discounting in response, as employed in London in recent years, whether successful or not, would probably lead to lower levels of employment and investment, and a deterioration in working conditions. Such a downward spiral would take years to reverse.

CONCLUSION

This concludes the review of the key trends and drivers affecting the sector, and of scenario work relating to the sector. The reader should have a better idea of what issues are driving the sector and of the paucity of scenario work relating to the sector. Having looked at the trends and scenarios and their implications, the third and last article in this series, Hotels and catering-policies, issues and the future, carries the discussion forward to look at major policy issues and challenges facing the sector. Consideration is given to their timeframe and the agents and regions affected.

7

Management of Hotels in India

INTRODUCTION

Spreading over 3m square kilometres, India rises in the snowy peaks of Kashmir in the north, and falls to the tropical shores of Kerala's southern tip. In the west the barren rocky deserts of Rajasthan provide an arid, hostile environment, while in Bengal to the east lush jungles create a haven for wildlife. India's size and diversity is matched by very few countries. Dotted across this vast and breathtaking countryside are huge metropolises, swelling secondary cities and many thriving regional centres, over 40 cities with populations 1m strong, all with their own particular industries and economies. But despite India's huge scale, contrasting regions and scattered cities, one thing does link this spectacular country, growth.

The figures are staggering. India contains over 1.13 billion people, and is predicted to become the world's most populous country by 2050, overtaking China as it swells to 1.6 billion. Three cities-Mumbai, Delhi and Kolkata-contain over 10m inhabitants, and those figures rise daily. The northerly state of Uttar Pradesh has a population of over 139m-approaching the 143m living in the whole of Russia and making it the most populated internal region in the world. Likewise, India's economy is growing at speed. Real gross domestic product (GDP) grew by 8.5% in 2005, a further 8.8% in 2006, and according to the Economist Intelligence Unit (EIU) this trend will continue in 2007-08. Yes, India is on the move and the hotel industry is not being left behind. Across India average room rates are sky-rocketing. In the twelve months to March

2007 average room rates have risen 28.7% to US$174, driving revenue per available room (revPAR) up 26.9% to US$122. The Indian hotel market however, does suffer from limited supply. There are an estimated 105,000 hotel rooms in India-a number comparable to that of Manhattan. This lack of supply, especially in the lower end of the market, combined with increased demand, is allowing hoteliers to push up average room rates.

For the first time India looks like becoming a major force in the world hotel industry. So what is fuelling this dramatic growth, and how sustainable is it? In this article we shall look at the factors defining this exciting period in India's history. To gauge these trends there are no better places to look than India's four major gateway cities-Delhi in the north, Chennai in the south, Kolkata in the east, and Mumbai in the west.

THE NEW TIGER ECONOMY

It has to be recognised that it is not India's hotel industry alone that is prospering. Across the country industries are booming, encouraged by a strong and apparently stable economy. The government is looking east, to their heavyweight partner China and the heavily Chinese influenced Association of South-East Asian Nations (ASEAN), for trade and investment. Combine this with an increasingly close relationships with the US, already excellent ties with the UK and an, albeit partial, thaw in tensions with neighbour Pakistan, and India's global network of friends looks pretty healthy. Key areas such as IT, pharmaceuticals and telecommunications have seen rapid expansion in recent years. Many companies outsource their operations to India, benefiting from a seemingly bottomless pool of skilled labour, cheap costs and hefty government incentives.

So what effect is this economic upsurge having on the hotel industry? Well, the EIU believes that approximately 80% of foreigners coming to India are there to do business. As business travel generally generates a higher spend than leisure tourism, it is plain to see why the Indian government is keen to promote this further. International tourism expenditure in India in 2006 was some US$8.7 billion, and is expected to rise to over

US$10 billion in 2008, with the lion's share of this being generated from the hotel sector.

It is no wonder therefore, that India's government is tearing down the barriers to potential inward investment and continued growth. The central government's expenditure tax is no longer applied to hotels and services charges have been slashed. The hotel industry is now classed as part of the country's infrastructure by the government, lowering borrowing costs. The government is also issuing new long-term tourist visas to the citizens of selected countries, including the UK, Japan, Germany, France, Switzerland and Brazil. The five-year validity of the visa sends out a clear message: encourage repeat visits from wealthy tourists.

Hotel Performance for Gateway Cities in India

	Occupancy (%)			Average Room Rate (US$)			RavPar (US$)		
	4/2006 to 3/2007	4/2005 to 3/206	Change %	4/2005 to 3/2007	4/2005 to 3/2006	Change %	4/2005 to 3/2007	4/2005 to 3/2006	Change %
All India	70.3	71.3	-1.4	174	135	28.7	122	96	26.9
Mumbai	75.9	73.1	3.8	202	149	35.6	153	109	40.8
Kolkata	71.3	71.3	-0.1	120	88	35.7	86	63	35.6
Delhi	74.8	79.4	-5.5	225	166	35.7	168	131	28.2
Chennai	75.2	78.3	-4.0	135	102	32.5	101	80	27.2

Source: HotelBenchmark Survey by Deloitte

ISLAND NATION

India can almost be considered an island, and in ancient times it was. Approximately 6m years ago the Indian continental plate crashed into the Eurasian continent, an impact so severe it created the largest visible mountain range on earth-the Himalayas. With such a formidable boundary to the north and two long coastlines tapering to the southern tip-where the Bay of Bengal and the Arabian Sea meet at the Indian Ocean-India can essentially only be reached by air. The volatile border regions with Pakistan and Myanmar only serve to limit land access further. With the existing road and rail network often considered time consuming, unreliable or even unsafe, and a growing number of private low-cost airlines entering the market, domestic air travel across this vast land is also becoming increasingly popular.

Given the scale of India, air travel is a key sector. Domestic air travel throughout the country is becoming a cheaper, more feasible option with private carriers Kingfisher, Jet, Air Sahara, Indigo, Spicejet and Deccan Airways all expanding their fleets and cutting fares. In response to this, the national carriers Indian Airlines and Air India are doing likewise.

The majority of international visitors arriving in India fly into one of the four gateway cities. So how are the hotel industries in these metropolises being affected by, and reacting to, the overriding nationwide trends?

THE CAPITAL

The gateway to the north of India, Delhi is the starting point for the majority of India's tourists. The apex of the revered Golden Triangle tourist track and capital of the ancient Mughal Empire, Delhi has enough attractions of its own to enjoy before tourists set off to Agra and Jaipur. However with thriving telecommunications, IT, banking and manufacturing industries, a key English-speaking work-force and a per-capita income more than twice the national average, Delhi is also a haven for business travel.

Delhi's relevance to the world of business is enhanced by the presence of many major multinational companies, with local government actively promoting this area as a counter to the Financial Centre of Mumbai. With the exception of the Taj Group, all hotel industry major players have based themselves here.

A dramatic 35.7% rise in the twelve months to March 2007 forced Delhi's average room rates up to an incredible US$225; the highest of all Indian cities. While occupancy levels decreased slightly to 74.8%. The main reason for this is under supply, especially in the lower end of market. As with all cities in India, the market in Delhi is dominated by 5-star and 5-star deluxe properties. Efforts are being made to solve this problem; with the local government introducing, as part of their Delhi Master Plan, a scheme intended to create a more even-spread accommodation hierarchy across the city, while also developing accessibility (road, footpaths, road bridges and parking). Another impetus for this is the fact that Delhi will host the forthcoming Commonwealth Games in 2010.

Between now and the Games, new developments in the National Capital Region (NCR-including Delhi and its suburban conurbations of Gurgaon and Noida) are set to include a 320-room Novotel, a 200-room Taj Hotel, three Starwood (the 300-room Westin New Delhi, the 97-room Westin Sohna-Gurgaon and the 220-room Sheraton New Delhi) and a 319-room Leela-Kempinski joint venture. The public sector is also playing a role with the state governments of Delhi, Haryana and Uttar Pradesh having ear-marked 75 potential NCR sites for hotel development.

Together with Mumbai, Delhi accounts for the bulk of inward arrivals. The modernisation plan for Indira Gandhi International Airport by its new private owners is already underway. This is expected to be completed by 2010 and will more than double its capacity.

FINANCIAL CENTRE

The capital of the western Maharashtra state, Mumbai was created as a deep water port by the British and Portuguese, and began to boom following the construction of the Suez Canal. It is now the financial capital of India, home to the Reserve Bank of India, the National Stock Exchange and the more traditional Bombay Stock Exchange, contributing an estimated 40% of India's foreign trade. Mumbai also has thriving industries revolving around IT, engineering and healthcare sectors. Most Indian conglomerates have their corporate offices here, including Tatas, Birlas and Reliance. This status makes Mumbai a haven for national and international business travel.

Mumbai experienced revPAR growth of 40.8% in the year to March 2007. This, again, is due to a sharp increase in average room rates, which rose 35.6% to US$202 over the same period. Occupancy for this period stands at 75.9%. Once again an extremely top-heavy market dominated by luxury properties, as well as a shortfall in supply, is forcing this trend. Increased capacity at Mumbai's Chatrapati Shivaji International Airport has exacerbated the problem and allowed hoteliers to force average room rates even higher. With the proposed, further expansion and modernisation of the airport by its new owners, and with the new airport planned in the eastern suburbs of Mumbai, the city looks set for an even greater increase in arrivals. Planned developments over the next two years by Marriott, Four Seasons and Accor's 300-room Sofitel Mumbai will help.

THE GROWTH CITY

The capital of West Bengal, Kolkata is the hub of trade into eastern India. As a traditionally socialist city, Kolkata had been unattractive to inward investment. The state government (the longest serving democratically elected communist government in the world) had long favoured trades' unions and workers' rights, and consequently the post-independence days had seen Kolkata lose out as international companies located elsewhere. However since 2000 with changed leadership, IT and manufacturing sectors are now revitalising the city. With its prime location for trade routes with China and the ASEAN countries, and direct flights to Brunei, Bangkok and Singapore, Kolkata looks set to grow and grow. Although revPAR remains the lowest of the gateway cities, Kolkata's rate of growth is among the country's highest. An average room rate rise of 35.7% in the year to March 2007 is on a par with Delhi. Average rates for this period stand at US$120, having hit a peak of US$160 in January 2007, while RevPAR grew 35.6% to US$83.

But as the city's status as a centre of industry grows in the coming years, will supply become increasingly outstripped by demand? In the hotel sector Marriott plan to open a new 250-room Courtyard property in the city by 2009, while Hilton, with its Indian development partner DLF Ltd, also has a new opening planned in the city. It remains to be seen however, if the supply of beds in the city can reach the necessary levels for the projected visitor boom.

THE RESORT

Despite the 12km-long Marina Beach that defines Chennai's eastern limits, the capital of Tamil Nadu state and the gateway to south India is no beach resort, but a major industrial centre. The traditional hub of India's automobile industry is also now becoming a major IT centre, housing manufacturing plants for companies such as Dell, Nokia, Samsung and Cisco. Naturally the meetings, incentives, conference and exhibitions (MICE) tourism is a major sector, with the 2,000-capacity Chennai Conference Centre providing an excellent facility. Many of the positive effects of Bangalore (India's Silicon Valley) have also rubbed off on Chennai, with many IT outfits reportedly considering Chennai more favourably due to the infrastructure that the city offers. With revPAR growth of 27.2% for the twelve months to March 2007, Chennai follows the pattern of India's gateways cities. Average room rates, rising 32.5% to US$135, accounted for this growth, while occupancy fell slightly to 75.2%. Direct air links with many ASEAN countries and the Middle East show strong potential for further growth through MICE tourism. Leela-Kempinski plan to open the 300-room Leela Palace Kempinski Chennai by 2008, while the 253-room Hilton Chennai is set to open in December 2007. Both hotels will include significant conference facilities, including a 1,600 square metre convention centre at the Leela-Kempinski.

THE AUTUMN EFFECT

The autumn time is always a good period for the Indian hotel industry. The searing temperatures of the summer months cool off to create a more visitor-friendly climate, and India's inbound tourist cycle begins. This starts in late September/ early October and runs through until February or March. Inbound tourism takes a significant leap around this time, and with the government's 'Incredible India' campaign compounding the already versed impacts of India's economic growth, and increased capacity at India's two main airports in Delhi and Mumbai, 2006 was an especially good autumn. A good conference season and the fact that cricket-crazy India was hosting the autumn ICC Champions Trophy led to the number of inbound tourists growing 13% to over 4.4m in 2006. The impact of this combination of factors saw hotels able to force room rates up dramatically.

Although previous year comparisons had been positive throughout 2006, momentum gathered in autumn and October saw room rates across India rise 36% to a national average of US$196. By November this had risen further to a staggering US$215, levelling at US$205 in December. The biggest individual impact of this autumnal boom was seen in Mumbai in November 2006, when the soaring average room rates and high occupancy levels saw revPAR swell to US$213-a staggering 83% rise from the previous year.

A False Dawn...?

'Make hay while the sun shines', appears to be the current motto of India's hoteliers. But can average room rates be forced higher in future years and if so, how high? Already Mumbai and Delhi have average room rates comparable to the traditionally most expensive cities in Asia. Delhi's average room rate for the April 2006 to March 2007 period (US$225) outstrips all its regional rivals, including Singapore (US$138), Shanghai (US$138), Hong Kong (US$190) and Tokyo (US$196). But how high can they go?

A hotel construction boom in years to come looks like resolving the supply problem in all sectors. India's budget sector in particular looks set to take off, with Accor and Hilton planning to launch their Ibis, Formule 1 and Hilton Garden Inn brands across the country.

Local operators are also expanding their portfolios, with Sarovar having launched its Hometel budget brand, and South-India based Choice Hotels looking to open 8-10 budget hotels a year in the next 3 years. And development is planned not only in the gateways cities, but new, rapidly growing metropolises such as Bangalore, Hyderabad, Pune, Chandigarh, Indore and Jaipur. Once this happens it is likely that the new competitive climate will force average room rates, even in the top end of the market, to plateau or fall.

A Bright Future

To maintain such growth, India's economy needs to continue its boom and the government continue to invest in the country's infrastructure. There seems no reason why, with India's wealth of resources and skilled labour, the economy cannot continue to grow at speed. With a booming IT sector, India is ideally placed to thrive in the 21st century. However justification of such high average room rates can be found only in world-class facilities and back-up services for the business traveller.

If the logistics of travel itself are troublesome, business people may be dissuaded from travelling to India. As India's cities attract increasing numbers of visitors, the surrounding services need to be improved.

However with the increasing supply of air travel it is becoming easy to travel around this vast, spectacular land. Whether you enter by the north, south, east or west-through Delhi, Chennai, Kolkata or Mumbai-India is now becoming more accessible. As urbanisation increases, from sprawling gateway metropolises, to the rapid-rising secondary cities, and small but swelling regional cities, the need for hotel rooms will keep pace. International chains have realised this great opportunity, and even although average room rates cannot continue to climb as steeply in future years as was seen in 2006-07, a large increase in supply will compensate for this. Growth is growth in any form.

PRESENT STATUS OF HOSPITALITY INDUSTRY

The hospitality industry is growing at a faster rate than ever envisaged and today it has no boundaries.

So high is the confidence in this industry that the only restriction is ambition. Over 250 million people around the world are estimated to be employed in this sector alone and the statistics indicate that one job is created in every two and a half seconds by the hospitality industry. Being a trade that encompasses industries like aviation, shipping, entertainment, catering, multiplexes, shopping malls, call centers and of course hotels and restaurants, the opportunities are pouring in with exciting career, assured job, handsome pay packets and above all international recognition and job satisfaction.

WHY HOTEL MANAGEMENT ?

For a professional this is a very lucrative segment capable of offering a long growth oriented career. The hotel sector itself requires a large amount of well trained manpower with excellent skill in housekeeping, food & beverage service and production, marketing, accounting, security, engineering, fire fighting, public relations and so on. A hospitality professional can find job opportunity in customer relations, sales and marketing and event management.

In this fast changing world, the hospitality industry has become the ideal place for those having an inborn talent to mingle with people, work with them and serve them. The young entrants have to come up with an open mind to explore the challenging world of hospitality business. They shall need to be multi skilled, talented and proactive not only to stay afloat but also to stay in demand in the challenging times that lie ahead.

ROYAL GROUP AND HOSPITALITY INDUSTRY

Hotel Division

The entry of Royal Group into the hospitality industry was by opening an ethnic village resort namely Royal Village in close harmony with the nature in the suburbs of Cochin. The century old traditional Farm House which stands as a testimony of ancient Kerala lifestyle attracting domestic and international tourists alike symbolizes the desire of the group to preserve and protect the culture and heritage of our country.

Munnar is best known for its personalized and intimate services offered. This luxury hotel with its exceptional five star facilities may be perhaps the only one of its kind in the state with state of the art Discotheque, star gaze gallery and many more making once stay highly enjoyable. All the above properties and their upcoming new proprieties in prime tourist locations in the state are together known as Royal Group of Hotels-for the rich and famous-which is well known in the fields of hotel, travel and tourism all over India and abroad.

Education

For Royal Group the field of education is not new. By the end of eighties before the policy of liberalization and globalization was heard, at a time when new products and technology with foreign tie ups were all poised to enter the Indian market and when there was acute shortage of trained manpower, Royal Group was quick to take initiative in establishing job oriented courses in the state.

Thus was born School of Engineering. By conducting Kerala Government Engineering courses in different streams at Trivandrum over a decade, the education division of Royal Group has marked their presence in the field of Technical Education.

Catering College, with its different divisions is functioning in a multi level operating system imparting courses in Hotel Management at various levels. The college has got approval from the All India

Council for Technical Education (AICTE) New Delhi and the Government of Kerala for conducting 3 year Diploma course in Hotel Management and Catering Technology at Munnar.

In association with the largest educational chain in the world-the Educational Institute of American Hotel & Lodging Association (AH&LA) USA the college offers specialized courses in Front Office Management, Housekeeping Management, Principles of Food Production, Food & Beverage Service and International Hotel Management in addition to Professional Cookery at their branches at Cochin, Calicut and Trivandrum also.

As a recognition of the facilities and the reputation, the renowned Punjab Technical University has approved Munnar Catering College as their outside study centre in conducting different Hotel Management courses at Diploma, Postgraduate Diploma, Degree and Postgraduate Degree level at their Cochin and Trivandrum branches. The educational division of the Royal

Group also conducts courses in Pharmaceutical Sciences with approval from the Government of Kerala, the Pharmacy Council of India and AICTE and Para Medical Courses in association with The Punjab Technical University under Distance Education Programme.

The Institute of Pharmaceutical Sciences established in the capital city of the state is now offering Diploma in Pharmacy for eligible candidate selected as per specified norms fixed for the purpose, whereas the Institute of Para Medical Sciences, Trivandrum offers courses for Diploma in Hospital Management, Diploma, P.G Diploma, B.Sc & M.Sc. degrees in Medical Laboratory Technology.

By conducting Kerala Government Engineering courses in different streams at Trivandrum over a decade, the education division of Royal Group has marked their presence in the field of Technical Education also.

On the Job Training

For developing competence in the operation of all departments of a hotel an unmatched opportunity is wide open for the students of Munnar Catering College to get trained at own hotel and resort which many other institutions cannot offer. Students of Munnar Catering College are offered on the job training in all the departments of own hotels under guidance and supervision of experienced and talented professionals exclusively appointed for the purpose.

In addition to this, to get a better understanding and first hand information of what is happening around in the hospitality industry the students are also sent for practical training during their course of study to other reputed hotels too, as part of their curriculum in Hotel Management.

HOTELS AND CATERING SECTOR-VISIONS OF THE FUTURE

This second article in the Sector Futures series on the hotels and catering sector looks at the trends and drivers affecting the sector, presents a framework to link them together and assesses their impact. The article also reviews some scenario work relating to the sector before concluding with an examination of the implications on the sector of the drivers and scenarios. Examples of the implications include better working conditions, consolidation and more consumer protection.

Following the overview of the sector and initial look at trends and drivers in the first article of this series, this article now examines these trends and drivers in more detail and reviews existing foresight research on the hotels and catering sector.

Trends and Drivers of Change

The discussion above identified and introduced several trends and drivers that are shaping the sector. In a STEEP (social, technological, economic, environmental and political) breakdown, the key social drivers were identified as ageing populations and changing lifestyles and tastes.

Information technologies, along with new production and kitchen technologies, were identified as the key technological drivers. Economic drivers included globalisation and low-cost travel, which in part raise issues about skill levels, migration and competition. Regarding environmental drivers, the main issues were identified as the direct impact of climate change on the sector as part of the tourist industry and the political desire to improve energy and resource efficiency across the economy.

The key political drivers are likely to be legislation to improve consumer and worker rights, along with the quality and labelling of food. Beyond that, the sector, as part of the tourist industry, remains sensitive to the impact of international relations on consumer behaviour. The links and interactions between these forces are shown in the schematic diagram below.

STEEP Analysis

The following table summarises the STEEP factors affecting, or expected to affect, the industry along with their possible impacts.

Table 1: STEEP analysis and possible future of hotels and catering industry

Trends and drivers	Possible future of hotels and catering industry
Social	
Ageing population	Ageing consumers create a new type of demand. Older workers push harder for better conditions and better-qualified young workers choose other careers. These pressures lead to more social dialogue and an improvement in working conditions.
Change in tastes and demands	More informed and flexible consumers demand more value and more personal service. Increase in niche markets, e.g. organic/ethical restaurants, health hotels, etc.; expansion of budget hotels.
Technological	
Information technologies	Leads to better resource management and more flexible service delivery. Consequently, creates demand for new IT skills and less demand for traditional skills. This may shift gender balance in the work-force.
New kitchen technology	Outsourcing and simplification of kitchen operations expected to turn kitchens into assembly lines, deskill staff and bring about lower wages. This may lead to higher margins for companies.
Internet	Expands the range of information providers and establishments on offer to consumers and leads to changes in shopping behaviour. For firms, it expands the customer base and creates new competition, raises the importance of presentation and quality of service and demands new marketing strategies.
Economic	
Low-cost air travel	More tourists and more trips taken, but expenditure patterns are unclear; expansion of services in new destinations. Long-term growth may be curbed by environmental concerns.

Globalisation	New geographic and consumer markets pose threats and opportunities to the sector. Likely to favour large enterprises and promote consolidation. Likely to stimulate debate on skill levels and migration.
Environmental	
Climate change	Negative impact on the industry in affected tourist areas. Policy on use of energy resources might bring about cultural and hardware changes.
Environmental awareness`	Increased focus on dealing with pollution and waste management results in more environmentally friendly resource use, which may raise costs.
Political	
Legislation	Improvements in working conditions, consumer protection and product information increase costs for businesses. Small businesses are the most affected, because the improvements encourage consolidation. Effects filter down the supply chain and could alter the products on offer.
EU enlargement	Within the EU, increased tourist demand, migration and competition.
Social dialogue	Better industrial relations and working conditions, with higher skill levels. Potential to reduce labour turnover.

ASSESSMENT OF THE TRENDS AND DRIVERS

Sociological Drivers

Sociological changes, such as changes in lifestyles, are driven by and affect consumers, and directly affect businesses. The temporal impact varies, but some changes, such as the increased use of the Internet for shopping, have had a profound impact on the industry. Such drivers require businesses to adapt in order to survive, for example, by reviewing their relationship with the customer and their marketing strategy. An ageing population will affect the composition of the workforce (as outlined in the first article) and may help improve working conditions; it is also likely to lead to a change in the composition of consumer demand. In addition, growing interest from consumers in the production and health aspects of food is increasing pressure on caterers to supply better-quality food, produced in socially responsible ways, and with information on its origins. Reluctance by the industry to act on these issues is leading to increased governmental involvement. Changes to the supply chain in response to these trends are likely to be long-lasting.

Technological Drivers

Technology has been a primary driving force of change among consumers and in the sector, thereby helping to globalise it. While it creates opportunities, technology is also a major threat to small enterprises in the sector. Because of their small size, it is much harder for them to generate economies of scale and recover the cost of investment in new technologies. However, if they do not invest in new technologies, they are likely to lose out to those who have. The increasing use of technology has led to a need to retrain existing staff. Some industry bodies have argued that technology poses a threat to employment by reducing staff hours (as seen in the fall in full-time employment) and thus will exert downward pressure on wages. The initial boom in the use of information technologies appears to be slowing, and while its use will continue to increase, it is likely to be at a more gradual pace.

Economic Drivers

Globalisation has affected all parties. It has pushed governments to cooperate and integrate more, and in doing so has made the world more accessible to all parties. Economically, it has reduced restrictions on the movement of capital, labour and resources. For the consumer, it has opened up new parts of the world, thus the hotels and restaurants most dependent on tourism face stiffer competition for their services, but they may also benefit from tourist visits from newly accessible regions. For companies, it opens up a larger market and offers the possibility of greater economies of scale that benefit larger chain groups and encourage consolidation. Recent trends show that many companies in the sector have chosen to expand by means of mergers or acquisitions as they become more aware of the need to pool resources in order to compete effectively in an expanding market.

The rise in low-cost air travel has above all benefited consumers, offering them more choice, flexibility and pricing options. While establishments are receiving increased numbers of visitors, it is not clear that the increase in visitor spending has been commensurate with the increase in numbers. Many tourists have become far more cost conscious, leading to a growing demand for budget, no-frills hotels. The EU market for low-cost travel still has some way to go before it reaches maturity, so the effects have probably not yet reached a plateau. However, with governments looking increasingly set to levy environmental taxes on air travel and with oil prices rising and staying high, ticket prices can be expected to rise also. The impact of this on consumer demand is uncertain, as it is not yet clear how sensitive consumers are to the pricing of budget air travel.

Environmental Drivers

In general, environmental drivers are likely to have a less immediate impact on the sector than the other drivers discussed. The most direct impact is likely to be felt by establishments that form part of the tourist industry in areas affected by climate change (coastal and ski resorts) and areas of environmental interest. However, the timeframe for such effects is likely to be further in the future than for other drivers. Although freak changes or storms may wreak havoc, the resultant damage they cause is often temporary, but the permanent damage, as from rising sea levels, is taking place as a slow, gradual process.

Nevertheless, the net impact on businesses in affected areas can be expected to be negative as the features that made them attractive in the first place are eroded. While some may be able to adapt to the new environment, their success is likely to depend on how consumers react. In other respects the impact of environmental changes is likely to be felt through policies to reduce emissions, to improve the use of all resources, especially energy resources, and to reduce pollution by improving waste management.

Although much of the focus has been on power generation plants, all companies are under pressure to be more energy efficient and such pressures are likely to increase in the medium term. Furthermore, the timeframe for these drivers may be longer than for others, as environmental concerns are often low on the political agenda, and it is not easy to reach political consensus on environment-energy policies when these are believed to curb growth. Any costs created by environmental policy can be expected to affect enterprises in the first place, and it will be up to them how to deal with this. The obvious choice is to pass it on to customers, but regardless of whether this is done or not, any additional costs are likely to favour larger enterprises that enjoy greater economies of scale and have more flexibility in absorbing costs.

Political Drivers

New legislation, such as smoking bans, changes to licensing laws and new regulations governing food safety, is partly a response to changes in people's tastes and lifestyles. However, new laws can bring great costs to businesses. The smoking ban, for example, has improved conditions for workers and customers, but at the same time there is evidence that it has reduced turnover and that this has translated into job losses. Over the medium term, firms are likely to face increased demands from consumers for more informative marking and higher-quality standards for food.

How governments will respond to such pressure from consumers is unclear. In the UK, for example, the quality of catered school meals became a hot topic in 2005 after the poor quality of such meals was highlighted by a high-profile chef on TV. One company supplying such meals (Compass) has suffered as a result, and the UK government is taking action to improve the quality of school meals. On the other hand, among the proposed EU laws recently scrapped by the EC president, José Barroso, there was one on food labelling. Nevertheless, governments may still be willing to take initiatives independently of EU legislation in order to satisfy their electorates.

The enlargement of the EU has positively impacted on the hotels and catering sector because the new Member States provide a new source of demand. However, migration from the new to the old Member States in pursuit of higher wages and a better standard of living is turning out to be lower than had been expected before accession. Moreover, because economic growth in the new Member States is expected to accelerate now that they are in the EU, rising wage levels and improved standards of living will probably make migration to EU15 countries less attractive.

New policies are helping to expand the scope of social dialogue within the hotels and catering sector. Social dialogue is becoming a major part of good governance because it allows all stakeholders to be part of policymaking within the firm and industry. On the other hand, union membership in this sector is comparatively low, making it difficult for workers to agree on objectives and to present a united front.

Scenarios for the Hotels and Catering Sector

In contrast to STEEP analysis, scenario work allows us to look beyond the familiar environment. It helps the industry to prepare for the consequences of unexpected events by asking the following questions:

- What if (X) happens?
- What would be the effects on the industry if (X) were to happen?
- What are the best ways of counteracting adverse effects?

The search for scenario work on hotels and restaurants failed to discover work related solely to hotels and restaurants. It was only as part of the tourist industry that hotels and catering received attention, and so the scenario analysis here is based primarily on foresight work related to tourism. Although hotels and restaurants are part of and rely on the tourist industry, their market is not confined just to tourists. Furthermore, the published scenario work was reactive, in that it was based on dramatic events in their immediate aftermath. It did not analyse the possible effects of hypothetical events or look at observable and more prosaic trends.

In recent years, there have been several unexpected events that have affected the hotels and catering industry, such as the 9/11 terrorist attacks, the outbreak of SARS, the foot and mouth epidemic in the UK and the bombings in Madrid and London. Such shocks have a low probability of occurrence, but their impact is high. Recently, however, such shocks have become more frequent and hence people are more inclined to believe that they will happen again. It is extremely difficult to predict these shocks, but good policies at all levels (European, national or firm) or any foresight work must not ignore their possible reoccurrence. Petersen (1997) refers to these shocks as 'wild cards'. He suggests that some shocks are imaginable, and if agents are well prepared, they could be turned into manageable events:

There is a general assumption that there is nothing to do about these huge surprises. However, not all wild cards are unimaginable and by identifying wild card events that may possibly occur in the future on a proactive rather than reactive matter, these can sometimes be converted into anticipated manageable events. The chance alone of averting a future catastrophe or at least preparing strategies to handle it may be reason enough to examine wild card possibilities. If not dealt with wild cards can trigger a chain of events much worse than the initial happening. A major natural disaster can for instance cause a global epidemic, which may lead to nations closing their borders in turn leading to a collapse of the airline industry and so forth. (1997, pp. 43-47)

Post-9/11 Scenarios

One topic that scenario work could not ignore was the impact of 9/11 on the travel and tourism industry. Two major scenarios were published shortly after the attack on New York. The World Travel and Tourism Council (WTTC) estimated at that time that there were 207 million people employed worldwide in the travel and tourism economy. Its 'best guess' was that the attacks would lead to 8.8 million job losses worldwide, of which 1.2 million would be in the EU.

Within six weeks of 11 September 2001, the International Labour Organisation (ILO) published the report The social impact on the hotel and tourism sector of events subsequent to 11 September 2001 (136kb), which outlined two possible scenarios:

THE BEST-CASE SCENARIO

Assumptions:

- 9/11 is a one-off;
- there are no other attacks in the United States (US);
- there are no other attacks in other parts of the world.

Travel to Europe, which before the attack was showing recovery from recession, would not be badly affected. Europeans would continue to travel within the continent, while travel to the Middle East was unlikely to revive in the short term. The European tourism industry would benefit as a substitute destination choice. However, US tourists, who account for a significant part of the demand in the industry, would not return to Europe for some time. The reduction in US tourists, who are recognised as big spenders, would affect upmarket restaurants and hotels the most.

The Worst-case Scenario

Assumptions:

- there are other major terrorist attacks in the US;
- there are outbreaks of terrorism in other countries;
- the ongoing war in Afghanistan spreads to other regions.

In this scenario, the tourist demand from Asia and North America would plummet. Within Europe, the travel pattern would also change depending on the scale and location of any attacks. Domestic travel would probably benefit, with demand shifting from the location of an attack to an alternative location. In the extreme position, personal or business holidays would come to a halt.

In the ILO's best-case scenario, the WTTC predictions were pessimistic. In the ILO's worst-case scenario, the consequences are far worse than the WTTC's predictions.

Iraq War Scenarios

When the US and the UK decided to invade Iraq in 2003, WTTC looked at the possible outcomes of the Iraq war and their consequences for the US tourist industry in its 2003 research on the United States-Travel and tourism, a world of opportunity (526kb, pp.18-21). The WTTC's scenario was informed by the experience of the 1991 Gulf war, the effects of which, according to the WTTC, were to limit economic growth through three main channels: higher oil prices, shattered consumer and business confidence and lower equity prices.

The base scenario: diplomatic solution or victory after a short, contained war

In the base case, the war is assumed to be short, contained and successful, and to remove global uncertainty. The effects on oil prices, confidence and equity prices are assumed to be very similar to what they would have been had there been a diplomatic solution to the crisis. In the short term, economic growth is assumed to be higher due to increased government spending. The difference in the effects on travel and tourism between no war and a speedy, contained war is therefore predicted to be small. However, the threat of war was assumed to undermine confidence and to reduce international travel, and this would affect the travel and tourism industry more than the rest of the economy.

Assumptions:

- quick, decisive victory or diplomatic solution;
- no use of weapons of mass destruction (WMD) against US troops, Israel or region;
- no reduction in OPEC oil production and exports;
- no challenges to Arab governments in region;
- new Iraqi government installed and in control;
- no damage to oil-producing capacity in Iraq or elsewhere.

The war scenario: victory with regional disruption. Under this scenario, a longer-lasting war results in persistently higher oil prices, with a deeper and longer fall in confidence and equity markets. The effects on the travel and tourism industry are expected to be more severe.

Assumptions:

- Iraq attacks oil facilities in region, with limited damage but political and economic knock-on effects;
- Iraq attacks Israel and US troops but not with WMD effective enough to trigger a major response or to have highly lethal effects;
- unexpected protracted Iraqi military resistance;
- limited Israeli intervention in war; rising political unrest in region;
- low-level civil tensions and clashes in Iraq after military conflict is over;
- some terrorist attacks on US interests.

These pressures were predicted to lead to a slowing of between 1% and 2% in GDP growth in the US and UK. The effects on the travel and tourism industry are more severe under the war scenario. In the US, under this scenario, in 2003 the travel and tourism industry would experience:

- 0.9% fall in industry demand;
- 3.7% fall in industry GDP;
- 8.9% fall in exports;
- loss of 449,100 jobs.

Climate Change Scenarios

Although the global climate has been changing for some time, there is uncertainty about its future path and patterns as well as the consequences. Research commissioned by the World Tourism Organisation (WTO) suggests two possible scenarios on global climate change, relating specifically to the tourist industry in Hungary, The responses of Lake Balaton to global cliamte change (299kb, Rátz, 2003).

Climate Zone Shift Scenario

Assumptions:

- The temperate climate zone covering Hungary shifts northward and is replaced by a warmer climate.

This would be expected to lead to a longer summer season with much higher temperatures. This could have benefits for the tourist industry, assuming the temperatures are not too high and droughts are infrequent. In contrast, winter sports tourism is likely to disappear under such a scenario.

Ice Caps Melt Scenario

Assumptions:

- Ice caps melt due to global warming.

Under this scenario, the Gulf Stream cools down and changes the climate in Europe. The Hungarian climate becomes colder and wetter. This would have a mainly negative impact on the tourism industry, as the summer season becomes shorter and wetter. However, it could lead to the further development of winter sports tourism.

Scenario Summary

Some scenario work relevant to the hotels and catering industry tends to focus on dramatic events. In some cases, the work is done after the shocks have occurred, with a best-case scenario assuming that these shocks are unique and the worst-case scenario assuming that they are not. In hindsight, it is easy to say that it is a pity such analysis was not conducted before the events occurred and that there were no plans to deal with the consequences of such events.

Regarding the climate change scenario, it should be emphasised that it related to Hungary only. Furthermore, the study's primary focus was not the effect of climate change on the hotels and catering sector; instead, it formed part of a wider discussion on the overall impact of climate change on the region. Since the concern here is the European hotels and catering sector, the major drawback of the Iraq war scenario is its focus on the US tourist industry.

Moreover, to date there appears to have been little work done on exploring the future of the industry through scenario planning in the light of the various current influences identified in the first two articles of this series. It may be more useful to project these current trends and drivers and identify possible outcomes and responses. Possible scenarios to consider are:

- What if the current weakness of the EU economy persists for much longer than expected?
- What if there is a collapse in the world financial market?
- What if there are more outbreaks of deadly viruses?
- What are the implications of developing countries becoming developed over the next 10 years?
- What would happen if the Internet ceased to exist, e.g. because of political censorship?
- What if the current skills gaps remain in 10 or 15 years' time?
- What will the role of information technologies be in the industry in the future, and how will this affect labour demand?
- What are the implications if the European Union breaks up?
- What are the implications of a Europe-wide zero immigration policy?
- What are the implications for labour supply if there are no government pensions?

Implications

As younger workers increasingly become more qualified, they are less likely to consider the hotels and catering industry, with its poorer working conditions, as a career option. This and the ageing of the population are likely to persuade businesses to employ older workers. Because of their circumstances, older workers are often less mobile and have other commitments. Consequently, they are likely to be more demanding about working conditions, to be more favourable to union membership and to become more involved in social dialogue.

Changing lifestyles and more demanding consumers are likely to promote the development of more specialised enterprises and broaden competition among hotels and restaurants. The more specialised nature of services should allow firms to charge a premium. These niche markets are likely to attract multinationals as other parts of the hotels and catering industry become commoditised and less profitable, Commoditisation exerts downward pressure on premiums and profits. In order to survive and make a profit, firms offering commoditised services can be expected to cut costs and homogenise the service/experience on offer.

On the supply side, the increasing use of technology will continue to help establishments better manage their resources and reduce spare capacity. A better knowledge of future demands has implications for staff, in that establishments are likely to seek more flexible working patterns to match demands. This in turn has implications for lifestyle and for where the savings go. On the demand side, the Internet, wireless computing and 3G mobile telephony all make it easier for consumers to obtain information, compare prices and value for money and shop around. This trend and the increasing use of the Internet as a marketing device by businesses will lead to more intense competition and make it harder to close a sale. Firms are increasingly likely to respond by seeking staff with skills in information and communication technologies (ICT), including marketing, sales and web design.

Any increase in outsourcing in the catering industry further separates the consumer from food producers, making it harder to check the origin of food. This implies a possible widening of the information gap and is likely to increase pressure on catering companies to provide information about the food they serve. Businesses can be expected to resist this because of the cost implications, so governments may intervene. The use of technology in the kitchen can be expected to raise productivity and lower labour demand. This again has implications for where the savings go. Increased productivity should see wages rise, but lower reliance on chefs' food preparation skills would have the opposite effect.

In the context of globalisation, EU enlargement offers a larger labour pool and facilitates migration. It is unclear to what extent this will help to fill the skills gap, as the tourist industry in most new Member States is small in comparison to that in France or the UK, for example. However, as long as relative wage differentials between regions are large enough, workers in poorer regions can be expected to move to richer regions for work. This can be expected to lower employment costs in the hotels and catering industry in richer regions. Furthermore, this is likely to attract the most skilled from the poorer regions, thus hindering the development of the industry there. At the same time, in enlarging the EU hotel and catering market and making it more accessible, globalisation has created an opportunity for companies to exploit substantial economies of scale. To what extent this could approach the scale seen in the US, for example, is unclear given the much wider cultural and language differences that exist in the EU. Nevertheless, it is still likely to lead to the increased presence of larger multinational hotel and catering chains, which is likely to fuel the demand for migrant labour in order to reduce employment costs. Customers may suffer if this leads to a homogenisation of service on offer, but brand names and reputations should ensure a higher-quality product. In order to maintain this, companies can be expected to recruit the best-skilled staff and improve working conditions in order to retain them.

The skills gap in the industry adversely affects the quality of service in the industry and damages the industry's reputation among travellers. This lessens establishments' pricing power and makes it harder to attract customers. This implies handsome rewards for companies that fill the gap (with good practice putting firms on a virtuous cycle) and premium wages for those with the necessary skills. The existence of the gap suggests that firms are unwilling to undertake training themselves and that working conditions need to be improved in order to attract and retain skilled staff. Establishments therefore have to take a more proactive and united approach.

Although low-cost airlines have increased the frequency of trips made by travellers, they often stay for a shorter duration and tend to be more cost-conscious. Furthermore, as profit-maximising companies independent of political or national influence, low-cost carriers will not hesitate to scrap unprofitable services. This has implications for policy as well as the hotels and catering industry's marketing strategy at a local level. In some regions, the rapid growth in the tourism and leisure industry is likely to work against raising levels of education or skills, while its effect on wages will depend on the industrial structure of the locality.

Legislation to improve the working environment, e.g. smoking bans in bars and restaurants and working time regulations, has negative implications for firms' margins and labour demand. In response, firms are likely to push for productivity gains and seek more cost-effective labour and a greater application of technology.

Political concern over consumer health and the content of food is increasing pressure on catering firms to reduce sugar and salt levels, for example, in prepared food. If catering firms respond to such concerns, this could create new demands for new tastes in food. If health problems such as diabetes and obesity become greater public health issues, then the prospect of health-related taxes on food must surely draw closer. Growing concern among consumers about the origin of their food and the production methods involved is largely a social trend, but it, too, is generating political pressure for more information and increased food labelling. This raises the prospect of legislation forcing the industry to inform consumers. The disclosure of more information and the demand for food produced in more socially responsible ways is likely to promote good practice in the food supply chain, and may lead to a shift away from low-end food establishments.

In the wake of the 9/11 attacks, the EU hotels and catering sector saw turnover growth slow dramatically. US visitor numbers to the EU are only now returning to the pre-9/11 levels. International relations remain fractured because of the US-led 'war on terror' and the Iraq war. The continuation of political and military hostilities and the continued involvement of EU nations mean that some EU Member States remain targets for terrorism, as seen in the Madrid and London bombings. US tourist confidence is therefore likely to remain fragile. High-profile marketing campaigns may be needed in the US to bolster confidence. That US visitor levels are recovering suggests terrorism has not inflicted long-lasting damage on the industry. Such damage could be caused, however, if one location were to suffer multiple attacks within a space of two or three years. While the industry is likely to be able to recover from this on an EU level, the impact on the affected region is likely to last longer. Heavy discounting in response, as employed in London in recent years, whether successful or not, would probably lead to lower levels of employment and investment, and a deterioration in working conditions. Such a downward spiral would take years to reverse.

Conclusion

This concludes the review of the key trends and drivers affecting the sector, and of scenario work relating to the sector. The reader should have a better idea of what issues are driving the sector and of the paucity of scenario work relating to the sector. Having looked at the trends and scenarios and their implications, the third and last article in this series, Hotels and catering-policies, issues and the future, carries the discussion forward to look at major policy issues and challenges facing the sector. Consideration is given to their timeframe and the agents and regions affected.

8

Restaurant and Hotel Management

TAJ HOTELS

Taj Hotels Resorts and Palaces is the largest Indian luxury hotel chain. A wholly owned subsidiary of the Tata Group, Taj Hotels Resort and Palaces comprises 57 hotels in 39 locations across India with an additional 18 international hotels in the Maldives, Mauritius, Malaysia, Seychelles, United Kingdom, United States of America, Bhutan, Sri Lanka, Africa, the Middle East and Australia. Their first and most well known property is the Taj Mahal Palace & Tower in Colaba, Mumbai. The Taj Mahal Palace & Tower, Mumbai was opened on December 16, 1903, by the founder of the Tata Group, Jamshetji Nusserwanji Tata. Taj President-a business hotel and Taj Land's End-an ultimate luxury boarding are also located in Mumbai. It operates TajAir, a luxury private jet operation with state-of-the-art Falcon 2000 aircraft designed by Dassault Aviation, France; and Taj Yachts, two 3-bedroom luxury yachts which can be used by guests in Mumbai and Kochi.

FALAKNUMA PALACE

Falaknuma Palace is situated on a hill 650 meters in height, in the Old City of Hyderabad, India. It was built by Nawab Vikar-ul-Umra. It was purchased by the then Nizam VI during 1897 for use as a royal guest house. The palace provides a good view of Hyderabad. The palace is spread out in a scorpion shape with two pincers spread out as wings on the north. The middle part occupies the main building. The Harem quarters and the kitchen stretch towards the south.

The palace was designed by an Italian architect. The palace boasts of lavishly decorated interiors made of the Italian marble, and follows a western architectural style. It took almost nine years to complete. This famous palace houses a large collection of rare treasures, paintings, statues, furniture, manuscripts and books collected by the Nizam. The jade collection displayed here is considered to be unique in the world. Some old models of artillery are also exhibited in the front.

The Palace is being converted into a heritage hotel by the Taj Hotels group.

HOTEL ORGANIZATION IN FUTURE

No hotel company operating today can be unaware of the swift pace of global change and its impact on every facet of the hospitality industry. With just five years left in this century, we can expect change to be the only constant. New business practices are evolving virtually as fast as our technologies, while resistance to change has become one of the primary causes of business failure. The specter of constant change raises fundamental questions as to the creation of shareholder wealth in a capital-constrained, highly competitive environment. How will hotel organizations build shareholder wealth, and what key drivers will result in success? What future products and services will be essential in a technology-driven, global environment marked by rising customer expectations? Moreover, what alternative approaches and skills must organizations develop to ensure market success?

The future success of hotel organizations will be driven in large part by the ability to foresee--and capitalize--on change. Beyond this truism, however, there is an urgent need to identify what will be required in the competitive environment of the future with its intense focus on serving customer needs. The hospitality industry–as is the case with business generally--is subject to deep currents of change set in motion as economic and social systems shaped in the industrial era evolve to a knowledge-based era driven by technology advances.

In this period of global transition, it behooves hotel organizations to examine the key factors that will not only define success, but the ability to survive in coming years. Many of these issues were spotlighted in a global study undertaken by the Economist Intelligence Unit and co-sponsored by Arthur Andersen. The Successful Corporation of the Year 2000 surveyed more than 600 senior executives around the world. Its mission was to identify the characteristics needed to lead successful businesses in the next century. These executives offer a number of compelling messages regarding the key success factors of the future.

Customers will have the strongest influence on the corporation in the year 2000. Indeed, these executives believe that the customer will be "king" in the new century. Exceptional leadership was by far the attribute most frequently cited by CEOs and senior executives; the consensus appears to be that successful companies in the year 2000 will be led by corporate visionaries. A strategic planning focus is not only essential, but must embody a concept of planning for the future that anticipates change, rather than being based exclusively on historical models. In structuring organizations for the future, companies must build management capabilities to deal with one of the most critical challenges–diversity in the marketplace. Employing information technology to drive business success in this information-driven era is not only the path of least resistance, but vital to virtually every aspect of operations.

The study's top-line results create an excellent backdrop to address key issues confronting the hotel industry, and what factors will lead to membership–rather than rejection–in the elite club of the world's corporate success stories in the year 2000.

FROM AN ASSET TO CUSTOMER FOCUS

Recognizing that the hotel industry has a somewhat split personality reflecting the inherent conflicts between its real estate and operational aspects, it is important to understand the industry's real estate origins and how they are shaping the challenges ahead. The origins of the industry's real estate persona are embodied in the classic theory of location-"if we build it, they will come." As a result of this "building" complex, the industry has tended to have a real estate and asset orientation, rather than a customer focus. From the hotel company perspective–especially that of the brand-oriented "chain"–the varied interests of a diffused property ownership group can be quite different than the singular interest of the chain that operates and markets the properties.

Even when the ownership of geographically dispersed hotel properties is controlled by a single hotel organization, the financial structuring tends to be property-specific. Corporate financial strategies are frequently subjugated to the needs of the last property deal brought into the company's fold. Each property in a so-called "chain," is frequently the subject of a unique and distinctive ownership and financial structure. This phenomenon–quite common in the real estate sector, but unusual for business enterprises generally–makes for elusive economies of scale in the structuring and financing of property-driven expansion.

Collectively, these factors have produced low comparative returns in real estate, although criticism levelled at commercial real estate returns is somewhat less germane to the hotel industry, where management and franchise fees can produce high returns for those companies where property ownership is held by third parties. Nevertheless, average returns in the real estate industry in the United States, for example, are just over 10 percent, compared to small company stock returns at almost 20 percent and large company stocks at an average of about 15 percent.

While hotel chains have adopted traditional corporate frameworks, there are a number of predominantly real estate-driven, family-owned businesses in the hotel sector that continue to operate as relatively unstructured organizations. In meeting the future, these businesses will need plans, people and processes in order to establish viable corporate forms that can compete in tomorrow's marketplace and capitalize upon its opportunities.

In today's changed environment, the hotel organization must deal with a number of new realities. Investors in our industry are no longer satisfied with long-term capital appreciation and psychic income that heretofore were often the justification for otherwise seemingly uneconomic investments in hotel property or, indeed, hotel chains. The first reality is that there is a very specific and identifiable relationship between bottom line performance and value. Improvements in business operations raises values. It is not surprising, therefore, that the new owners attracted to this industry in recent years have new sets of demands. This transformation from an old-guard group of investors and owners to income and return-driven newcomers has meant that the once "quiet enjoyment" of operators in their management of hotels for third parties is being disturbed, interrupted and overturned.

These challenges all take place in an environment where capital has become extremely selective in markets that have little stability. A global shortage of capital will not remain a short-term problem, and future hotel organizations must have a stronger alignment to capital providers–a critical "customer" group. Hotel companies will need to compete by offering better returns and performance than in the past. Hotel chains have found their development timetables quashed in recent years, making it difficult to achieve goals of critical mass often required to improve performance. These factors are driving consolidation in the brand "sweepstakes." Capital markets, therefore, continue to favour well-established companies, a reality that must drive entrepreneurial organizations to meet the future now by planning for an evolving corporate context in which to operate.

KEY SUCCESS FACTORS-THE FUTURE

Within this broad context, hotel developers, owners and management companies will all need to develop new strategies, skills and processes that look forward to the competitive demands of the future. These ultimately must address issues related to vision and planning, as well as organizational skill sets and processes to attract and retain customers. To stake a claim in the future, current business practices should be examined in light of what can be expected to be the key success factors in the year 2000.

Embrace a global change orientation. As the information age produces greater worldwide integration of business activities, a global knowledge base will become invaluable. Success in local and regional hotel markets will be shaped decisively by a global business environment that defines capital movement, customer expectations and applications of new technologies.

Focus on the Customer

If the customer is "king" in the 21st century, hotel organizations will be best served by focusing less on their hotel assets as measures of success, and more on their customers.

This involves a fundamental shift in viewing the real estate asset as the wealth creator--to the customer as the key to building shareholder wealth. A customer focus must imbue business decisions at all levels of developing and operating a hotel organization. Pursuing such a course will inevitably impact shareholder wealth. To accomplish this, however, customers need to participate in the product development process.

Fully realizing a customer focus in the industry poses a significant challenge. The hotel industry must confront problems due to conflicts between operational needs and real estate goals. Quite simply, an operator must remain customer-focused, but the short-term strategies to meet these needs may be inconsistent with the long-term objectives of property owners. Balancing those goals will be essential. A customer focus implies a significant shift in what drives hotel development--placing primary emphasis on the customer with the locations to follow. Nevertheless, a hotel organization with its large investment in fixed assets--the real estate--can never be as nimble as a consumer products company in adjusting products and services to match rapid shifts in the marketplace.

The Japanese taught us that the concept of "zero defects" in products and services can yield tremendous benefits. But today an even more rigorous standard dominates--quality that surprises. In practical terms, the hotel industry finds it extremely difficult to meet the standard of zero defects in service. Hotel services are based primarily on people, not computers or other equipment. Quality that surprises takes the concept of zero defects a step further. Yesterday's surprising product or service is today's status quo. Twenty years ago, a business executive did not expect a consistent and predictable level of service wherever he or she travelled in the world. Today that is a standard--not the exception--as is the expectation for sophisticated technology in hotel rooms to support business needs. With customer discrimination so acute, it is not surprising that brand loyalty is a diminishing "commodity" in the hotel industry.

Find the Ingredients for Visionary Leadership

Today's hotel organizations need to recognize the need for visionary leadership. The ability to forecast the future--to anticipate change rather than react to it--will be one of the single greatest determinants of market dominance in the years ahead. The old "command and control" model of leadership is giving way to a focus on leadership in ideas, information, inspiration, vision and teamwork. Warren Bennis, an authority on leadership in the U.S., puts it this way--"For the most part, failing organizations tend to be over-managed and under-led. The leader sets the tone for the moral character, the vision, the corporate culture and the fiber of the institution."

While visionary leadership is essential, it must be linked to business operations and foster a risk bias, rather than a procedural bias. This will allow the organization to stretch and, in turn, change. And it must be shared by empowered professionals and staff throughout the organization, including those who meet the customer. Overcoming the resistance to change can be a daunting task, particularly in large hotel organizations in which diversions from the status quo may threaten established management lines.

It suggests that a culture based on conformance may need to be replaced by an emphasis on flexibility, learning and cooperation. Management competencies will need to be aligned in order to achieve the desired result. For many organizations, this may mean a shift from traditional hierarchies typical of companies in an industrial era to a flatter organization with a more transparent interface between leadership, organizational functions and employees.

Create a defensible position through corporate strategy. For many of the industry's leaders, vision is driven by the strategic planning process, a function which has become critical for success.

Strategic planning, however, has at times been a step-child in the hotel industry, and it is often the first to be cut when organizations are downsized. It is clearly in transition. There also has been a tendency to decentralize and simplify this function--both actions of potential benefit. Strategic planning must be led by the top people in the organization--the CEO and COO. On the other hand, it should be close enough to the customer to ensure that planners can "listen" to and be influenced by customer needs.

Empower Management

Beyond the ability to envision the future, core management capabilities will make the difference--they are essential. A clear vision without the management skills to support it cannot be a recipe for success. First and foremost, hotel management must have strategic development skills and the ability to integrate complex factors affecting success. Market volatility has become the norm, in part caused by the rapidly changing tastes of customers. Customers are increasingly approaching the hotel industry with widely different social, economic and political backgrounds, to say nothing of employees. Being able to deal with these diversities in a positive and constructive fashion that capitalizes on the differences, rather than working to find ways to mitigate them, is the clear path for successful management in the future.

The organization will also need to be imbued with a sense of entrepreneurship that reacts proactively to the market's diversity. Traditional organizations that follow well-documented rules must give way to leaders who can balance a sense of discipline with that of flexibility. Talent and resources must be marshalled and leveraged. In an industry with high fixed costs and labour intensity, the concept of leverage in the hotel business is an all-important one. Improving labour productivity through technology must be a goal for today's forward-looking hotel organization. Management must also be able to narrow the gap between the employer and the employee, forcing a flatter organization in the process. This will put management closer to the customer and speed the two-way communication process up and down the organization.

Be in the Information Fast Lane

The traditional role of information technology (IT) as a back office support for accounting and bookkeeping has clearly moved front and centre stage. IT today influences all aspects of business from corporate strategies to organizational structure--and from the very business processes it is designed to support to performance measurement. In a world where the customer is "king," IT must also deliver in two critical areas: sales and marketing and customer service.

Technology was once viewed as a way to reduce costs by replacing people. That attitude has been firmly supplanted by one that seeks IT support for the creative work that all organizations must pursue. IT must allow organizations to react more speedily to market needs and, of course, produce the fulfilment of customer demands both quickly and accurately. To do this IT must operate on a decentralized basis. IT delivers, but it has to be the right information to the right people, and it needs to be done on a timely basis.

IMPROVING THE MANAGEMENT PROJECT

Improving Management of NGO and Privately Owned Nature Reserves and High Biodiversity Islands in Seychelles Project funded by the Global Environment Facility through the World Bank

The Seychelles is known world wide as a storehouse of rare biodiversity. Historically, most of the islands and ecosystems have been severely impacted by human activities. Nevertheless, a few examples of whole island ecosystems have been protected and restored. These islands are Cousin, Cousine, Aride, Fregate and Aldabra, all managed, surprisingly, by civil society organisations. Nevertheless, there are significant barriers to sustainability of conservation efforts by these organisations.

The focus of the project is two islands, Cousin and Cousine, which are host to numerous rare and endemic species, and immense biodiversity. These include shared resources such as 10 species of breeding seabirds, 5 species of endemic land birds, rare floral species, 8 species of reptiles and hundreds species of invertebrates, the most important population of hawksbill turtles in the Western Indian Ocean and the highest biomass of reef fish in the granitic islands of Seychelles. The project is to ensure the islands' function as a reserve for the preservation of globally important biodiversity through understanding processes and changes in sites, species and habitats in the islands for better management and decision-making on activities to preserve this globally important biodiversity.

Cousin and Cousine are adjacent to Praslin-the second most populous island of the Seychelles. Cousin was purchased in the 1960's through a world wide appeal at a time when unique biodiversity in Seychelles was in jeopardy. An international NGO held the title to the island because land tenureship was the only method of securing the island for perpetuity and thereby restoring the ecosystems. This NGOs also assisted the previous owners of Cousine in the early years to conserve its biodiversity. This proved to be a very wise move because the islands are remarkable in that unlike other granitic islands of Seychelles, endemic and globally important fauna and flora have been saved.

They have been protected by NGO/private resources and management, and at least for Cousin, through national legislation and policy. The ownership and management regimes by civil society organisations and the relative remoteness, which are the main reasons why biodiversity has been saved, are now proving to be constraints for not only continuing with established activities but also for initiating new programs; the civil society organisations cannot source adequate resources from the local private sector, governmental or international sources. In addition, anthropogenic impacts and lack of knowledge of ecosystem-level changes, all mean that science and conservation action on each of them cannot move beyond present capacity and limits.

The project assumption is that conservation of island biodiversity can be sustained and at the same time greatly improved through an inter-island integrated and collaborative approach geared to clear management outcomes and also to the development of public education and community buy-in. The project recognises the importance of developing financial sustainability to maintain these conservation programs. The project intends to build long-term capacity for sustainable conservation and use of island biodiversity through program and capacity building, infrastructure acquisition and installation, co-management, and education and advocacy.

The two islands are small, close to each other, and share similar and sensitive ecosystems, associated conservation activities and problems. They are both focused on biodiversity conservation, chiefly concerning globally threatened endemic land birds and internationally important colonies of breeding seabirds. Each island also hosts similar important reptile, botanical and invertebrate species. Both islands have a distinguished conservation history and offer a slightly different model and philosophy for biodiversity conservation. Cousin Island is owned by an international NGO but managed by an independent, locally registered, not-for-profit Association. Cousine Island is owned and managed by a private limited company registered in Seychelles. Management of the islands are supposed to be undertaken with in-country resources.

PROJECT VISION

The project will remove barriers that currently prevent civil society organisations from augmenting and enhancing their capacity to conserve and restore species, sites and habitats.

The project will aims to create partnerships between neighbouring islands which have shared globally important biodiversity and similar environmental issues. This will be done through a substantial number of new and improved linked programs, the creation of a common resource and management center, institutional strengthening and capacity building, and public education and advocacy. The ultimate aim of this model partnership is to catalyze further collaboration and public buy-in, to remove other barriers and to mitigate negative ecosystem changes. The process set in motion by the project will improve the management of high biodiversity islands as well as increase the number of managed conservation sites in Seychelles. This project will thus have global biodiversity benefits, lead to greater sustainability of biodiversity and permit the sharing of these benefits to be directed principally at local levels. The vision mirrors the three principal objectives of the 1992 Convention of Biological Diversity.

OVERALL GOAL OF THE PROJECT

The Goal of the project is to improve management of biodiversity-rich islands by installing a shared multi-pronged programme framework and infrastructure for enhanced and sustainable conservation, financing and use of biodiversity.

The project vision and overall goal will be delivered through two principal components namely Small Island Ecosystem Management, and Public Education and Advocacy.:.

Component 1: Small Island Ecosystem Management

A. Improved management of terrestrial and marine habitats and important species.

B. Establish collaborative management and resource center on Praslin

C. Institutional strengthening

D. Capacity building and training

Component 2: Public Education and Advocacy

A. Develop biodiversity awareness and advocacy programs

B. Establish community outreach, partnerships and stakeholder participation programs

PROJECT PARTNERS

Nature Seychelles, formerly known as BirdLife Seychelles, is a local not-for-profit association registered in Seychelles.

It is currently the largest independent environment organisation in Seychelles. The association is involved in a suite of activities including species and habit conservation, monitoring, research, island restoration, eco-tourism, education and awareness and advocacy.

Nature Seychelles manages Cousin Island Special Reserve and has a presence on several other islands. It has a multi-stakeholder and result-oriented approach through its programs such as the Seychelles Magpie-robin Recovery Team (SMART) and the Seychelles Seabird Group (SSG) as well with other organisations such as the WildLife Clubs of Seychelles, Ministry of Environment and Ministry of Education.

Its donors and partners include the World Bank/GEF and the Royal Society for Protection of Birds. It is a member of the BirdLife International network, WIOMSA, the African Bird Club and IUCN, works in close collaboration with WWF, the Mauritian WildLife Foundation and many others.

Cousine Island LTD (Owner and Manger of Cousine Island): is a private limited company registered in the Seychelles. The company has built a very small and ecologically friendly luxury hotel. The island is not legally protected and the owner is not obliged to conserve its biodiversity. The company has voluntarily put in a system for biodiversity conservation using its own resources. It delegates management responsibility for the island to a Conservation Warden. The Warden works in close collaboration with the hotel manager. The purpose of setting up the small hotel is to bring in sufficient revenues to maintain the conservation and research programs on the island and to maintain it as a high biodiversity area. The company supports other conservation programs in Seychelles, for example the Magpie Robin Recovery Program and the Seychelles Rare Birds Committee.

LANDMARKS ACHIEVEMENTS

Hotel Association of India, established on 24th October 1996, within a short span of less than a decade of its inception, has successfully provided an integrated hospitality platform produced ground breaking results and recorded several notable 'firsts' for the hospitality industry described in the ensuing pages:-

Export House Status for Tourism and Hospitality Industry

Among the path breaking industry 'first' initiatives of Hotel Association of India is the unique recognition secured for tourism and hospitality sectors in India as 'export industries'. This was an unparelled achievement of the Association which undertook the entire groundwork and created consensus in support of according export status for hospitality industries. HAI organized series of inter-active meetings with the concerned Ministries of the Government of India, culminating in a high level Conclave presided over by Shri Ramakrishna Hegde, then Hon'ble Minister of Commerce, Government of India, on 16th July 1998 at the Oberoi Hotel, New Delhi which cleared the decks for the action plan blue-printed by HAI receiving the official seal of approval of the Government of India manifested in the a Gazette Notification of November 26th, 1998 declaring Hotels and Tourism Units eligible for the benefits of Service Export House/International Service Export House/International Star Service Export House/International Super Star Service Export House categories on the basis of their quantum of foreign exchange earnings. This extraordinary recognition placed hotels and tourism units on par with industries engaged in export of products for imports of projects and products against their foreign exchange entitlements and facilitated hotels in acquiring competitive edge vis-à-vis hotels overseas in providing world class facilities.

Tourism Export Promotion Council

Another notable first for hospitality and tourism industries, synchronizing with the grant of Export House Status, was notched by the Hotel Association of India by formulating the Constitution of the Tourism Export Promotion Council (TEPC) on 20th November 1998. The approval of the Company Law Board was also secured for the new body under Section 25 of the Companies Act 1956. TEPC represented an unique experiment in bringing together for the first time all constituents of the tourism sector-hotels, travel agents, tour operators, transporters, airlines, tourism finance companies-under a single umbrella on a common platform.

Establishment of SAARC Hotel Association

HAI reached beyond the national boundaries to provide regional co-operation aiming hotels in South Asia and became the prime mover in the formation of the SAARC Hotel Association. This was achieved by developing close synergy between the hospitality industry organizations of Bangladesh, Bhutan, India, Maldives, Nepal, Pakistan and Sri Lanka. The SAARC Hotel Association was formally launched at Mumbai on 7th April 1999 with Nepal being assigned the responsibility of hosting the SAARC body for its initial two years and later by rotation by other member countries.

International Code of Conduct to Govern Relations Between Hoteliers, Travel Agents and Tour Operators

For the first time in the history of travel trade in India on 28.4.2000, HAI successfully evolved consensus among the Travel Agents Association of India (TAAI) and the Indian Association of Tour Operators (IATO) and the Hotel Association of India (HAl) resulting in the signing of the International Code of Practice governing the relations between Hoteliers, Travel Agents and Tour Operators. The code represents a watershed for the tourism and travel industry in India, as protracted negotiations for adopting a code of practice for over three decades had not yielded any results till HAl took the lead and crafted consensus in favour of adopting the global practice. It's signing by the three national bodies signalled to the international travel fraternity and business travellers that India had opted for internationally approved policies of hotel bookings, cancellations, refunds, claims etc.

Legal 'First' For Hotel Industry

The Hotel Association of India took the lead in invoking the intervention of the High Court of Delhi in protecting the interests of hospitality industry in India on a matter of vital importance to the hotels as well as to the foreign and domestic tourist staying in hotels. Hotel Association of India filed a writ in the High Court Delhi against an arbitrary and ad'hoc administrative directive requiring the hotels in approved categories, classified by the Ministry of Tourism, to follow a Single Tariff system. The directive would have proved detrimental and counter productive to national tourism interests.

The industry perspective presented by HAI was accepted by the High Court of Delhi which granted a Stay in favour of hotel industry, signifying an unique legal validation of hospitality industry system of operation across the country.

Seeking Repeal of Anti-women Legislation

The Punjab Excise Act enacted during the British rule in India in 1914 contains an archaic and anti-women provision prohibiting the employment of women in licenced premises, i.e., bars and restaurants in hotels.

The Hotel Association of India challenged the validity of this ancient legislation before the Hon'ble High Court to protect the interest of women. The HAI's Writ against the constitutional validity of the provisions of the Punjab Excise Act, 1914

Media Centric Initiatives

The large number of foreign correspondents stationed in India, representing powerful and popular foreign publications, newspapers, journals, T. V. Channels, Broadcasters play a major role in making or marring the image of India as a peaceful tourists destination country through their news reports and dispatches. HAI took the lead in organizing the first ever hospitality industry meeting with the foreign correspondent stationed in New Delhi.

The event was organized with the objective to discuss adverse the impact of Travel Advisories issued by foreign Governments on the State of Indian hospitality and tourism industry and correct their perspective to restore consumer confidence in travel, tourism and hospitality sectors adversely affected by global events of preceding years. Because of the unique nature of the special event and its potential for future tourists arrivals in India, the Ministry of Tourism fully associated with HAI.

Survey on the Impact of Travel Advisories in Hospitality Industry

Foreign Embassies and Missions are often instrumental in advising their respective countries to issue "Travel Advisories" to caution their citizens from undertaking visits to specific countries owing to adverse conditions of safety and security. Travel Advisories against visiting India were issued by several countries following global events like the terrorist attacks on 9/11 in USA and 13/12 in New Delhi, War in Afghanistan and tension on Indo-Pak borders etc. The adverse travel advisories affected tourists arrivals to India over a prolonged period.

The Hotel Association of India stepped in by organizing an innovative Survey among foreign tourists staying in hotels to obtain their reactions to such advisories issued by the foreign governments. The HAI Survey brought out that a preponderant majority of tourists declared India as a safe and peaceful destination and foreign travellers viewed the travel advisories and warnings as "coloured by political considerations" and based on "inadequate knowledge of ground realities". Some of them opined that they found New Delhi "safer than Manhattan". HAI Survey facilitated the Governments of the respective countries in reviewing and withdrawing the adverse travel advisories and re-assured tourists of their safety and security in India.

Setting Up of Confederation of Indian Travel and Tourism Industry

Another first initiative mooted by the Association related to the need for creating a Confederation of Indian Travel and Tourism Industry (CITTI) as an umbrella organization to represent all components of the Travel & Travel industry in India. Unlike other industries, there has never been an umbrella organization in the tourism industry. To fill this gap, HAI proposed the setting up of CITTI which would address the policy issues and concerns of the industry. The Constitution of the proposed new body has been drawn up and made available to all sectoral associations to facilitate its establishment in the future.

Study of Tariff System in Hotels

The first ever 'While Paper' on Tariff Systems in Hotels in India, produced by a Central Government Autonomous Organisation the National Institute of Public Finance and Policy (NIPFP), was undertaken at the behest of the Hotel Association of India. The NIPFP headed by eminent economists of the standing of Dr. Raja J Chelliah, former Chief Economic Advisor of the Government of India and Dr. C. Rangarajan, former Governor of the Reserve Bank of India, provided the Indian hospitality industry with its most appropriate perspective and authentic study of tariff systems.

First Afro-Asian Infotech Hotels Expo

HAI-led initiative resulted in Afro-Asian Region's first Conference-cum-Exposition on Information Technology being institutionalized as 'an annual event in New Delhi for countries in the South Asian Region. The first Conference-cum-Expo organized by HAl on April 10-11, 2000 at the ITC Maurya Sheraton Hotel, New Delhi received support from the United Nations Economic and Social Commission for Asia and the Pacific, and the SAARC Tourism Council. The Ministries of Tourism and Information Technology, Government of India, extended official support to HAl as Co-sponsors of the event.

Second Afro-Asian Infotech-hotels Expo

The Second Conference-cum-Exposition on Information Technology in Hotels was organized on March 15-16, 2001 at the Taj Palace Hotel, New Delhi. This Afro-Asian conference was supported by United Nation Economic and Social Commission for Asia and like the front conference the Pacific (UN-ESCAP); Ministry of Tourism, Ministry of Information Technology, Government of India, SAARC Tourism Council and SAARC Hotel Association, Pacific Asia Travel Association (PATA) and International Hotel & Restaurant Association (IH&RA).

Creating a National Network of HAI Chapters

The Hotel Association of India, established in April 1997, enlisted co-operation on a voluntary basis of professional hoteliers in twenty five State and fifty three cities to monitor hospitality related developments to enable the Association to address the concerns of the hospitality industry at the grass-roots level.

Going Global With Knowledge Exchange Partners

Knowledge Exchange partnerships were formed with international organization such as the World Travel and Tourism Council (WTTC); the Pacific Asia Travel Association (PATA); World Tourism Organisation (WTO); the International Hotel and Restaurant Association (IH&RA); the United Nation Economic and Social Commission for Asia and the Pacific (UN-ESCAP); the South Asia Association of Regional Countries (SAARC), the World Health Organisation (WHO) and the European Union's South Asia Integrated Tourism Human Resource Development Programme (EU-SAITHRDP)

Inter-sectoral Linkages with Apex National Fora

At the National level working partnerships were established with apex industry for a like the Federation of Indian Chamber of Commerce and Industry (FICCI); Associated Chamber of Commerce and Industry of India (ASSOCHAM); Confederation of Indian Industry (CII); to provide hospitality industry perspective in the formation of national industrial policies and development.

Affiliation with World Health Organisation (WHO)

HAI's pioneered the concept of 'Healthy Hotels' in line with WHO's 'Healthy Cities' campaign by initiating programmes for the hospitality industry on 'Hygiene Management in Hotels' at Agra in 1997. The WHO representative in India delivered the keynote address at the First Hygiene Management Seminar.

Innovative-"India Quiz Contest" at ITB Berlin 2002

A new promotional first was scored by the HAI at ITB Berlin, held from 16th to 20th March 2002. This was the first time 25 leading Indián hotels were brought together by HAI on the industry net to sponsor prizes of FAM Holiday Tours to Travel Trade visitors at the ITB.

The India Quiz Contest brochure of HAI provided a high visibility to the Indian hospitality industry products among visitor to the ITB, Berlin. The participating hotels received excellent marketing exposure of their properties in the Quiz brochure. This also offered unique opportunities for prospective agents and operator for the familiarization and experience of the hotels.

Guidelines for Provision of Disabled Friendly Facilities in Hotels

The Association undertook a pioneering role in formulating a comprehensive set of Guidelines for provision of Disabled Friendly facilities in Hotels, especially in parking and Approach Areas, Lobbies, Public Areas, Lifts, Rooms, Bathrooms and to install special Fire Prevention measures for the disabled.

Promoting Public-Private Partnership

The Association in a step towards promoting the public-private partnership called upon its members to extend their full corporation to the Archeological Survey of India in the maintenance of the National monuments, which has translated into following public-private sector partnership:-

(i) Illumination of Humayun's Tomb at Delhi by the Oberoi Group of Hotels.

(ii) Development of facilities for visitors at the Agra Fort by the ITC Hotels Ltd.

(iii) Main entrance of the Jantar Mantar observatory at New Delhi by the Apeejay Surrendra Park Hotels Pvt. Ltd.

(iv) Illumination of the Safdarjung Tomb, New Delhi by the Grand Group of

Special Promotional Packages in Hotels

A major initiative undertaken by HAI galvanized the entire Indian hospitality industry to come together under the Association's banner to offer for the first time in the history of the industry as many as 62 special promotional packages in hotels for marketing averages in association with Air India.

Memorandum of Undertakings Signed With the Hotel Association of Nepal and the Uganda Investment Authority

The Hotel Association of India signed two Memorandum of Understanding which aimed at fostering and promoting tourism in their respective countries by inter alia agreeing to exchange information in respect to development and trend in the fields of tourism, hospitality and hotel sectors and encourage interaction between their respective hotels and Hospitality Association of India for Tourism Promotion and exploring investment opportunities in these sectors.

India Quiz Contest Brochure at 51st PATA Annual Conference

Encouraged by the overwhelming response received from the ITB Berlin, HAI launched its exclusive India Quiz Contest at the 51st PATA Annual Conference held in New Delhi from 14.04.2002 to 18.04.2002 offering opportunities of FAM Holiday in 14 leading Hotels.

Study Project on Management of Cross-cultural Tourists Movements in Hospitality Sector

HAI initiated a study project on Management of cross-cultural tourism movements in hospitality sector to assess and promote awareness among staff in smaller hotel and upgrade their knowledge and skills for handling of foreign tourists.

Grant of Fiscal Benefits to the Hospitality Industry

For the first time the tourism industry's aspirations elaborated in the Hotel Association of India's various memoranda to the Central Government were translated into "tourism-friendly", measures in the Union Budget of 2003-04.

These measures were aimed at making India more affordable destination, fuelling growth of hospitality infrastructure, facilitating business re-organisation, re-structuring hospitality industry and motivating State Governments to rationalize tourism tax regime. The major incentives extended to hospitality industries included and exemption of Service tax in hotels relating to Conference and Banquet business, which have been excluded from the service tax net.

Encouraging Investments

Hotel Association of India orchestrated the strategy leading to announcement in the Union Budget 2003 of benefits under Section 10(23) (g) on loans to hotels (3 star and above categories) for increasing the availability of funds for the hotel industry.

This provision has allowed lending institutions to make available funds to hotel projects at reduced rates of interest. The financial institutions will get a tax break on the interest income they earn on loans extended to such borrowers.

Inclusion of finance to the hotel projects of three star category and above for the first time under Section 10 (23)(g) of the Income Tax Act "signals" the positioning of hotels on the threshold of securing full infrastructure status as granted to other industries. HAI is now carrying this agenda forward to securing the wider benefits of infrastructure under Section 84 I/A of Income Tax Act.

Restructuring Hospitality Business

Amalgamation and Merger

It is at the behest of HAI that the Finance Ministry constituted a Working group under Chief Commissioner of Income Tax Mumbai which recommended the grant of benefits under Section 72 A of the Income Tax Act (which relates to the set-off of accumulated losses and depreciation on amalgamation), for the hotel industry to help loss-making hotel companies in re-organising their business.

The facility of mergers and acquisitions was hitherto available only to industrial undertakings and manufacturing units. With its extension to hotel companies, it has facilitated moves towards consolidation with the hospitality industry and releasing of resources blocked in non-performing assets.

This measure has now enabled smaller hotel units to enter into franchisee arrangements with established hotel groups/

chains which in turn has led to improvements in occupancy levels and service standards.

Zero Duty Facility for Imports by Hotels

HAI pursued with the Ministry of Commerce, Government of India for grant of the zero duty import facility to hotels and stand alone restaurants. The Industry has now been granted under the "Served from India Scheme", the zero duty facility to all hotels including one star, two star hotels for import of food items and alcoholic beverages sell which would make India an affordable destination.

HAI Directory of Hotels Going Global

The exclusive HAI Directory of Hotels is an annual publication promoted with a singular aim of fulfilling the promotional need for tourists and visitor coming to India for an authentic compendium of leading Indian hotels recognized by the Ministry of Tourism. For the first time in 2005 the Directory was utilized by the Ministry of Tourism for distribution among foreign travel agents and tour operators in 12 countries through the Government of India's Tourist Offices abroad.

World Tourism Day Celebartion

A new promotional first was scored by HAI for creating awareness about the World Tourism Day on 27th Sept. 2005 amongst not only the member-hotels but also the school children.

To encourage and facilitate the member-hotels in celebrating the World Tourism Day on 27th September 2005, HAI outlined a bouquet of activities to be organized by the member-hotels. The member-hotels came forward in large numbers and organized the activities with enthusiasm and excitement. In New Delhi, HAI collaborated with the Sanskriti School to launch a Quiz Contest on Tourism for school children on the World Tourism Day.

Members Services

Variety of professional member-services are provided by HAI to its members these include:-

(i) INFORMATION BULLETINS sent out regularly with updates on latest developments concerning hotel industries, policy changes and pronouncements by Ministry of Tourism, Ministry of Finance, Ministry of Commerce, CBEC, CBDT, State Governments and affiliate international organizations such as WTTC, IH&RA, WTO etc.;

(ii) HAI TODAY-the first hospitality industry magazine of its kind in India;

(iii) HAI DIRECTORY OF HOTELS-an exclusive high quality reference manual of recognized hotels in India;

(iv) HAI PRIVILEGE CARDS which are offered to members in the Gold and Silver Categories entitling them to discounts on hotel room tariffs and restaurants outlets in all member hotels on reciprocal basis;

(v) HAI LEGAL SERVICES which enables members to avail benefits of highest calibre legal advice on issues of concern them and interventions on their behalf in courts.

GREEN WEEKS OF THE HAI

HAI has successfully institutionalized the concept of celebrating annual green weeks in hotels to exhibit its commitment to conservation of environment through use of bio-degradable and environment-friendly products by efficient management of waste generated and by adopting measures for efficient utilization of day light to conserve upon electricity etc. HAI has this year celebrated its ninth annual green week, reaching out to large number of tourists, employees, their families, school children and society with its environment message.

Fundamentals Of Revenue Management Will Be Revealed In A Special Report Commissioned By HSMAI Special Interest Group

MCLEAN, VA The Hospitality Sales & Marketing Association International (HSMAI) Revenue Management Special Interest Group has taken on an ambitious project to produce the first-ever comprehensive "Fundamentals of Revenue Management" special report.

The report will be a practitioner-friendly publication that addresses the fundamentals of revenue management for a broad audience of hospitality professionals. With comprehensive content that is both readable and actionable, it will deliver tools and information for revenue management education, incorporating expert advice from interviews with industry executives and educators, case studies, and practical checklists for implementing successful revenue management strategies at the property level.

"Creating relevance for members and the industry at large through ground-breaking initiatives such as this Revenue Management Special Report is in keeping with HSMAI's mission to be the leading source for sales and marketing information, knowledge and business development for professionals in tourism, travel, and hospitality," states Robert A. Gilbert, CHME, CHA, president and CEO of HSMAI.

"We are very excited about this debut project, and expect it will be a springboard for other initiatives including certification and revenue management research," notes Tim Wiersma, vice president of revenue management for Host Marriott and chair of HSMAI's Revenue Management Tangible Resources Committee.

The publication will be produced in a manner similar to the recent special report produced by HSMAI and TIG Global entitled DeMystifying Distribution, widely praised by the industry for its insight, accuracy and comprehensive coverage of the topic.

The commissioned report, which will be released at the third annual HSMAI Revenue Management Strategy Conference on June 19, 2005 in Minneapolis, will be co-authored by Caryl Helsel and Kathleen Cullen of the Solutionz Group, a business development and strategic consulting group based in Florida. Helsel heads the hospitality practice and previously held executive positions with Kimpton Hotels, Pegasus Solutions and Mandarin Oriental Hotel Group, and is the former president of the Hotel Electronic Distribution Network Association (HEDNA). Cullen is a lead consultant on the hospitality team and is a hospitality revenue management and distribution veteran, holding executive positions with Swissotel and Raffles Hotels, as well as past vice president of HEDNA. Delving deep into the fundamentals, nuances and specifics of revenue management, the special report will address the following:

- Ideas and initiatives to maximize revenue opportunities, optimize profits by managing revenues and develop an infrastructure (strategies, policies, procedures, reports, etc.) to make informed decisions about accepting or rejecting business.
- An overview of the external market such as segmentation, demand forecasting, revenue strategy, operational forecast, interdepartmental integration, strategic pricing, inventory control strategies and internal performance analysis.
- Tactics including rate-level maintenance, inventory management and rate offer assessment (for group and negotiated rates).
- The optimal environment, characteristics and descriptors.

Bibliography

Ashworth, Gregory J.: *Marketing Tourism Places*, London, Routledge, 1990.

Bryson, McDowell: *Concierge: Key to Hospitality: A Training Manual*, New York, Wiley, 1992.

Clark, Mona: *Interpersonal Skills for Hospitality Managers*, London, Chapman Hill, 1995.

Clough, Richard: *Construction Project Management*, New York, John Wiley & Son, 2000.

Donald, M.: *Customer Service in the Hospitality and Tourism Industry*, Englewood Cliffs, Prentice Hall, 1994.

Hubert, B.: *A Host of Opportunities: An Introduction to Hospitality Management*, Chicago, Irwin, 1996.

Ireland, Lewis: *Quality Management for Projects and Programs*, Upper Darby, PMI, 1991.

John Bowen, and James Makens: *Marketing for Hospitality and Tourism*: New Jersey, Prentice-Hall, 1998.

Kotler, Philip: *Marketing for Hospitality and Tourism*: New Jersey, Prentice-Hall, 1998.

Marjorie, E.: *Careers in Travel, Tourism, and Hospitality*, Lincolnwood, VGM Career Horizons, 1997.

Nancy, N.: *Choosing a Career in Hotels, Motels, and Resorts*, New York, Rosen Pub. Group, 1997.

Nelson, Bob and Economy, Peter: *Managing for Dummies*, Foster City, IDG Books, 1996.

Robert, C.: *Cases in Hospitality Marketing and Management*, New York, John Wiley, 1997.

Rosenzweig, J. E.: *Organisation and Management*, New York, McGraw Hill International, 1963.

Thomas, F.: *Introduction to Management in the Hospitality Industry*, New York, Wiley, 1995.

Index

◆◆◆